THE WAR AGAINST EAST TIMOR

Carmel Budiardjo and Liem Soei Liong

Zed Books Ltd
57, Caledonian Road,
London N1 9BU

Marram Books
101, Kilburn Square,
London NW6 6PS

Pluto Press Australia
PO Box 199,
Leichhardt,
NSW 2040

In de Knipscheer
PO Box 6107,
2001 HC Haarlem,
Netherlands

The War Against East Timor was first published in 1984.

In the United Kingdom
Zed Books Ltd.
57 Caledonian Road, London N1 9BU

Marram Books
101 Kilburn Square, London NW6 6PS

In the Netherlands
In de Knipscheer, PO Box 6107, 2001 HC Haarlem, Netherlands

In Australia
Pluto Press Australia, PO Box 199, Leichhardt, NSW 2040, Australia

Copyright © Carmel Budiardjo and Liem Soei Liong

Typeset by Grassroots, London
Cover design by Len Breen
Printed by The Pitman Press, Bath, UK

All rights reserved

> British Library Cataloguing in Publication Data
> Budiardjo, Carmel
>   The War against East Timor
>   1. Timor Timur (Indonesia)—Politics and government
>   I. Title   II. Liong, Liem Soei
>   959.8'6   DS646.57
> ISBN 0 86232 228 6
> ISBN 0 86232 229 4 pbk

NL ISBN 90 6265 170 4

US Distributor:
Biblio Distributor Center, 81 Adams Drive, Totowa, New Jersey 07512.

About the authors

Carmel Budiardjo has worked for TAPOL, the British Campaign for the Defence of Political Prisoners and Human Rights in Indonesia, for the past ten years. Before that, she experienced three years political imprisonment in Indonesia. She is the joint author of *West Papua: The Obliteration of a People*.

Liem Soei Liong is an Indonesian who now lives in the Netherlands where he contributes to *Feiten en Meningen*, the publication of the Dutch Indonesia Committee. He has also worked for the Education Division of the Royal Tropical Institute.

Contents

Map v
Glossary vi
Chronology viii
Background xv
Preface xvi

PART I: The War Against East Timor
1. **Self-Determination** 3
2. **The War** 15
3. **Resistance and the Struggle for National Liberation** 52
4. **The Population Uprooted** 74
5. **The Indonesianization of East Timor** 96
6. **Atrocities and Violations** 127
7. **The Struggle for Self-Determination Continues** 139
Photos 157
Notes 161

PART II: The Indonesian Army's Secret Instructions for Counter-Insurgency Operations in East Timor
Introduction 169
Document 1 176
Instruction Manual on the Way for Village Guidance Officers or Teams to Expose/Break up GPK Support Networks
Document 2 183
Instruction Manual on the System of Security in Towns and Resettlement Areas
Document 3 193
Established Procedure for Territorial Intelligence Activities in East Timor
Document 4 211
Instruction Manual on The Village as the Focal Point of Attention and How to Guide It Comprehensively

Document 5 216
Instruction Manual on How to Protect the Community from the Influence of GPK Propaganda

Document 6 223
Instruction Manual on Village Guidance Officer/Village Guidance Team Activity in Developing and Organising Trained People's Resistance Forces

Document 7 228
Established Procedure for Conducting Razzias (Raids) on Settlement Areas

Document 8 233
Established Procedure for the Interrogation of Prisoners

Document 9 238
Plan to Re-structure the Trained People's Forces (Ratih)

Bibliography 245
Index 249

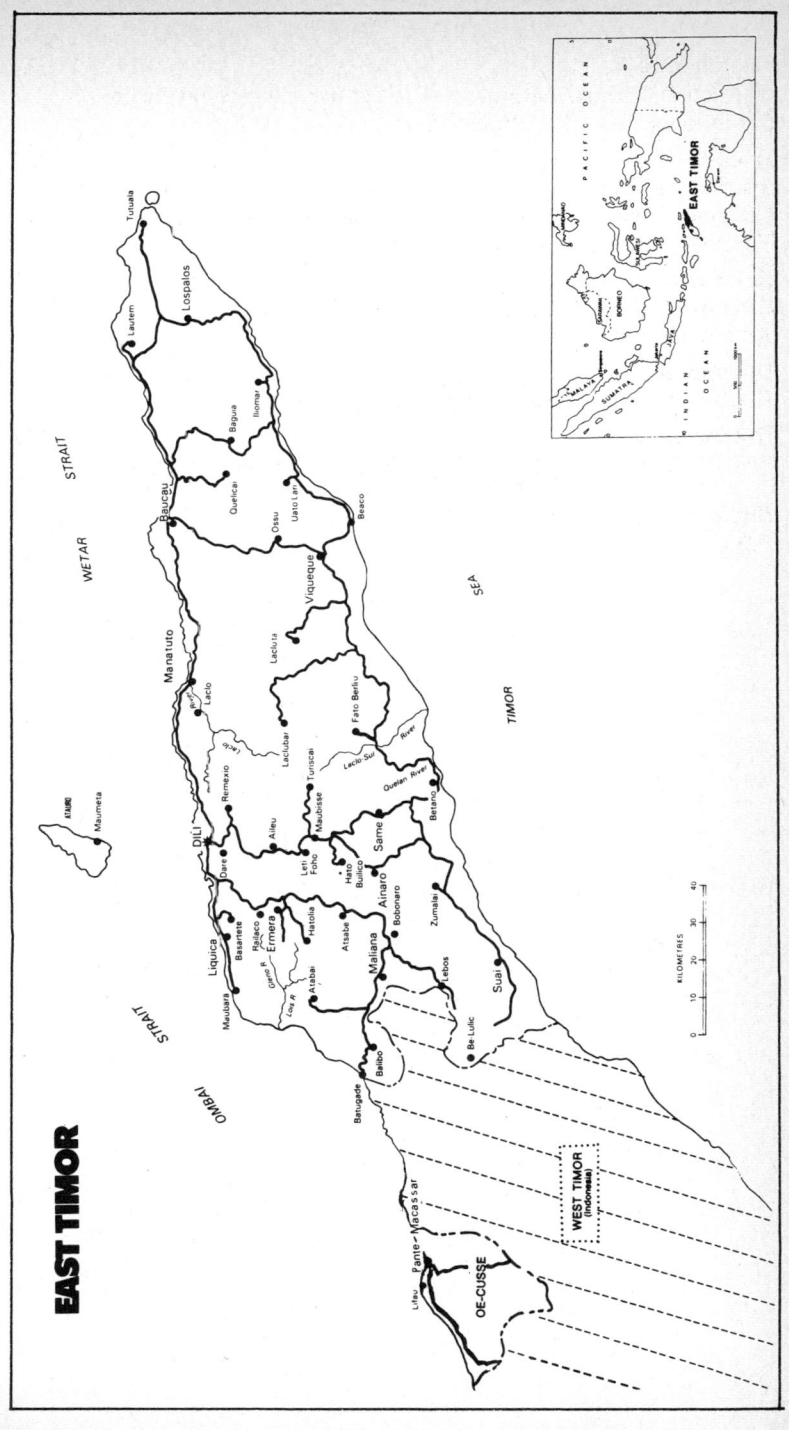

Glossary

ABRI/TNI	Indonesian Armed Forces/Indonesian Army.
Apter	Territorial apparatus.
Babinsa	Village guidance NCO.
Binpolda	Local police officer.
Bupati	Head of District.
Camat	Head of Sub-district.
Cernak	Centre for National Resistance (part of the guerrilla movement).
GPK	*Gerombolan Pengacau Keamanan*, or Security Disruptor Gangs, the term officially used in Indonesia for Fretilin, the East Timor resistance movement.
Hansip	Civil Guard.
Kabupaten	District, in Indonesia's local administration.
Kamra	People's security.
Kecamatan	Sub-district, in Indonesia's local administration.
Kelurahan	Village administrative unit.
Kodam	Regional Military Command. The country is divided into 17 Kodams.
Kodim	District Military Command.
Koramil	Sub-district Military Command
Korem	Sub-regional Military Command.
Kosek	Section Police Command.
Kowilhan	Territorial Defence Command. The country is divided into 4 Kowilhans
Liurai	Traditional Timorese chieftain.
Miplin	Popular Militia of National Liberation (part of the guerrilla movement).
Muspida	Regional leadership consultative body, comprised of all leading figures in the military, police and local government apparatus.
Nurep	Popular Resistance Nucleus (part of the guerrilla movement).
Protap	Established Procedure.
Operasi Komodo	*Komodo* ('Giant Lizard') Operation.

Operasi Kikis	The 'Chipping-Away' Operation.
Operasi Keamanan	Operation Security.
Railakang	Rear-theatre artillery.
Rakyat	People.
Ratih	Trained People's Unit.
Satgas	Special Unit.
Satgas Intel.	Special Intelligence Unit.
Satpur	Combat Units.
TBO	Operational Support Forces.
Team Pembina Desa (TPD)	Village Guidance Team.
Tripida	Tripartite Regional leadership (of military, police and civilian heads).
Wanra	Another term for *Hansip*, or Civil Guard.

Chronology

1974

25 April — Armed Forces Movement overthrows fascist regime in Lisbon. This opens the way for decolonization in East Timor.

11 May — ANP, the official party of the colonial fascist regime, reconstitutes itself as the *União Democratica Timorense* (UDT).

20 May — The *Associacão Social Democratica Timorense* is founded in Dili out of clandestine organization, *Core*

17 June — ASDT is given a written assurance by Indonesia's Foreign Minister that Indonesia respects East Timor's right to self-determination.

5 September — President Suharto discusses East Timor with Australian Prime Minister Whitlam who agrees with Suharto that an independent East Timor would not be viable.

11 September — ASDT renamed *Frente Revolucionaria de Timor-Leste Independente, Fretilin.*

October — Indonesia sets up *Operasi Komodo* to destabilize East Timor and facilitate its annexation.

November — New Portuguese governor of East Timor who says he is committed to decolonization is appointed.

December — Fretilin initiates anti-illiteracy programme and sets up co-operatives in the countryside.

1975

21 January — Fretilin enters coalition with UDT which formerly favoured union with Portugal. The coalition calls for independence and rejects integration with Indonesia.

Early February — Indonesian troops carry out manoeuvres in South Sumatra, reported as being a pre-invasion exercise.

May — UDT quits the coalition, and comes under increasing pressure from Indonesia to oppose Fretilin.

June — Portugal holds talks on decolonization in Macau, attended by UDT and Apodeti, a party created by Indonesian intelligence. Fretilin refuses to attend as integration with Indonesia is included on agenda.

11 August	After visiting Jakarta, UDT leaders launch a coup in Dili aimed at eliminating Fretilin whose popular support has grown enormously.
27 August	Portuguese governor abandons Dili as civil war rages, and goes to Atauro island, north of the capital.
28 August	Fretilin gains control, but urges Portuguese administration to return and complete the decolonization process. This plea is ignored.
September	UDT and the pro-Indonesian Apodeti set up an 'Anti-Communist Revolutionary Movement' with two other miniscule groups, Kota and Trabalhista.
September–November	Indonesian troops make military incursions across the border from West Timor. Batugade captured (7 October). Maliana captured (14 October).
16 October	Five TV journalists from Australia killed by Indonesian troops as they capture Balibo. Australian government fails to protest.
24 November	Fretilin addresses urgent appeal to UN after fall of Atabae.
28 November	Fretilin declares independence and proclaims the Democratic Republic of East Timor.
5-6 December	President Ford and Secretary of State Kissinger visit Indonesia.
7 December	Indonesia invades Dili. *Operasi Komodo* dissolved and Seroja Joint Command takes charge of operations.
12 December	UN General Assembly (72 to 9 with 44 abstentions) calls for Indonesian withdrawal from East Timor.
17 December	The four pro-Indonesian parties set up 'Provisional Government of East Timor' on board an Indonesian warship.
22 December	UN Security Council unanimously condemns invasion and instructs Secretary-General to send a special representative to East Timor.
25 December	15,000-20,000 additional troops join the invasion. Indonesia still controls only a few towns.
1976	
20-23 January	UN special representative in East Timor visits only three towns.
1 February	UN representative's attempts in Darwin to visit Fretilin-controlled areas sabotaged by Indonesian and Australian governments.
13 February	Lopez da Cruz of the 'Provisional Government of East Timor' states that 60,000 have died in East Timor.
22 April	UN Security Council (12 to none with 2 abstentions) again calls for Indonesian withdrawal.
15 May–2 June	Fretilin National Conference held to mobilise nationwide resistance.

31 May	Indonesian-sponsored 'People's Assembly' unanimously decides to integrate with Indonesia.
17 July	President Suharto signs Bill of Integration.
September	The first US-manufactured OV-10 Bronco counter-insurgency aircraft sent to Indonesia.
Sept-Oct	Many Timorese being herded into 'guarded camps', the beginnings of Indonesia's population-control strategy.
October	Transmitter in Darwin, in radio contact with Fretilin, seized by Australian police. Australia gives *de facto* recognition to integration.
November	Indonesian church document estimates 100,000 killed in East Timor.
1 December	UN General Assembly (75 to 20, with 52 abstentions) rejects integration and calls for an act of self-determination.

1977

17 January	Indonesian Minister of the Interior announces that 1977 general elections cannot be held in East Timor as conditions are not 'suitable'.
February	Jim Dunn, a former Australian Consul in Dili, publicizes details of Indonesian atrocities in Dili based on interviews of Timorese refugees in Lisbon.
23 March	Dunn testifies to US Congressional Sub-Committee.
1 April	Following publicity given to Dunn's testimony, Indonesian Foreign Minister Adam Malik says: '50,000 or perhaps 80,000 might have been killed in East Timor... It was war... Then what is the big fuss?'
16 August	Suharto offers 'amnesty' to Fretilin fighters, as the prelude to a new offensive, the encirclement and annihilation operation.
7 September	Fretilin President, Xavier do Amaral, is arrested by Fretilin leadership for pursuing a policy of compromise with the enemy and trying to undermine armed resistance.
September	Indonesia launches first stage of encirclement and annihilation operation.
16 October	Nicolau Lobato unanimously elected as Fretilin's new president.
28 November	UN General Assembly (67 to 26 with 47 abstentions) repeats the call for self-determination in East Timor.
1 December	Amnesty International criticises Indonesia for not allowing International Red Cross to operate in East Timor.

1978

20 January	Australia gives *de jure* recognition of integration.
February	Strong criticism at US congressional hearing of US military supplies to Indonesia since the start of the invasion.

March	General Yusuf appointed Minister of Defence and Commander of the Armed Forces, and takes over command of Indonesian military operations in East Timor.
4 April	British Aerospace announces the sale of eight Hawk ground-attack aircraft to Indonesia.
Mid-year	Special Co-ordinating Team for East Timor, chaired by Brigadier-General Benny Murdani, set up by Ministry of Defence.
May	Encirclement and annihilation operation Stage II commences.
5-7 May	US Vice-President, Walter Mondale, in Jakarta, confirms sale of 16 A4-Skyhawks to Indonesia.
20 June	Australia announces supply of Nomad reconnaisance aircraft to Indonesia.
16-17 July	Suharto visits East Timor, only going to Dili and Maliana. Opens TV transmitter in Dili.
30 August	Amaral surrenders to Indonesian troops some weeks after his guards were captured.
September	Encirclement and annihilation operation Stage III commences.
7-9 September	Visiting journalists and ambassadors shocked by famine and high death rate among Timorese in camps.
October	Australian parliamentarians call for International Red Cross to be allowed into East Timor.
22 November	Fretilin's last support base in Matabian in the eastern zone falls.
3 December	Fretilin loses radio link with outside world after surrender and defection of Information Minister, Alarico Fernandes.
13 December	UN General Assembly (59 to 30, with 46 abstentions) again asserts East Timor's right to self-determination.
31 December	Fretilin President, Nicolau Lobato, shot dead by Indonesian troops.
1979	
Early months	Many more concentration camps established for people forced down from the mountains by bombings.
26 March	Indonesia's Seroja Joint Command, in charge of military operations since the invasion, is disbanded.
20 May	International meeting of solidarity with East Timor held in Lisbon.
October	After being kept out of East Timor since the invasion, the International Red Cross is allowed back in. Together with the Catholic Relief Services, it commences large-scale relief programmes to halt 'Biafra-scale famine'.
1 November	Report and photos of famine-striken Timorese given wide coverage in world press.
21 November	UN General Asembly (62 to 31, with 45 abstentions) again calls for self-determination in East Timor.

1980

6 February — US ambassador to Jakarta accused at US congressional sub-committee of remaining silent over food disaster in East Timor.

10 June — Fretilin attacks Indonesia's television transmitter in Dili and several military targets.

8 November — *Documents on Australian Defence and Foreign Policy 1968-1975*, disclosing secret western support in mid 1975 for Indonesia's plans to annex East Timor, is banned after Australian Government injunction.

11 November — UN General Assembly (58 to 35, with 46 abstentions) again calls for self-determination for East Timor.

1981

1-8 March — Nationwide conference convened by Fretilin for national re-organization of the resistance. The Revolutionary Council for National Resistance is set up and a new leadership is elected with Kay Rala Xanana Gusmão as Chairman.

15 April — International Red Cross is forced to leave as Indonesia plans new offensive against resurgent Fretilin forces.

May — Operation Security launched. Tens of thousands of Timorese forced to participate. This Operation lasts till September.

19-21 May — Permanent People's Tribunal in Lisbon finds Indonesia guilty of violating the UN Charter on self-determination and armed aggression.

3 June — Indonesian-appointed Regional Assembly of East Timor complains bitterly to President Suharto about exploitation, corruption and widespread human rights violations.

September — Hundreds of villagers massacred in Lakluta as part of Operation Security. Many thousands exiled to Atauro island.

18 October — The two signatories of Regional Assembly Report are arrested after Report is published abroad.

24 October — UN General Assembly (54 to 42, with 46 abstentions) again calls for self-determination in East Timor.

26 October — Australian Senate decides to hold inquiry on East Timor.

End October — Catholic religious in East Timor complain about universal church's silence on the tragic sufferings of people of East Timor.

1982

11 January — Australian press publish warning from Bishop of Dili regarding the grave food situation.

14 April — International Red Cross permitted to resume food and medical programme.

12 May — Australian Senate Inquiry hearings commence.

28 May	A *Philadelphia Inquirer* article discloses widespread malnutrition and worsening conditions in East Timor.
Early July	Australian Labour Party adopts a policy supporting self-determination in East Timor and a halt to Australian military supplies while Indonesian troops remain in East Timor.
13-14 October	Suharto visits Washington. Many US newspapers criticise Indonesia's annexation of East Timor. Nearly a hundred members of Congress call for action on East Timor.
4 November	UN General Assembly (50 to 46, with 50 abstentions) again re-asserts self-determination in East Timor. It instructs the UN Secretary-General to initiate discussions 'with all parties directly concerned' and to report to the 1983 General Assembly.

1983

16 February	UN Human Rights Commission (16 to 14, with 10 abstentions) supports self-determination for East Timor and condemns human rights abuses.
5 March	Australian Labour Party returned to power.
23 March	Indonesian commander in East Timor, Colonel Purwanto, enters into negotiations with Fretilin leader, Kay Rala Xanana, who demands withdrawal of Indonesian troops and a UN-supervised act of self-determination. A ceasefire comes into effect.
End March	General Benny Murdani, who was responsible for planning and commanding the 1975 invasion, is appointed Commander-in-Chief of Indonesian Armed Forces.
May	Centre for Defence Information, Washington, identifies war in East Timor as having second highest death toll worldwide after Kampuchea.
10 May	Mgr da Costa Lopes, Bishop of Dili, an outspoken critic of the Indonesian administration, is forced to resign.
June	Australian Prime Minister Hawke, in Jakarta, says 'East Timor must be put behind us'.
26 June	General Murdani warns Fretilin leader, Xanana to surrender or be crushed.
Late July	International Red Cross halts operations again in mainland East Timor as Indonesia withdraws facilities, in preparation for new offensive.
20 July	Amnesty International exposes Indonesian military document authorising torture in East Timor.
29 July	Declaration of 170 West European parliamentarians calls for self-determination in East Timor.
30 July-3 Aug	Australian Parliamentary Delegation visits East Timor.
8 August	Indonesian troops killed in clash with Fretilin. Over 200 villagers killed in reprisal attack.
16 August	Murdani announces that resistance in East Timor will be crushed 'without mercy'.

1 September	20,000 Indonesian troops launched new offensive.
Mid-September	Australian Parliamentary Delegation to East Timor supports integration. Australian Senate Inquiry Report, in contrast, rejects integration. Both reports are accompanied by dissenting reports.
22 September	UN General Assembly East Timor resolution deferred till 1984 after UN Secretary-General announces that his report on consultations regarding East Timor requested by the General Assembly in 1983 will be delayed for a year.
25 December	Armed Forces Commander-in-Chief, General Benny Murdani, visits East Timor to boost morale of his troops. Fresh elite troops also arrive.
1984	
6 January	Alarming reports from Jakarta (*AFP* and *Sinar Harapan*) about grave food shortages in East Timor caused by Indonesian military operations.
18 January	A Fretilin communique, released in Lisbon, reports guerrilla attacks in various parts of the country.
29 January	The Angolan Information Minister attending the Conference of Information Ministers of the Non-Alligned Countries holds a press conference in Jakarta on East Timor. Indonesian journalists banned from attending.
19 February	*AFP* in Jakarta reports heavy Indonesian casualties in East Timor.
21 February	Indonesian is denounced by the UN Human Rights Commission in Geneva for human rights violations in East Timor. The Commission hears testimony from the former Bishop of Dili.
Early March	12 Timorese are tried in Dili for 'treason', all receiving heavy sentences. Many more will also be tried, according to press reports from Jakarta.
16 March	The International Red Cross is allowed to visit prisoners in Dili but is still prevented from resuming its food aid programme in mainland East Timor.
16-18 March	The Revolutionary Council of National Resistance (CRRN), meeting in East Timor, declares that the Indonesians are 'growing more and more demoralised by the fact that our activities cover almost the whole country'. (*Canberra Times*, 17 April, 1984)
25 March	Fretilin Peace Plan is announced in Lisbon, following an international solidarity conference there.
30 March	President Eanes of Portugal convenes the Council of State to press the government to work for a just solution in East Timor.
3 May	The Bishop of Dili, Mgr Belo says ten battalions are being deployed by Indonesia in the eastern sector alone 'but there is no end in sight to the military operation'. (*The Guardian*, London)

Background

• East Timor is a country of about 19,000 square kilometres and is located at the eastern extremity of the Indonesian archipelago, between 8°15' and 10°30' S longitude and 123°20' and 127°10' E latitude. The crocodile-shaped island of which East Timor is the eastern half is dominated by an east-west mountain range which has been decisive in conditioning the way of life of the people of East Timor.
• Weather conditions vary enormously due largely to the influence of the mountain range on winds and rainfall. The island has the longest dry season in South East Asia with rainfall distribution dividing the country into four rainfall zones. The southern coastal plain catches two wet seasons making two harvests possible, but conditions in the north are much drier making only one harvest possible.
• The main cash crops are coffee and sandalwood. Food crops include corn, rice, wheat, potatoes, sweet potatoes, cassava, sago and a variety of vegetables, tubers, and tropical fruit.
• The island of Timor is a racial meeting point, populated by waves of migrants who were prodominantly Malay and Melanesian. In the past two centuries, Arab, Chinese and African faces have also become part of the Timorese crowd.

Before the Indonesian invasion in 1975

• The last pre-invasion population figure was 688,711, the figure of the Catholic church published in 1974. The official language was Portuguese, whilst Tetum had become a sort of *lingua franca* in East Timor.
• The majority of Timorese still adhered to their traditional beliefs. After the arrival of the Portuguese, many were converted to Catholicism. By the 1970s, about thirty per cent of the population were Catholics.
• Before the first Europeans arrived in Timor, the island was divided into many small kingdoms; the rulers were called *liurais* (mainly in the east) or *rajas* (mainly in the west). Long before the Europeans appeared, Chinese, Arab and Gujerati traders had frequently visited East Timor, especially in search of sandalwood.
• Although the Portuguese were the first Europeans to arrive in East and Southeast Asia, the Dutch followed soon after and succeeded in gaining control almost everywhere. The only places where the Dutch failed to expel the Portuguese were Macao and Timor. In 1702, the Portuguese started to set up a colonial administration in Timor but it was not until the middle of the nineteenth century that the struggle between the Portuguese and the Dutch for control of the sandalwood trade was more or less settled. The Dutch ruled in the western half of the island which became Indonesian West Timor after the Republic of Indonesia was established. The Portuguese remained in control of East Timor until the Democratic Republic of East Timor was set up on 28 November, 1975.

Preface

One-third of East Timor's population—about 200,000 people—have been killed in the war that has raged since Indonesian troops invaded in late 1975. According to *A World at War, 1983* published by the Washington-based Centre for Defence Information, the Indonesian aggressors have caused more deaths that any other conflagration then in progress, with the single exception of the killings in Kampuchea, Yet of all the many wars with huge death tolls referred to in that report, the war against East Timor is certainly the least known and the least understood. The reason is not hard to find: the people of East Timor are the victims of one of the West's most favoured Third World dictatorships, the Suharto military regime in Indonesia.

After the invasion in December 1975, a world-wide solidarity movement grew, stretching from Australia and New Zealand, throughout western Europe to the USA. Numerous solidarity actions were launched for the first few years of the war, while most of the press and most political circles showed no interest at all. The western powers not only remained silent as the killings intensified, but even stepped up supplies of counter-insurgency aircraft and military equipment to Indonesia, providing the troops with the hardware they needed to fight the resistance, a war against the entire population. Complicity and support have turned these western governments into accomplices in Indonesia's attempt to annihilate an entire people.

After the resistance in East Timor, under the leadership of Fretilin (*Frente Revolucionaria de Timor Leste Independente*, the Revolutionary Front for an Independent East Timor), suffered a series of devastating defeats in 1977 and 1978, the flow of information about the war virtually dried up. Most of the subsequent information smuggled out spoke of violent abuses of human rights and the catastrophic impact of the Indonesian occupation on the living conditions of the population. These were the issues that were to become the focus of international solidarity for the next few years, together with efforts to maintain support for East Timor's right to self-determination at the UN.

Little was heard about military activities until the second half of 1981 when news came of an Indonesian campaign, using tens of thousands of Timorese, to 'round up Fretilin remnants'. Only much later did it become clear that these were not 'remnants' but a resurgent resistance movement challenging the forces of occupation not only in the bush but right inside the towns controlled by the troops. Fretilin's 'year of the strategic counter-offensive' 1982, was also the year in which information began to seep out. News emerged about the years of silence which suggested that a new analysis and historical account of the war and the nature of Indonesia's colonial regime was urgently needed as the basis for renewed solidarity with the victims of Indonesian aggression.

The documents that have provided the basis for the present analysis come from a variety of sources. In the first place, Fretilin has produced several invaluable reports. In October 1982, Xanana, president of the Revolutionary Council of National Resistance, sent a message to the UN General Assembly outlining the history of the war and the appalling atrocities committed by Indonesia against the population of East Timor. Then, in the middle of 1983, Fretilin prepared two well-researched reports, one on social and economic conditions in the Indonesian concentration camps where most of the surviving East Timorese are now forced to live, and one on human rights violations and atrocities committed by Indonesian troops. Information on Fretilin's National Conference held in March 1981 was also received.

Other documents, used extensively in this analysis, have been made available thanks to the persistent work of activists in Australia whose interest in East Timor has never flagged. The *Dossier on East Timor* (1982) published by the Australian Council for Overseas Aid brought together a wealth of information about conditions in occupied East Timor collected from East Timorese living or studying in Jakarta or stranded there as they waited to join their families abroad. The Australian Senate Inquiry (1982) heard evidence from witnesses who provided new insights into many aspects of life inside the country, all of which became available in the verbatim records of the Inquiry. And from Australia too came *The Timor Papers* published in the middle of 1982 by *The National Times*, giving lengthy extracts from daily CIA reports on the progress of Indonesian military operations before and after the invasion in December 1975.

The Indonesian press is rarely allowed to report anything on East Timor. Of all the issues that are subjected to censorship by the Jakarta military regime, the war in East Timor is by far the most heavily-guarded secret. However the few occasions when Indonesian journalists were able to visit the territory have provided additional information of considerable value to the present analysis.

By far the most important source of all from the Indonesian side has been the set of secret instructions on counter-insurgency operations issued to the troops in 1982 which were contained in a folder captured in December that year by Fretilin guerrillas. These documents, which are reproduced *in extenso* at the end of this book provide irrefutable proof that, whatever lies are told to the Indonesian people and to the world at large, the forces of occupation are well aware that they confront a well-organized and powerful adversary in East Timor.

The war against the people of East Timor and Indonesia's desperate attempts to Indonesianize its '27th province' have failed to crush the will to resist of a population almost totally isolated from international contact; a population that has been decimated and savaged by a military power that enjoys enormous superiority in numbers, in military equipment and in international assistance. The tenacity of the people of East Timor in face of such adversity has been a constant source of admiration and inspiration, and it is to them that this work is dedicated.

Carmel Budiardjo
Liem Soei Liong

PART I
THE WAR AGAINST EAST TIMOR

1. Self-Determination

The people of East Timor exercised their right to self-determination on 28 November 1975 when a *de facto* Fretilin government unilaterally declared independence and proclaimed the establishment of the Democratic Republic of East Timor. Nine days later on 7 December, Indonesia launched an all-out attack on the capital of East Timor, Dili. The December invasion and the armed incursions that preceded it were the culmination of a campaign initiated more than a year before by the Suharto military regime to prevent the emergence of an independent state in place of the Portuguese colonial regime that had maintained control of the eastern half of the island of Timor since the 16th Century.

Portuguese traders had been attracted to the island by its rich abundance of sandalwood. In the face of Dutch colonial expansion throughout the Indonesian archipelago, the Portuguese only succeeded in hanging on to the eastern half of the island. Until the early 20th Century, the Portuguese colonial administration functioned by indirect control; the traditional structure of *reinos* or kingdoms under their *liurais* served the regime by collecting taxes and recruiting forced labour for colonial projects. In 1910, a number of *liurais* rose up against the Portuguese in protest against the imposition of new tax burdens. The Great Rebellion (1910-12) led by Dom Boaventura, the liurai of Manufuhi (Same), was put down with a great deal of bloodshed only after thousands of troops had been brought to the colony from other parts of the Portuguese empire in Africa.

The Great Rebellion led the Portuguese to restructure their administration of the colony and weaken the role of the *liurais*. The *reinos* were abolished; the colony was now administered by *sucos*, smaller units consisting of a handful of tiny, dispersed hamlets. The *chefes de suco* were now to become the channel through which taxation and forced labour exactions were imposed, and the *chefes* were chosen locally subject to Portuguese approval. Many *liurais* continued to occupy positions of traditional authority, but the hereditary line of those who had been involved in the Great Rebellion was cut to ensure that succession fell into the hands of people more pliable to colonial interests.

During the Second World War, the Allied Command in the Pacific decided to send Australian troops to East Timor to prevent it from becoming a stepping-stone for Japanese expansionism south to Australia.

Without this intervention, the Portuguese colony might have remained neutral like Macau but the presence of Australian troops transformed East Timor into a major war zone; 20,000 Japanese troops landed and fought a bitter year-long campaign. Many hundreds of Timorese fought tenaciously alongside the Australian commandos, giving them invaluable support in a difficult terrain that neither the Australians nor the Japanese could master. When the Australian commandos were forced eventually to evacuate, the Timorese resistance continued. The Japanese forces of occupation took revenge on the Timorese for rallying to the Allied cause. Many thousands lost their lives and many more died of starvation.

Jim Dunn's account of the Allied campaign in East Timor and its devastating consequences for the Timorese people is the best available. He describes the East Timor campaign as 'one of the great catastrophes of World War Two in terms of relative loss of life.'

> The war had a devastating effect on the livelihood of the Timorese. Many farms were abandoned, especially in the fighting zones, and most of what little food production there was went in forced deliveries to the Japanese. In addition to the destruction caused by the war and by the looting of the occupiers, the Timorese had to endure devastating bombing raids by Allied aircraft operaton out of Darwin.[1]

The Australians lost forty of a total of four hundred commandos; by the end of the war; Timorese losses are estimated to have exceeded 40,000.

Immediately after the cessation of hostilities, Portuguese colonial rule was reimposed 'vigorously and at times ruthlessly, especially in those areas where loyalty to the Portuguese flag had been undermined'.[2] After the devastation of the war years, the Portuguese rebuilt some towns and villages, particularly Ermera, the centre of the coffee-growing area, as well as Dili and Baucau, but

> beyond the towns and adminstrative villages lived more than eighty per cent of the population in the hundreds of tiny hamlets, in conditions that had endured with little change since the beginning of Portuguese colonialisation.[3]

The Indonesian Republic which came into existence in 1945 never laid any claim to East Timor, nor did it challenge Portuguese colonial rule in the territory at the United Nations or elsewhere. On the contrary, during the 1950s and 1960s when Indonesia was pressing hard its claim to West Papua (West New Guinea), it made a point of denying any interest in this Portuguese-held territory and insisted that its claim to West Papua was based on the territory's former position within the Dutch East Indies. There was one short-lived uprising in East Timor against Portuguese colonialism in 1959 but this won no sympathy from Jakarta. In fact, the uprising was partly instigated by refugees from Indonesia who had been involved in a regional revolt based in Sulawesi. The uprising was ruthlessly crushed; over 150 Timorese were killed and about sixty were exiled to Angola and Mozambique.

The Struggle for Self-Determination

East Timor's protracted struggle for self-determination started after the overthrow of the Salazar regime in Portugal in April 1974. With the lifting of political repression in the colony, several political parties came into existence. The *União Democratica Timorense* (UDT) was set up in place of the ANP, the official party of the fascist regime, and had a following among the colony's small elite, high-ranking colonial officials, plantation owners and regional chieftains. Fretilin (*Frente Revolucionaria de Timor Leste Independente*) had its origins in clandestine groups in existence prior to April 1974 that were inspired by the liberation movements in Portugal's African colonies. UDT initially advocated continued association with Portugal but towards the end of 1974 it switched to a policy of supporting independence. Fretilin consistently demanded complete independence and rejected any form of special relationship either with Portugal or Indonesia. Apodeti, a party which strongly advocated integration with Indonesia, had virtually no social basis in East Timor, though its fortunes were actively promoted by the Indonesian authorities.

As these changes in political circumstances took shape in East Timor, it was clear that the Indonesian military regime viewed the prospect of an independent East Timor with deep apprehension. Although Indonesia's Foreign Minister, Adam Malik, gave Fretilin a written assurance, in June 1974, that 'independence of every country is the right of every nation, with no exception for the people of Timor' and that 'the Government and the people of Indonesia have no intention to increase or to expand their territory or to occupy other territories, other than what is stipulated in their Constitution', by September that year, Indonesia was actively intervening in East Timor's internal affairs. The Indonesian Consul in Dili was doing everything possible to promote Apodeti's fortunes while Radio Kupang in West Timor was broadcasting almost daily commentaries branding Fretilin as 'communist' and UDT as 'neo-facist'. Contradicting his earlier assurance, Foreign Minister Adam Malik declared in December 1974 that there were only two options open to East Timor, union with Indonesia or continuation of Portugal's control. The third option of independence was 'not realistic' in view of 'the backwardness and economic weakness of the population', he said.

All this was generated by the activities of Indonesia's Special Operations command, OPSUS, under its commander Major-Gen. Ali Murtopo, who set up *Operasi Komodo* (Komodo Operation)* in October 1974. This operation was aimed at creating political destabilization in East Timor through infiltration and intelligence activities. At the same time, preparations

---

* *komodo*: a giant lizard.

for a full-scale military operation were being made. Already in early 1975, military reinforcements were being sent to Indonesian West Timor for deployment along the border. West Timor was declared out of bounds to Indonesian and foreign journalists by the Indonesian High Command. In March 1974 news leaked out that a new road was being constructed linking the West Timor capital of Kupang with the border.

Early in 1975, not long after UDT switched to supporting independence, it entered into a coalition with Fretilin, aimed at pressing the Portuguese authorities to facilitate the process of decolonization and self-determination. By this time, Apodeti was totally isolated and enjoyed only the support of the authorities in Jakarta. The Indonesians then decided to try and use UDT as their vehicle by playing upon its prejudices against the far more radical Fretilin. During discussions with UDT leaders in Jakarta, Indonesian officials asserted that Indonesia could only tolerate independence for East Timor if Fretilin had first been destroyed. Persuaded by such assurances, UDT quit the coalition with Fretilin in May. Three months later they launched a coup in Dili, hoping to wrest control from the Portuguese administrators and eliminate Fretilin as a political force. But the scheme backfired. By this time Fretilin enjoyed wide support throughout the country. It had also won the support of Timorese troops in the Portuguese colonial army. After two weeks of bitter fighting, UDT was routed. Many of its leaders and members fled to West Timor, together with thousands of refugees fleeing from the areas of conflict. The Indonesians took advantage of the UDT leaders plight and forced them to sign declarations in support of integration with Indonesia before allowing them and the refugees to enter Indonesian territory.

As the political situation deteriorated during 1975, the Portuguese colonial administration in Dili received no guidance from Lisbon on how to implement the policy of decolonization that had been enshrined in Portuguese law after the April revolution in 1974. Some senior Portuguese officials in Lisbon even responded positively to Indonesian approaches, aimed at getting Lisbon to formally acknowledge that Indonesia should have a role in determining East Timor's future. In response to the political confusion in Lisbon, the Portuguese governor of East Timor and his entire staff abandoned their responsibilities, when the civil war broke out in August 1975. They quit the capital and fled to the island of Atauro. The Governor even refused to return to Dili after hostilities ceased, despite repeated calls from Fretilin leaders, who continued to regard the Portuguese administrators as being responsible for carrying out the country's decolonization. As a consequence, Fretilin found itself in *de facto* control of the country from September 1975.

With Apodeti a spent force, UDT roundly defeated and Fretilin in full control, Indonesia stepped up its military intervention. It launched a series of armed incursions across the border backed by sea and aerial bombardments of border towns in the north and south. This placed East Timor's territorial integrity under grave threat. The refusal of the Portuguese administration to return and the growing menace from Indonesia hastened Fretilin's decision to declare independence. The Democratic

Republic of East Timor was proclaimed on 28 November 1975. The establishment of this independent state would enable East Timor to issue a direct appeal to the international community for action by the United Nations to halt Indonesian aggression.

> **Declaration of Independence**
>
> Expressing the highest aspirations of the people of East Timor and to safeguard the most legitimate interests of national sovereignty, the Central Committee of Fretilin decrees by proclamation, unilaterally, the independence of East Timor, from 00.00 hours today, declaring the state of the Democratic Republic of East Timor, anti-colonialist and anti-imperialist. Long live the Democratic Republic of East Timor! Long live the people of East Timor, free and independent! Long live Fretilin!
>
> 28 November 1975

Indonesia's hostility towards the establishment of an independent East Timor stems from the military regime's perpetual paranoia over security. The prospect of sharing borders with a potentially democratic, non-aligned state was seen from the beginning as a grave threat to its own security. This was not based on the remote possibility that a tiny population might threaten Indonesia's territorial integrity, but it was feared that a neighbouring state, run along democratic lines, could set an example to people living across the border in West Timor or in other nearby Indonesian islands living under an authoritarian and brutally repressive regime.

Indonesia's interest in East Timor... indicated a deep apprehension at a possible threat to the security of the Republic which might arise from uncertain change in the adjoining colony. It is possible that the Suharto administration would have been opposed to the emergence of any independent state in succession to Portuguese rule. The advent in mid-May 1974 of a radical political movement with a measure of popular support generated an anxiety at the prospect of having to share a common border with an independent state of an unacceptable political identity. Its external affiliations could pose a challenge to Indonesia's interests through its very presence at the margin of a fissiparous archipelago.[4]

America's defeat in Indochina in April 1975 had created a situation in which Vietnam, the beneficiary of a huge arsenal of arms left behind by US troops, could be presented as a potential threat to 'stability' in South East Asia. Jakarta made good use of this in its propaganda war against East Timor and Fretilin. Frequently, baseless reports about Vietnam's links with the fast-growing independence movement were spread.

Stories about covert weapons supplies from Vietnam and Soviet submarines snooping around in the waters off East Timor abounded. There was even a report that several dozen Vietnamese troops 'disguised as Chinese' had arrived in Dili in mid-1975 to help train Fretilin troops.[5] This story also helped Jakarta's campaign to persuade UDT leaders to launch their coup in August 1975.

The new situation in South East Asia which followed the US withdrawal from Indochina helped create an atmosphere which favoured Indonesia's move against East Timor.

> All the governments in the non-communist world of importance to Indonesia, namely the Western Europeans, the United States, India, Japan and the ASEAN states, were at the outset motivated by a desire to sympathize with Jakarta's security anxieties in the uncertain aftermath of the withdrawal of the Americans from Vietnam.[6]

Western Responses

All major western governments have established close economic ties with Indonesia since the military coup in 1965. The Inter-Governmental Group on Indonesia (IGGI) was set up in 1967 on the initiative of Japan, who has become Indonesia's chief trading partner and primary source of capital investment. It has met annually in the Netherlands ever since to coordinate economic support for the military regime on the basis of the assessments and advice of the World Bank and the International Monetary Fund. The other members of the IGGI are the USA, Japan, Australia, New Zealand, Canada and almost all the Western Europe governments. The IGGI's deliberations have remained totally unaffected by Indonesia's invasion of East Timor: the level of western aid and investment steadily increased throughout the 1970s and into the 1980s.

Military support has also grown substantially since 1975, with the USA being the major western supplier. Others include Australia, the Netherlands, Britain, West Germany, France and Sweden. No country has allowed Indonesia's naked aggression to stand in the way of selling weapons, aircraft and naval vessels, as Indonesia modernizes its Armed Forces thereby strengthening their capacity to cope with a protracted war against East Timor.

The western powers most directly concerned, the USA and Australia, had made up their minds well before the invasion to give Indonesia a free hand. The communications that flowed to and from western embassies in Jakarta in July and August 1975 prove that western governments had decided to adopt a poilicy of complicity and condonation. This has continued to characterize western attitudes during the eight-year long war in East Timor. A number of confidential cables were published by G.J. Munster and J.R. Walsh in 1980.[7] Their book proved so embarrassing to the Australian Government that it was immediately impounded and withdrawn from circulation. Some of the cables it brought to light reveal just how far states like Australia, the USA and Britain were prepared to go to avoid doing anything to obstruct Indonesia's aggressive intentions.

On 17 August 1975, the Australian ambassador in Jakarta, Richard Woolcott advised the Department of Foreign Affairs in Canberra that:

> The situation in Portuguese Timor is going to be a mess for some time. From here, I would suggest that our policies should be based on disengaging ourselves as far as possible from the Timor question; getting Australians presently there out of Timor; leave events to take their course; and if and when Indonesia does intervene, act in a way which would be designed to minimise the public impact in Australia and show privately understanding to Indonesia of their problems. Perhaps we should also make an effort to secure through Parliament and the media a greater understanding of our policy, and Indonesia's, although we do not want to become apologists for Indonesia...[8]

Washington's views in mid 1975 were described in the same cable:

> (US) Ambassador Newsom told me last night that he is under instructions from Kissinger personally not to involve himself in discussions on Timor with the Indonesians on the grounds that the United States is involved in enough problems of greater importance overseas at present. The State Department has, we understand, instructed the (US) embassy to cut down its reporting on Timor... Newsom's present attitude is that the United States should keep out of the Portuguese Timor situation and allow events to take their course. His somewhat cynical comment to me was that if Indonesia were to intervene, the United States would hope they would do so 'effectively, quickly, and not use our equipment'.[9]

Of course Washington knew very well that their equipment would be used; by 1975, 90% of the military equipment being used by the Indonesian army was supplied by the USA.

The invasion actually took place a day after President Gerald Ford and Secretary of State Henry Kissinger completed a state visit to Jakarta. In fact, the invasion was postponed for a few days so as not to embarrass the visiting US head of state. Henry Kissinger told the press in Jakarta that 'the US understands Indonesia's position on the (Timor) question'.[10]

In January 1976, a US State Department official was quoted as saying:

> ... the United States wants to keep its relationship with Indonesia close and friendly. We regard Indonesia as a friendly, non-aligned state—a nation we do a lot of business with. In terms of bilateral relations between the US and Indonesia, we are more or less condoning the incursion into East Timor.[11]

An important strategic factor—control of the Ombai-Wetar Straits—has also guided Washington's support for Indonesia's seizure of East Timor. The Straits is one of four waterways linking the Indian Ocean to the Pacific, the others being the Malacca, Lombok and Sunda Straits. These straits are crucial to the Pentagon for passage by its Poseidon and Polaris nuclear submarine fleets through a zone completed dominated by the Indonesian archipelago. Jill Jolliffe has drawn attention to a paper produced in 1977 by R.G. Boyd of the Canadian Defence Department on the military importance of the Ombai-Wetar Straits.

> The Malacca and Sunda passages are not reliable because they are too shallow, and Malacca is overcrowded with sea traffic. This makes Ombai-Wetar and Lombok essential to US strategy. He rated them, with Gibraltar, as the most crucial deep-water straits in the world in American defence planning.
>
> The Ombai-Wetar Straits run within the boundaries of the former Portuguese territory of East Timor. During the Salazar dictatorship, the Pentagon had no concern about their security... Portugal's 1974 revolution aroused fears that the influence of revolutionary Portuguese officers, close to the pro-Moscow Portuguese Communist Party, might take root in an independent Timor threatening the secure passage of their submarines. This is one of the reasons the US and its regional ally Australia refused from the outset to contemplate self-deternimation for East Timor although Fretilin has consistently espoused a foreign policy of non-alignment and peaceful coexistence with Jakarta.[12]

British diplomats in Jakarta in mid-1975 adopted a similar attitude to their American and Australian counterparts. The documents published by Munster and Walsh also included a confidential letter sent by Sir John Ford, the British Ambassador in Jakarta, to the Foreign Office in London in July 1975:

> The people of Portuguese Timor are in no condition to exercise the right to self-determination... The territory seems likely to become steadily more of a problem child, and the arguments in favour of its integration into Indonesia are all the stronger. Though it still remains in our interest to steer clear of becoming involved in its future, developments in Lisbon now seem to argue in favour of greater sympathy towards Indonesia should the Indonesian Government feel forced to take strong action by the deteriorating situation in Portuguese Timor. Certainly as seen from here, it is in Britain's interest that Indonesia should absorb the territory as soon and as unobstrusively as possible, and that if it should come to the crunch and there is a row in the United Nations, we should keep our heads down and avoid taking sides against the Indonesian Government.[13]

The British Government and indeed all the governments of Western Europe have consistently pursued the policy outlined so cynically by the British ambassador more than eight years ago. Yet none has found it possible to acknowledge Indonesia's claim that an act of self-determination has ever taken place in East Timor. This rests on a petition for integration submitted by a 'People's Assembly' to the Jakarta Government in June 1976 and the preposterous claim that this assembly had been 'duly elected'.[14] The governments of Western Europe have, on the diplomatic front, found it impossible to support Indonesia's annual case in the UN when the General Assembly has voted on a resolution calling for an act of self-determination to take place in East Timor. They have chosen the path of abstaining so as to 'avoid taking sides against the Indonesian Government' while at the same time strengthening their ties with Indonesia in the real world of commerce, investment and military collaboration.

The US Government and the Question of Self-Determination in East Timor

The following exchange took place between John Holbridge, Assistant Secretary of State for East Asian and Pacific Affairs and Congressmen Solarz, Chairman of the Congressional Subcommittee on Asian and Pacific Affairs during a hearing on East Timor, held on September, 1982:

Solarz: You said in your testimony, 'We accept the incorporation of East Timor into Indonesia without recognising that a valid act of self-determination has taken place there.' Why don't you recognise that a valid act of self-determination has taken place there?

John Holbridge: Because one has not taken place, Mr Chairman. There has been no referendum or anything of that sort. On the other hand, as a practical matter, as I say, the Portuguese simply marched out and left a vacuum behind there. There was fighting that occurred before the Indonesians moved in, the Indonesians did move in and we consider that as, in fact, a fait accompli.

Solarz: Does the Government of Indonesia claim that an act of self-determination has taken place?

Holbridge: There was an act—you might say that the election of May 1982... shows an adjustment to the situation in which the people of East Timor have had a chance to participate in a democratic exercise in which they have elected four representatives from the GOLKAR (the Army-backed government party) to the National Assembly.

Solarz: Does the Government of Indonesia specifically claim that an act of self-determination has taken palce?

Holbridge: Yes.

Solarz: Our position is that one has not taken place?

Holbridge: But we don't challenge the incorporation of East Timor into Indonesia.

Solarz: You say we accept the incorporation of East Timor into Indonesia?

Holbridge: That is correct, and we have since 1976.

Solarz: Even though a valid act of self-determination has not taken place? So, my next question is, if a valid act of self-determination has not taken place, why do we accept its incorporation?

Holbridge: As I told you, as a practical matter, you are not going to find there is going to be a reversal of the situation there.

* * *

Solarz: I suspect that as a practical matter, Mr Secretary, you could say the exact same thing about Cambodia.

Holbridge: Well, in Cambodia, there was an administration that was there challenging the advent of the Vietnamese act of aggression. There was nothing similar in Timor. There was an absolute political void when the Portuguese marched out.

* * *

Solarz: Do you consider the Fretilin to be representative of the people of East Timor?

Holbridge: I wouldn't want to make any such judgement at all. I don't know who the Fretilin represents, but my guess is that they are not necessarily representative of the entire body politic of East Timor.

Solarz: But you think the opposition in Cambodia is more representative of the Cambodian people than the Fretilin is of the Timorese people?

Holbridge: Unquestionably because there has been this continuity since the very beginning.

Solarz: I have here a document from the Indonesian Embassy which says that the right to self-determination on East Timor was exercised in a free and democratic manner by the people of East Timor in accordance with their traditional practices and customs. The decision for independence through integration with the Republic of Indonesia was taken by the East Timor People's Assembly on May 31, 1976. Now, you have said that we don't recognise a valid act of self-determination has taken place there. Are we aware of this claim?

Holbridge: We are aware of that. That is an Indonesian position.

Solarz: We don't accept it?

Holbridge: I will fall back. We simply say that in our judgement, a valid act of self-determination has not occurred.

Solarz: Why isn't this valid? They say it. I am just trying to find out as a poor country boy from Brooklyn.

Holbridge: The provincial parliament was appointed by the Indonesians and was not elected.

Solarz: I see, so, in other words, this parliament was appointed after the Portuguese had left.
Holbridge: After the Indonesians had, in effect, arrived on the scene.
Solarz: And they appointed a parliament and this parliament voted for affiliation with Indonesia.
Holbridge: The provincial assembly yes.

From the Hearing of the Subcommittee on Asian and Pacific Affairs of the UN House of Representatives Committee on Foreign Affairs, 14 September, 1982.

Other Responses

At the time of the establishment of the Democratic Republic of East Timor, altogether fifteen states accorded it formal recognition. Foremost among them were the five former Portuguese colonies in Africa, Mozambique, Angola, Guinea-Bissau, Cape Verde and Sao Tome and Principe, all of whom have continued to give East Timor every possible assistance in its diplomatic struggle for the withdrawal of Indonesian troops and for an act of self-determination. The other countries which accorded recognition were Albania, Benin, Cambodia, China, Congo (Brazzaville), Guinea, the Democratic Republic of Korea, Laos, Tanzania and Vietnam.[15]

Although the UN General Assembly adopted resolutions every year, from 1975 till 1982, supporting self-determination for East Timor, the votes in favour have progressively fallen. However, the large number of abstentions means that not more than a third of UN members were prepared to support Indonesia, even seven years after its enforced integration of East Timor. Although the Soviet Union has voted against Indonesia throughout, several countries of East Europe have abstained or in more recent years, have not bothered to vote. Support for East Timor has largely come from African countries; the oil-producing states of the Middle East have generally supported Indonesia. Pacific countries have tended to support East Timor although several were persuaded in 1982 to change their votes as a result of active lobbying by the Australian delegation. Australia has voted with Indonesia since 1978. In Latin America, Brazil has supported East Timor every year, because of a shared Portuguese tradition, while several Caribbean countries have also supported East Timor, notably Cuba as well as Nicaragua and Grenada following the coming to power of progressive regimes. In 1983, Indonesia vigorously lobbied several Pacific states to counteract the growing movement of solidarity in the Pacific with liberation movements, including Fretilin.

Up until 1979, the Conference of Non-Aligned States supported East Timor but all reference to the issue was removed from the Final Declaration of the Non-Aligned Conference in 1983, held in India. The host country tends to exert a major influence over the contents of the Declaration;

India has supported Indonesia on the issue of East Timor since the very first UN vote in December 1975.

As for Indonesia's immediate neighbours in South East Asia, the countries of the ASEAN alliance, Malaysia, Thailand, the Philippines and Singapore, have with one exception voted solidly in favour of Indonesia. Singapore was the exception which cast its vote with the abstentions in December 1975, then failed to vote in 1976, but has supported Indonesia ever since.

Of all the ASEAN members, Malaysia has gone out of its way to help Indonesia in its aggressive designs on East Timor. When UDT leaders were under strong pressure from Jakarta in mid-1975 to launch a strike against Fretilin, a member of the Malaysian Government added weight to the pressure by contacting the UDT leaders and warning them that ASEAN countries would not accept the emergence of an independent state in the region that was under leftwing domination. Malaysia has also acted as the conduit for arms supplies to Indonesia in order to conceal the true origin of the equipment in question. The first occasion was in September 1975, when Indonesian troops were mounting operations against East Timor along the border with West Timor. The CIA's *National Intelligence Daily* reported on 26 September 1975 that

> Vastly increased Indonesian involvement is now proposed; special troops armed with weapons that cannot be traced to Jakarta will be used. Malaysia has reportedly agreed in principle to supply such weapons.[16]

Malaysia performed a similar service in early 1977 when it agreed to hand over at least four Sabre jets to Indonesia. The jets were in fact being supplied by Australia. Writing of this transfer, Michael Richardson reported that the Australian Government wanted the deal to be kept secret, thinking that the Sabres may be used in East Timor.[17]

2. The War

On 7 December 1975, Indonesia launched a full-scale invasion of East Timor, with a massive attack on the capital, Dili. On 8 December, the CIA's newspaper, the *National Intelligence Daily* reported:

> Indonesian troops have captured Dili, the capital of Portuguese Timor. Yesterday, marine and airborne troops equipped with US weapons mounted a full scale attack against the city.[1]

On the day of the invasion, journalists monitoring a radio post in Darwin, Australia heard the following broadcast from Fretilin's radio in Dili:

> The Indonesian forces are killing indiscriminately. Women and children are being shot in the streets. We are all going to be killed. I repeat, we are all going to be killed... This is an appeal for international help. Please do something to stop this invasion.[2]

On Christmas Day 1975, Indonesia landed a further fifteen to twenty thousand troops in Dili. The first months of Indonesia's war set the genocidal pattern which has continued to characterise the invasion of East Timor. The brutal results were soon revealed when a news report from Jakarta stated that sixty thousand East Timorese had been killed by mid-February 1976. The figure was given in a statement made on 13 February 1976 by Lopes da Cruz who had been appointed Vice-Chairman of the 'Provisional Government of East Timor' by the Indonesians.

When the invasion code-named Operasi Seroja (Operation Lotus) was lauched in 1975, the Indonesian generals expected victory in a matter of days. Now, eight years later, the national resistance, led by Fretilin and supported by virtually the entire people of East Timor has fought thirty to fifty thousand occupying Indonesian troops to a stalemate. As in other guerrilla wars, the key to Fretilin's success lies primarily in its popular support. It was this which the Indonesian generals underestimated.

The Timor Papers

In 1982, the *National Times* (Sydney) obtained access to a large range of classified US documents providing detailed information about Indonesia's war in East Timor. This material, published under the title *The Timor Papers*, appeared in two issues on 30 May – 5 June, and 6 – 12 June, 1982.

The material was drawn primarily from the Central Intelligence Agency, its military counterpart the Defence Intelligence Agency, the super-secret National Security Agency, and the State Department. Most of the extracts published appeared in the National Intelligence Daily, a newsheet published by the Director of the CIA for an elite, specially-cleared audience in Washington, and was regularly on the President's desk every morning. Under intelligence-sharing arrangements with Australia, a large part of this information was passed on to Canberra. As the *National Times* points out, much of the intercepted communications that formed the core of the US intelligence came from radio antennae at the base run by the Australian Defence Signals Directorate at Coonawarra, near Darwin.

The Timor Papers, the publication of which passed virtually unnoticed by the world's press, not only provide irrefutable evidence of Indonesia's war preparations and clandestine activities in the period leading up to its all-out invasion of East Timor. They also show how US and Australian intelligence and the governments of these two countries knew in detail about these activities. Other western governments such as the British government must also have know what was going on since they have intelligence-sharing arrangements with Australia or the USA or with both these powers.

Preparation for the Invasion

For months before the invasion took place, Indonesian troops had been waging a clandestine war against East Timor from Indonesian West Timor. The deployment of Indonesian troops along the border area was first noticed in August 1975. By that time, the Indonesian generals had already decided that a speedy military invasion of East Timor was the only way to annex East Timor and prevent its emergence as a free democratic and independent state. The destabilization activities of *Operasi Komodo*, started in 1974 by Major-General Ali Murtopo, were failing to produce the desired results. The rapid growth in support for Fretilin in contrast to UDT's declining popularity and the virtual elmination of the pro-Indonesian Apodeti frustrated the intelligence operation's objectives.

Pressure was mounting among the Indonesian generals for an immediate invasion. According to Hamish McDonald, leading generals, among them the Minister of Defence, General Panggabean, Deputy Chief of the Armed Forces, Lieutenant-General Surono, and intelligence chief, Major-General Benny Murdani, were urging President Suharto to order an invasion.[3] The decision certainly rested with Suharto but he was not yet ready to give his approval. He knew only too well that his Armed Forces were heavily dependent on military supplies from the West; he needed to be sure that reactions of countries that were major military suppliers, such as the USA and Australia, would be muted enough to safeguard future supplies.

Fretilin's swift and decisive victory only a few weeks after the UDT launched its coup in Dili on 11 August was the final blow for *Operasi Komodo*. The chances of limiting Indonesia's role to one of political intervention had been eliminated; military invasion was now the only alternative. The plans for this had already been laid, as is clear from a report contained in the CIA's *National Intelligence Daily* on 29 August 1975:

> Indonesia's preparation for an invasion, originally discussed by Suharto and his military commanders on 8 August, now are expected to be complete by 31 August. The plan calls for a three-pronged attack on the north coast of the island.
>
> Two battalions are to launch a combined assault against Dili. The larger force of some 6,000 infantry will land at Atapupu in Indonesian Timor and then drive north into the Portuguese half of the island. One battalion will also land to secure the coastal strip extending eastward from Dili to Tutuala on the eastern tip of the island. The forces then are to link up and secure control of the complete north coast from Atapupu to Tutuala.
>
> The Indonesians expect some stiff resistance, but are confident they will be successful. Once the north coast of the island is secured, the Indonesian plan to withdraw most of their regular forces. They also plan to leave commando units of ethnic Timorese to establish control over the central part of the island to contend with any guerrilla units that may be operating there.[4]

Creeping Military Operations

From the end of August until the Indonesian invasion was launched on 7 December, Indonesian troops were engaged in a number of military operations across the border from West Timor, under the guise of counter-attacks by UDT and Apodeti forces. As these operations intensified, naval and aerial bombardments were launched against regions on the East Timor side of the border. Already on 13 September, the CIA daily report was declaring:

> Meanwhile, an Indonesian press report says that western districts of the territory (of East Timor) have proclaimed merger with Indonesia. This is the area where Indonesian special forces are taking control of towns with the intention of handing them over to Indonesian-trained Timorese refugees.[5]

During the following weeks, reports of heavy fighting in the border region regularly appeared in the press. Subsequent accounts of this period generally suggest that the military operations commenced in early or mid October, although in fact they had already begun by the beginning of September. A report of the earliest fighting became available recently when a Timorese refugee, Neobere, who had participated in the resistance in the southern border region of Suai, gave the following account:

> In the border region of the Suai district where I was (near the south coast), the Indonesian troops started coming across the border already in September. They used bazookas and hand-grenades and burnt down houses. They entered the towns—Tilomar for instance—and shot people. Some Fretilin soldiers, members of Falintil (the armed forces of Fretilin), were shot dead in these encounters. The Indonesians came across at night and returned to Indonesian territory the next morning. A man I knew named Manuel was killed on 18 September.
>
> In fact, I even remember an incident in the area before the beginning of September when some Indonesian soldiers were killed. I captured documents from an Indonesian soldier at the time. In that encounter, two Fretilin soldiers and four Indonesians were killed. So you see, throughout September and October, there was heavy fighting.[6]

While these military operations were in progress, Indonesia's propaganda and lobby machinery was accelerated. Leading newspapers in Jakarta joined in a campaign slandering Fretilin as 'communist terrorists', claiming that Fretilin only controlled Dili and Baucau, and asserting that it was completely isolated by UDT and Apodeti troops. The propaganda campaign was then injected with more sensationalist claims which suggested Vietnamese and Chinese involvement in East Timor. On the 28 September, Associated Press reported the Commander of the Java and

Bali (Second) Territorial Defence Command (Kowilhan II), General Widodo's statement that Fretilin's skill with modern weapons indicated that it had received outside assistance.[7] Foreign journalists also began to pick up these fabricated lies. An Australian commentator, Dennis Warner wrote on 5 September:

> The Indonesians believe, whether rightly or wrongly, that some Chinese communists who fled from Indonesia in the bloodbath that followed the September 30 affair in 1965 have established themselves in Portuguese Timor as a springboard for new adventures in the archipelago.[8]

Rumours deliberately fostered by Jakarta had convinced many people that after the military takeover in 1965, many members of the Indonesian Armed Forces who were supporters of the former President Sukarno had gone into hiding in the jungles of East Java, and had managed to get to East Timor and join forces with Fretilin after their victory in August 1975.

Why did President Suharto delay the invasion of East Timor until 7 December? Why was the period from the end of August when Fretilin assumed complete control of the country up to early December marked only by military operations and provocations across the border? Is it true, as some observers believe, that Suharto was showing a reluctance to pursue the option of all-out military invasion, that he was, as it were, withstanding the 'hawkish' demands of his generals? The answer lies firstly in the fragile position of Indonesia's Armed Forces with regard to its military equipment, and its total reliance on supplies from abroad. On 8 September, the CIA reported:

> Suharto is also concerned about the impact on Indonesia's bilateral relations with Australia and the US. In both cases, he is worried about the loss of military assistance which he badly wants to improve Indonesia's outdated equipment.[9]

Suharto therefore needed to proceed with caution so as to ensure at least the silent approval of the major western powers. He needed to be sure that military action would not endanger future military supplies. His cautious approach was characteristic of the political cunning he used to undermine and destroy President Sukarno's position following the events of late 1965, when the military under Suharto took power.

The border incidents were also an integral part of the preparations being made by the Indonesian general staff for the invasion, under Suharto's guidance. Troops occupying towns in the border region were expected to join up with the troops that would be landed farther east along the north coast when Suharto considered such landings opportune.

On 7 October, elite Indonesian troops moved into the northern border village of Batugade. The operation was led by Colonel Dading Kalbuadi who later took command of Indonesia's second invasion of East Timor in 1977. On 14 October, Indonesian troops launched an artillery and rocket attack; this time, the important regional centre of Maliana was assaulted. Two days later Balibo, some miles to the north was attacked. During this attack five television journalists from Australia were killed by Indonesian troops. The journalists' murder was picked up by the international press and produced widespread outrage; yet the Australian government made no protest. Revelations since then have proved conclusively that both Australian and American intelligence were closely monitoring events along the border and knew precisely what was going on. As neither the border operations nor the murder of the journalists led to protests by western powers, Suharto could feel confident there would be no international outcry.

CIA reports, monitoring events in East Timor, reveal that Indonesian military operations continued relentlessly throughout November, and are evidence that the US administration was kept informed daily. The following are some of the highlights from the CIA's monitoring service:

October 17: All Indonesian forces in the area were recently subordinated to a Joint Task Force Command, and the 'exercise' cover for the buildup has been abandoned.

October 18: Indonesian troops... have succeeded in occupying five border towns... Fretilin forces are putting up stiff resistance. The commander of the force has asked for reinforcements and a helicopter gunship to provide air support...

October 20: Indonesian commanders are continuing to complain about the poor quality of their supporting fire. An intercepted message revealed... that 70% of the Indonesian mortars were duds. The Indonesian high command has approved the commitment of another infantry battalion... (T)he loose naval blockade around the island should soon begin to have an effect on the Timorese...

October 24: By early last week, Indonesia had massed about 3,500 troops along the border. Some 1,500—supported at times by a B-26 bomber, a C-47 gunship and a few armed helicopters—attacked a number of Fretilin-held towns.

October 28: A second infantry battalion from Java has been dispatched to Timor. Jakarta has consistently underestimated the strength of the Timorese leftists, and further reinforcements may be necessary.

October 31: Despite increasingly visible military activities, Jakarta continues to deny its involvement... President Suharto remains concerned about international reaction...

November 6: The Indonesian combined task forces commander [Colonel Dading Kalbuadi]... plans to establish a supply base in Indonesian Timor in anticipation of heavier fighting and a lengthy military campaign. He has requested provisions and ammunition for a force of 13,000 allied Timorese partisans and Indonesian troops for a two- to three-month operation.

November 7: Indonesia has had increasing difficulties in maintaining a low profile on Timor as its limited military intervention there has expanded... Indonesian forces now control most of the border area and at least five towns inside Portuguese Timor and they are attempting to consolidate their positions.

November 26: After nearly five weeks of inactivity because of heavy rain. Indonesian air and naval units began bombarding several towns on the Portuguese side of the island. Ground forces simultaneously launched attacks and reportedly have captured Fatularan about five miles south of Atabae which is still in Fretilin hands.[10]

In fact, Atabae had been under attack since the middle of November. The situation there had become so serious by 24 November that the Fretilin central command addressed an urgent appeal to the UN Security Council and to world leaders including the Foreign Ministers of Papua New Guinea and Australia:

We inform you that the Indonesian forces with the support of eleven warships and approximately ten aircraft and infantry forces have attacked the border zone of Atabae for the past five days. The area is still under Fretilin control but the situation has reached crisis point today.[11]

The world community ignored this plea, just as they had refused to respond to the acts of aggression that Indonesia had already committed.

Faced with this serious military situation and in an attempt to strengthen its international position, East Timor was declared independent on 28 November. The fact that Indonesia had its invasion plans ready immediately is evident from a report in the US *National Intelligence Daily*, 1 December:

According to a reliable source, Indonesia will not initiate large-scale military action against Portuguese Timor until after President Ford completes his visit on December 7.[12]

To save the US President the embarrassment of visiting a close ally openly engaged in aggression, the invasion was postponed a few days. When President Ford was asked in Hawaii, the day after leaving Jakarta, for his reaction to the invasion of East Timor, '...he smiled and said: "We'll talk about that later." '[13]

James Dunn aptly analysed western response to Indonesia's brutal aggression:

...the forces against (the Timorese people) were not merely a paranoid group of Indonesian generals. The Timorese were unknowns, innocents, in a cynical world in which the fortunes of the weak and unimportant mattered little. In Washington, Tokyo, or

Canberra, the issue of the rights of the Timorese, it seemed, paled into insignificance when compared with the perceived aims and aspirations of Indonesia, an important player in the international power game.[14]

The First Period of the War

Indonesia's war against the people of East Timor can be divided into three periods. The first period lasted from December 1975 until August 1977, the second from September 1977 until mid-1983 while the third period commenced in August 1983.

The invasion of East Timor was the biggest military operation ever to have been mounted by the Indonesian Armed Forces. Elite troops were used in each initial assault, and regular troops were brought in to establish control and pacify an area. The elite troops deployed consisted of the red-beret Kopassandha para-commandos, the Marines with violet berets and the Air Forces' Kopasgat, the rapid deployment troops, who wear orange berets. Two Javanese territorial divisions also sent troops to East Timor, the West Java Siliwangi Division and the East Java Brawijaya Division.

An Indonesian writing shortly after the invasion was launched said that

> In the early hours of that day (7 December), fifteen Indonesian aircraft left their base in Jogjakarta, Central Java. Nine were bound for Dili, six for Baucau. At the border area, the 3,500 Indonesian troops under the disposal of Colonel Dading started to move in two directions overland in coordination with the paratroopers landing in Dili and Baucau, one direction pushing from Atabae where support troops could be provided by naval transport, the other went to Atsabe moving to Dili.[15]

Major-General Benny Murdani, then chief of Armed Forces intelligence, was the man responsible for the detailed preparations of *Operasi Seroja*. David Jenkins reported that in August 1975,

> when the non-military options had not been exhausted, Suharto was treated to a full-dress briefing by the then defence minister, General Maraden Panggabean, on how Indonesia proposed to subjugate East Timor. There were maps and charts on every wall of the briefing room, as well as details of the tides and where the various units would land.
>
> Suharto, somewhat taken aback, asked Panggabean who had prepared all these plans, only to be told it was Benny. The president shook his head. 'Benny!' he exclaimed. 'If you listen to Benny, you'll be in a war every day.'[16]

Eight years later, Murdani, now a full general and Commander-in-Chief of the Armed Forces, launched Indonesia's third all-out offensive against East Timor.

The 1975 invasion consisted of a series of landings and assaults, on Dili, Baucau, Liquica and Maubara on the north coast, on Los Palos in the east, and on Suai in the south, near the border with West Timor. There was a steady build-up in troop numbers, several thousand on the first day, and ten or fifteen thousand more by the end of 1975. According to the Australian MP, Ken Fry, who testified before the UN Security Council on 14 April 1976, Australian intelligence put the number of Indonesian troops in East Timor at the time at 32,000 plus another 10,000 being held in reserve in West Timor.

Yet, despite the huge number of troops, backed by sea and air strikes, the Indonesians made very slow progress. The US Defence Intelligence Agency on 13 February 1976 referred to 'several months of advancing into Eastern Timor at a snail's pace'.[17] After four months of heavy fighting, the invading forces had only gained control of the major towns and some regional centres and villages and had established corridors connecting these pockets of occupation. By August 1976, eight months after the first all-out strike, areas under Indonesian occupation consisted of several corridors, none of which provided safe travel for the Indonesian troops; movement between occupied centres could only take place under heavy armed escort.

Position of Invasion Forces in August 1976

Shaded ribbons indicate Indonesian control of roads and villages along those roads. Indonesian positions were subject to frequent guerrilla attacks by the East Timorese forces.

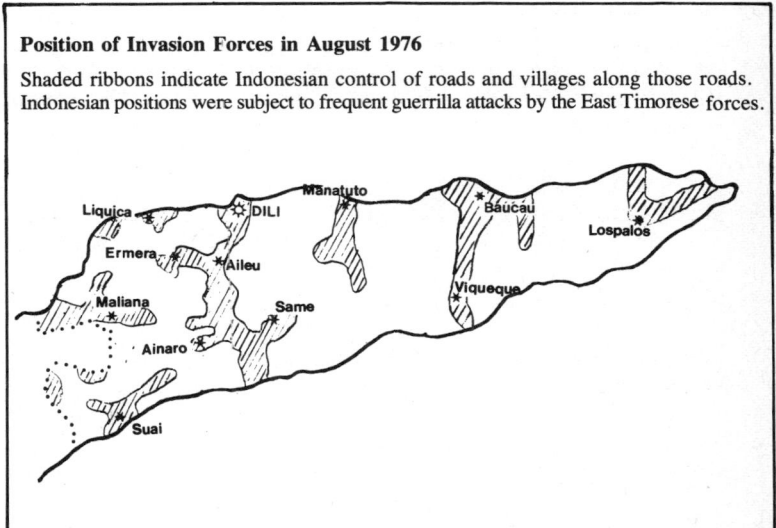

As a military operation, *Operasi Seroja* was a disaster. US defence planners later spoke of the military performance of their Indonesian allies as 'woeful'. From the very beginning, the operation was marred by lack of coordination and a series of miscalculations. Some Kopassandha troops were dropped short and fell into the sea where they drowned under the weight of their heavy equipment. Others were shelled on the coast from Indonesian naval vessels.

> *Operasi Seroja*... turned out (to be) a clumsy exercise which caused great civilian suffering and vastly worsened already large diplomatic problems for Jakarta. The first operations test of the new integrated armed forces structure, it was marked by poor co-ordination and showed up serious deficiencies in the discipline, training and equipment of some of Indonesia's best units. Kostrad (Strategic Army Command) Eighteenth Brigade troops were dropped on top of Fretilin forces withdrawing from the town (Dili), instead of behind to block off their retreat. After taking heavy casualties from Fretilin, the paratroops then came under fire from an Indonesian marine force driving inland. The remnants of the paratroops then rampaged through the town, killing and looting at random.[18]

During the first months of 1976, it was clear that Falintil forces had survived the massive onslaught and were reassessing their military strategy. In May and June many battles were fought, villages were captured and recaptured, in the north-west, in the Suai area and around Laklubar. Meanwhile the failure of the Indonesian military adventure had become increasingly clear to a number of well-informed observers. The Institute for Strategic Studies in London commented:

> If Fretilin can find the psychological resources, the military skills and popular support to sustain guerrilla warfare, Indonesian forces may find themselves engaged in a lengthy and difficult campaign.[19]

As events turned out, Fretilin was successful in all areas for a considerable time to come.

The casualties among Indonesian troops grew enormously. Fretilin's Radio Maubere, which was then regularly beaming reports abroad, claimed that during the period, 20 January to 3 April, 845 Indonesian soldiers were killed. In a letter from Indonesia, dated 7 April 1976, written by an Indonesian opponent of the war, the following picture of the effect of the war on Indonesian troops was given:

> Actually it (the war) is no secret any more in Indonesia, especially in Jakarta where the Army hospital (*Rumah Sakit Gatot Subroto*) and the Air Force Hospital in the Halim airbase is (sic) overflowed with war victims. And what makes it more tragic is that the families— even their wives—are not allowed to visit their husbands in hospital. At the same time, news that many Indonesian soldiers were killed by

the Timorese is just trickling down in Jakarta and whole (sic) Java. So, knowing that your husband, son or father has to go to Timor is nearly as shocking as a death/trial penalty.[20]

Falintil, which came into existence only half a year before the invasion, had gained enormous experience resisting Colonel Dading's covert operations across the border during the closing months of 1975. It had become conditioned to artillery, mortar and rocket-fire. It had also gained vital experience in the guerrilla warfare suitable to their territorial conditions. Although none of Falintil's commanders had been trained professionally in military strategy or tactics, they quickly emerged as dedicated, skilled and inspiring leaders of a people's army. The present Fretilin leader, Kay·Rala Xanana gives an account of this period of the war in a message sent to the United Nations on 14 October 1982.

The glorious Falintil combatted the enemy offensive while the people of East Timor actively participated in the resistance war, whenever possible with traditional weapons. Because of its superior numbers and weapons, the enemy was able to control the villages of the north coast, whose population were prevented from leaving. The enemy also cordoned off the corridors Dili-Betano and Baucau-Viqueque. A few villages fell under the control of the Indonesians, who repopulated them with people captured during military operations. They then moved to control the corridors Dili-Bobonaro and Lautem-Los Palos.

The powerful enemy, who came full of force and pride began to find a series of obstacles affecting his ambitious design of annexation, faced with the determination and courage of the armed Maubere* people who inflicted heavy casualties on their enemy and repelled them with tenacity when they raided Maubere bases. Poor planning by the militarist Jakarta regime, confronted by the tenacious resistance of the Maubere people, left them trying to find a solution to justify their weakness in face of their anxiety to impose domination.[21]

In 1976, a non-Fretilin source confirmed this assessment. In a report that reached the outside world from Indonesian Catholic relief sources, it was stated that beyond the towns and villages occupied by Indonesian military forces, there was no man's land 'where security is not guaranteed because of Fretilin raids'. About 150,000 people were estimated to be under Indonesian control in the occupied areas while some 500,000 were living in the eighty per cent of the country outside Indonesian control.[22]

Meanwhile enormous domestic difficulties prevented the military

---

* *Maubere people*: Mau Bere is a common Mambai name, held in contempt in colonial days. Fretilin adopted it as the name for the people of East Timor, turning contempt into pride.

government in Jakarta from stepping up operations in East Timor. In early 1976, it became public knowledge that the state petroleum company Pertamina had defaulted on a number of short-term debts, pushing it to the verge of bankruptcy. The financial crisis provoked by a ten billion dollar debt, incurred by the company's free-wheeling director, General Ibnu Sutowo, required months of negotiation before a rescue operation was agreed to by major financial institutions in the West. At the same time, growing criticism of corruption at the highest levels of the regime caused serious internal divisions within Jakarta's ruling elite.

> ### Indonesian Morale
>
> Further evidence of Indonesian setbacks comes from a recent American visitor to Indonesia who held extensive, informal conversations with officers in the Armed Forces of Indonesia.
>
> 'Military men say that Indonesian troops are reluctant to leave Dili, particularly after dark,' the visitor noted. 'Officers relax in European-style cafes, rather than lead assaults into Fretilin-held territory. Troop morale is low, and the officers know it. Fretilin forces have been tougher than anyone ever expected, and casualties have been heavy on the Indonesian side. 'Families of soldiers killed and wounded in East Timor receive no pensions; to keep news of the war from the Indonesian public, no military funerals are held; families of the wounded are discouraged from visiting their loved ones in the military hospitals.'
>
> My sources say that a demonstration of war widows was recently held at the home of the mayor of Jakarta, demanding compensation for the loss of their husbands. The wives have no choice; starvation is the only other choice for them and their families.
>
> All told, according to Indonesian military men, the invasion of East Timor has been a real fiasco, worse than anyone thought.
>
> Arnold Kohen, *Timor Information Project* (US),
> 16 November 1976

In contrast the pattern of armed Timorese resistance began to change after the first six months of fighting. In May 1976, Fretilin was able to convene a nation-wide congress to discuss the war situation, at which it was concluded that it would be suicidal to continue to engage in frontal combat against the numerically superior and much better equipped Indonesian army units. As a result the leadership decided to switch to more appropriate guerrilla tactics. It soon became evident to Indonesia's military leaders that clear-cut victory by means of ground combat was unattainable. Fretilin's guerrilla tactics could be sustained indefinitely because of the wide-spread popular support it enjoyed and the favourable geographic conditions for such warfare. Victory for the invaders could only be won at the cost of literally exterminating the country's entire population. This would require a totally different operation than the one which had already killed tens of thousands of Timorese. The Indonesian Armed Forces were forced to reassess their military and political strategy which led to a new phase of the war from mid-1977.

The Second Period of the War

In order to launch a new offensive against continuing Fretilin resistance, Indonesia needed massive supplies of military equipment, in particular counter-insurgency aircraft. As retired US Rear Admiral Gene R. La Roque has said, the delivery of OV10 Bronco planes in 1976 and 1977 from the USA 'changed the entire nature of the war'.[23] In addition to the 16 Broncos that were delivered as the new offensive got under way, Washington supplied three Lockheed C-130 transport aircraft and 45 Cadillac Cage V-150 Commando armoured cars, which carry up to 12 combat troops and are each equipped with machine-guns, an 81mm mortar, a 20mm cannon, and smoke and tear-gas launchers. US war deliveries also included M-16 rifles, pistols, mortars, machine-guns, recoilless rifles and extensive communications equipment. These deliveries contributed significantly to the military successes of the Indonesian Armed Forces in their 1977-79 offensive, spreading death and disaster among the people.

As far as the Indonesian troops were concerned, tens of thousands of whom were to be used during the 1977-79 offensive, the question of morale was a continuing problem. Major-General Benny Murdani candidly admitted to a Western diplomat that due to the unpopularity of the war, most units were rotated quickly, spending only two to four months in East Timor.[24] But as an incentive there was the chance of quicker promotion for those having served in the East Timor campaign. In addition, promotions were to be had, as Fretilin leaders were later to report, in return for acts of savagery against the Timorese population. Extra allowances were also given to troops, while there were plenty of opportunities to profit from petty corruption and the exploitation of the Timorese under their military control. For all the hardships, East Timor offered the enterprising soldier many attractions.

Indonesia's second military invasion of East Timor consisted of three massive offensives lasting from September 1977 until March 1979. For 18 months the population of East Timor were the victims of a campaign of encirclement and annihilation. The operation commenced with a major offensive in the border and coastal regions, which moved inwards towards the centre of the country, using ground troops on a huge scale to undertake search and destroy operations against the population in the mountainous regions after aerial bombardment had pulverized the area.

The encirclement and annihilation campaign had two objectives: to destroy the Fretilin leadership; and to force the population living in the mountainous interior to abandon their homes and make for the lowlands, thus coming under Indonesian control. This was to be achieved by the destruction of the agricultural system that had remained intact since before the first invasion of 1975. Indonesian claims that most people were forced to accompany Fretilin into the interior are absurd: the vast majority of Timorese peasants had always lived in the mountains although thousands more from the lowland towns and villages joined them as Indonesian troops advanced during the earlier stage of the war.

The first phase of the 18-month offensive was preceded by President Suharto's much-publicized amnesty offer to resistance fighters, during his speech to mark Indonesia's independence day on 17 August. The operations launched in September 1977 were under the command of Major-General Benny Murdani, the man who had plotted and commanded the first invasion in 1975. The other constant figure in military operations against East Timor, Dading Kalbuadi, was now a Brigadier-General in command of the XVIth Regional Command based in Bali including the East Timor military command. The East Timor commander was Colonel Sinaga, who earned the nickname, 'the black god', for his acts of brutality.

Military operations during the first phase were concentrated in the South Border Area of Bobonaro and the North West Sector of Liquica. A journalist from *Paris Match*, Denis Reichle, who managed to get across to the border region from West Timor, reported that 30,000 troops were engaged in the operations and that they 'were "systematically wiping out" the populations of villages largely known or suspected to be Fretilin supporters and destroying Fretilin supply lines and sources.'[25] On his return to Indonesian Timor, Reichle was arrested by Indonesian troops, his cameras and film destroyed, and deported.

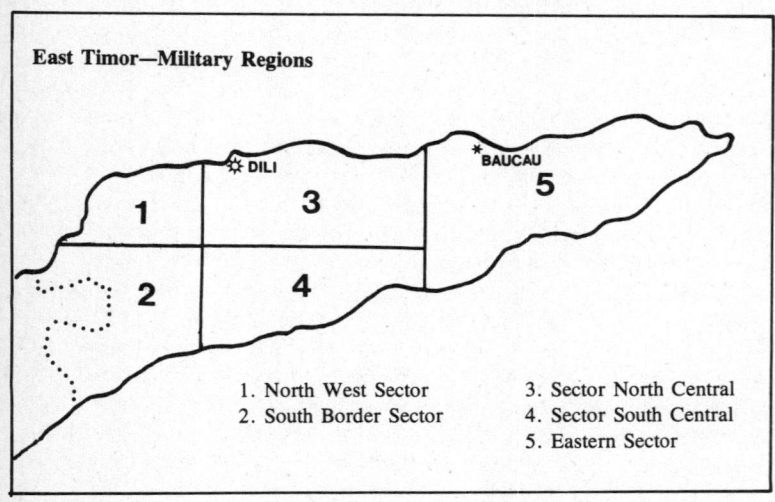

Kay Rala Xanana, the Fretilin leader, described this period of the war:

> ...they sent 50 battalions, with berets of all colours, from commandos to infantry, from paratroopers to marines, and with a whole diversity of material, from AR-15 and MU-2 and Kalashnikov rifles, from light Herstal to heavy rocket mortars, cannons and bazookas, to tanks and armoured cars and helicopters, anti-guerrilla aircraft and ships. They began the destruction of the support bases, where the popular resistance was consolidated against the invaders.[26]

Heavy pounding from the air and the sea continued for several months: Indonesian ground troops kept up their operations against the Fretilin support bases even after the wet season commenced in November. The support bases consisted of hundreds of small agricultural plots which provided food and other essential supplies for the beleaguered Timorese in the mountains. In November 1977, the South Border Sector became the centre of Indonesian operations, and in January 1978, new attacks were launched in the North West Sector. On 15 January, Radio Maubere reported that fierce fighting was taking place in the Liquica-Bazartete area along the north coast, and in the Aileu and Same regions south of Dili. The aim of the Indonesian operations was to drive the population in the border areas eastward and push the population in the southern coastal area northwards so as to encircle them and to herd them into the concentration camps that became the central feature of Indonesia's radical recasting of population patterns and control.

Although the first campaign inflicted heavy casualties on the population, the military objective remained unachieved. Radio Maubere reported on 19 January 1978 that Indonesian troops had failed to capture extensive liberated areas estimated to contain between 150,000 and 200,000 Timorese people in one of the country's most densely populated regions. Fretilin also reported that some 2,000 Indonesian troops were put out of action while 2,000 Timorese civilians were killed in intensive air, naval and land bombardment of the area. The attempted encirclement had been defeated 'because the Timorese fought with all weapons available and escaped to a "safe place".' At the same time however, hundreds of Timorese were captured.[27] Later reports indicated that Fretilin forces had even been able to re-capture a number of strategic positions in the Fatululic region (South Border Sector). Moreover the wet season was by now in full swing, making conditions unfavourable for Indonesian troops to continue operations on the ground.

In May 1978, as soon as the dry season commenced, a new military operation was launched, concentrated in the area south of Dili, most of which was still in Fretilin hands. This time, the operation was under the direct command of General Yusuf, who had been appointed the previous month as Minister of Defence and Commander-in-Chief of the Armed Forces. A loyal Suharto man, General Yusuf had spend twelve years out of active service as Minister of Industries. He was appointed to lead the Armed Forces in Suharto's new Cabinet, formed at the start of his third term as President, in March 1978. General Yusuf's return to active service took everyone by surprise; no one connected it at the time with the East Timor operations yet he had considerable field experience and had successfully directed the military campaign against the Kahar Muzakar rebellion in South Sulawesi in the early 1960s. However General Yusuf played a major role in East Timor operations throughout his term of office until March 1983. The notable failure of the operation launched in September 1977 under Major-General Benny Murdani and Brigadier-General Dading Kalbuadi had apparently convinced Suharto that a more competent officer was needed to take charge.

The changeover in Armed Forces leadership immediately led to a vigorous programme to re-equip and modernize the Armed Forces. As military operations in East Timor intensified, a deal with British Aerospace for the purchase of eight ground-attack Hawk aircraft was concluded. The deal, signed in April 1978, was welcomed by the company's director as 'superb news' and 'a real breakthrough into the Southeast Asia market'.[28] A month later, US Vice-President Walter Mondale visited Jakarta to finalize details of the sale of sixteen A-4 Skyhawk aircraft to Indonesia. Even as war was raging in East Timor, Mondale felt able to commend the military rulers of Indonesia on their human rights record because they had at last decided to implement a programme to release tens of thousands of political prisoners who had been held for nearly 13 years without trial. 'Warplanes have been bartered for political prisoners,' wrote the *TAPOL Bulletin* in June 1978. 'East Timor is ignored.' The A-4 Skyhawk was the mainstay of the US arsenal in the Indo-China War. It is particularly suited for bombing missions against guerrillas and the capacity to spray wide areas with weapon fire and high explosives, causing high civilian casualties. At the same time Dutch shipyards were building three corvettes for delivery to Indonesia in 1979 and 1980; the Dutch government ignored the insistent demands of many groups in Holland that the corvette deal be cancelled because of the continuing carnage in East Timor. Australia also stepped up the supply of military aircraft to Indonesia in 1978. In March, the government announced a gift of twelve Bell Sioux helicopters, plus facilities for the training of twenty-four Indonesian servicemen in Australia for the operation and upkeep of these aircraft. Three months later, in June, it was announced that six Nomad Searchmaster planes, fitted with ground and sea surveillance radar would be given to Indonesia, in addition to six previously donated. A year before, Australian parliamentarian Ken Fry warned that Searchmasters were being used in East Timor 'for "offensive surveillance" to search out Fretilin'.[29] In September 1980, the French Foreign Minister, de Guiringaud visited Jakarta to arrange for sales of military aircraft and other military equipment to Indonesia and for the eventual establishment of a plant to manufacture light automatic weapons.

The second encirclement and annihilation campaign commenced with a major build-up of troops in East Timor, in May 1978. There was an added urgency to this campaign as preparations were under way for Suharto to make his first visit to East Timor. This visit was intended to be a public assertion of Indonesia's control of the territory, two and a half years after the invasion. Suharto planned to visit Dili and Maliana, near the border with West Timor. The first major attack in this stage of the campaign took place in Lekidoe, ten miles south of the capital, on 13 June. Eight days later operations spread to the villages of Remexio, eight miles south-east of Dili. Yusuf had 15,000 fresh troops at his disposal, and quickly succeeded in taking control of the Fretilin-held village of Remexio, though fighting continued in the immediate vicinity well into July.

The Suharto visit took place on 16-17 July. He arrived in East Timor in a DC-10, a mammoth aircraft which had never previously been used in presidential visits to other parts of the country.[30] Baucau airfield had been greatly expanded to provide facilities for major aerial operations since Indonesia took control in December 1975. Besides an impressive array of senior government and military officials, Suharto was accompanied by the largest group of journalists ever to have joined a regional visit of this nature. Yet, the military authorities were far from satisfied with security conditions in East Timor for none of the journalists was permitted to leave Dili. As for Suharto, he briefly visited Maliana, returned to Dili and flew back to Jakarta, all within a day.

Two months later conditions in Remexio received international attention as the result of a visit by a group of foreign diplomats, including the US ambassador, Edward Masters in September 1978. Reporter David Jenkins who accompanied the visit described the results of the Indonesian operations in the following terms:

> In Remexio, as in most other towns, the people are stunned, sullen and dispirited. Emaciated as a result of deprivation and hardship, they are struggling to make sense of the nightmarish interlude in which as much as half of the population has been uprooted.[31]

He described the inhabitants as 'undernourished and desperately in need of medical attention. Many have come in from the surrounding hills where they barely survived on tapioca, leaves and poisonous berries'.[32] Although during this trip to Remexio, outsiders were given a brief glimpse of appalling conditions which the latest Indonesian operations had inflicted on the population, it was more than a year later before anything was done, with the help of international relief agencies, to alleviate the suffering. Security conditions in East Timor were still far too unsatisfactory for the Indonesian military to allow any external intervention.

The September 1978 Attack

The third and final stage of the encirclement and annihilation campaign began in September 1978. This time the area of concentration was the Matabian mountain range, south-east of Baucau and the lowland coastal plain of Natarbora to the west. An East Timorese refugee now living in Australia provided a comprehensive account of the operations in Matabian:

> The Indonesian campaign of encirclement and annihilation at Mount Matabian began around September 1978. Some 16 Indonesian battalions were involved. East Timorese civilians were obliged to walk in front of the advancing Indonesian troops. Fretilin leaders in the area were aware that the operation was about to begin... (They) advised the population of its imminence. The population was invited to go to the protected areas or to remain where they were. A very large number (according to this source, 140,000) chose to go to the protected areas. Many of this number eventually moved on to the Matabian Range where Fretilin had organised an extensive food store.
>
> Indonesian forces moved towards Matabian from a number of surrounding points. Frontline Fretilin forces... reported the burning of abandoned villages and surrounding food crops by the Indonesian troops. Fretilin forces resisted the advance from the base of Mount Matabian; the population remained behind the lines on the mountain. Indonesian forces employed naval and aerial bombardment of the mountain itself as well as the base. Direct fighting continued for some weeks, but by the end of November 1978, Fretilin forces had suffered many losses and morale was low. They retreated on to the mountain.
>
> Indonesian forces broke through the mountain defences and the population began to move off the mountain. A large number were captured at this time. Once off the mountain, there was no food for the resistance or the population. Because of this depletion of their forces and continued Indonesian bombardment, Fretilin leaders advised the population to surrender. Many refused and insisted on staying with the East Timorese troops. Many did surrender.[33]

Another Timorese refugee who testified before the Australian Senate Inquiry *in camera* gave a moving account of life in Fretilin-controlled areas during this period of intensive Indonesian operations:

> It was necessary to leave the villages in the daytime to hide from the aeroplanes that would drop bombs. The land would shake because of the bombs dropping, there was noise all the time and the bombs would make huge holes in the ground.
>
> So in the morning at first light we would move back into the hills leaving behind the old and sick who could run no more. Pregnant women kept running, only stopping to give birth, and then they would continue to run. Sometimes even during the night we would be woken up and have to move back into the bush.
>
> It was the bombs that weakened the resistance. They dropped every day. 1978 was the worst year. Aeroplanes flew from 8am till

midday and then again in the afternoon. Firstly an aeroplane came to check; if there was any smoke, a couple of minutes later the bombers would come and drop bombs, wiping out whole villages. We wouldn't go back to a village once it had been bombed because there was no more shelter.[34]

According to a priest who was with the resistance in this area up to the last, there were two major concentrations of population, many of them people who had escaped encirclement during earlier Indonesian operations farther to the west. About 30,000 people were contained within the Matabian mountain range, and 60,000 more were in the Natarbora plain. They were hemmed in by Indonesian troops approaching from the west, the north and the east. Falintil troops in Natarbora were under Mau Lear and Sahe, and in the east, they were under Xanana, based in Matabian.

The main Indonesian attack was launched against Matabian which was strongly defended. During the first weeks of the campaign, Indonesia sustained heavy losses; according to people who were in the region at the time, five battalions were destroyed. But the Matabian base, the last support base to be defended, fell on 22 November. Natarbora, which was not defended, was overrun by Indonesian troops in December, 1978. By this time, the food situation was desperate and sickness was widespread, so the encircled population had no alternative but to surrender.

Many guerrillas were captured and killed during the 'mopping up operations' that lasted until March 1979. There was a great slaughter of Fretilin Central Committee members and activists and of Falintil commanders and members. The death toll among the people herded into camps in conditions of great distress was very high indeed.

A 'Difficult and Pitiful Period'

It was not until November 1978 that the vandal occupiers were able to destroy the last remaining resistance of the Maubere people on the tip of the island.

This was a painful period for the Maubere people! With their land burnt, their homes destroyed, their possessions plundered, their animals machine-gunned, the Maubere people, in their great and heroic march for the defence of their country, also saw their children, their invalids, their elderly become a human column massacred by constant bombardment and strafing from the air. But rather than surrender, these people were determined.to die for their sacred native land. Disembowelled bodies, bodies blown to pieces by bombs, human bodies in unrecognizable shapes, burnt by napalm; innocent children, riddled by the bullets of the assassins fired from the air, held in the arms of their agonised mothers, leaving red trails of blood as they made their way to safety not stopping to bury the dead. These were the signs of pain and suffering and of the mortal hatred for the enemy, this was the heroic image of that difficult and pitiful period.

Badly beaten and sick, yet determined and fixed in their goal, the Maubere people had to agree to enter into the control of the aggressor, as the condition for developing a new form of resistance.[35]

Indeed 1978 was the most difficult year in the liberation struggle of the Maubere people. The deliberate campaign of starvation, the relentless aerial bombardments, the destruction of the agricultural system brought untold suffering for the Timorese people. Despite the resistance movement's successes in the early stages of the encirclement and annihilation campaign, which thwarted the Indonesian advance in the west for a while, the steady onslaught from land, sea and air brought most of the country under Indonesian military control.

The resistance movement was in disarray, its lines of communication disrupted. Many Fretilin leaders had been killed or captured, or had surrendered in the face of tremendous odds. Under these pressures, difficulties began to emerge within the Fretilin leadership. Already in 1975, Xavier do Amaral, the president, had suggested that contact be made with the Indonesians. The conflict intensified as the war escalated and when it was discussed in May 1977 a split occurred in the Fretilin Central Committee. Amaral was removed as President and held in

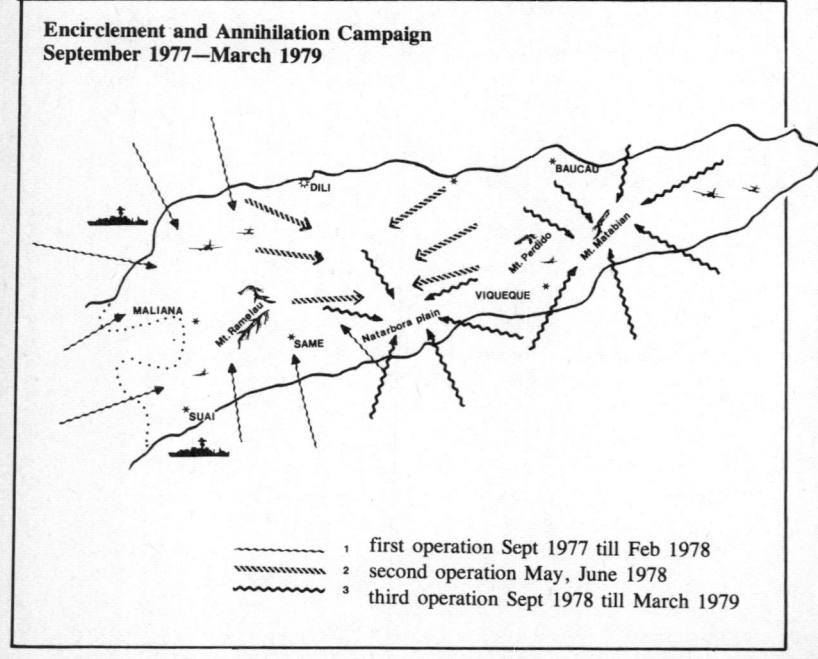

custody. In August 1978, during an Indonesian attack in Viqueque near the south coast, Amaral's guards were captured. He himself escaped arrest but then surrendered to the Indonesians a few days later and was one of the few members of the old Fretilin leadership not killed after surrendering. He became the personal captive of his former enemy Brigadier-General Dading Kalbuadi, working as his gardener and stableboy, first in Bali, and when Dading was promoted to the top leadership of the Armed Forces in 1983, Amaral was taken to Jakarta.

The Use of Chemical Weapons

The encirclement and annihilation campaign was heavily concentrated on destroying the food resources being produced by the hundreds of thousands of East Timorese then living in the interior. It was inevitable that chemical weapons and napalm would be used, in addition to the tactic of keeping the population continually on the run by constant, heavy bombardment. Radio Maubere reported the use of defoliants by the Indonesian forces on a number of occasions. In September 1977 it reported that 'a poisonous powder (was) being dropped by aircraft on crops in the liberated areas' (*Timor Information Service*, No. 22, 1977), and two months later, that 'chemical agents being sprayed by Indonesian aircraft (were) causing damage along the body and dangerously for the eyes' (*Timor Information Service*, No. 24, 1977).

Reports of the use of napalm in East Timor in late 1977, led to questions being asked in the Australian Parliament, although nothing more than assurances that the Foreign Ministry would consider the complaints were obtained at the time. (*Canberra Times*, 19 October 1977). In 1982, a Timorese who was interviewed in Jakarta confirmed that napalm bombs had been used. The Timorese, who was identified only as 'K' said:

> When they (the bombs) hit, they would cause fire and devastate the surroundings. A friend who was captured, who had had experience of napalm bombs in Africa where he served as a soldier, said the effect of the bombs used by the Indonesians was the same. (*Dossier on East Timor, 1982*)

The former Biship of Dili, Monsignor Martinhu da Costa Lopes has also spoken of evidence that napalm bombs must have been used. 'I do know that sometimes when bombs were dropped, they emitted a stream of fire which burnt everything in its path, all the vegetation. Perhaps these were napalm bombs. I have seen the effects but I can't classify the weapons.' (*TAPOL Bulletin* No. 59, September 1983).

An East Timorese refugee in Lisbon, Neobere who spent three an a half years with the resistance in the interior also spoke of the use of defoliants:

> 'In some places that were bombed, everything got burnt as a result; gardens as well as houses. In some places, a day or two after a bombing raid, a plague of maggots would come and destroy our crops. The Indonesians must have dropped things that hatched into insects to destroy our crops. Or sometimes after a bombing raid, many people had violent attacks of vomitting and dysentery from the drinking water. This kind of thing happened in the Matabian region in 1977 and 1978.' (*TAPOL Bulletin* No. 60, November, 1983)

A month after Amaral's surrender, Alarico Fernandes, Fretilin's Minister of Information and Internal Security, who was responsible for Radio Maubere, agreed to collaborate with the Indonesian intelligence in their Operation Skylight aimed at persuading Fretilin leaders to surrender. In September 1978, he announced his own breakaway from the Fretilin leadership and surrendered. As a result, Fretilin's radio communication with the outside world was severed. While Fernandes may have expected some reward from his former enemies, circumstances turned out to be even less favourable for him than for Amaral and his wife and daughter were raped by Indonesian soldiers in his presence. He was later exiled on the Indonesian island of Sumba. All the others who surrendered with him were executed.

Towards the end of 1978, the fragile lines of communication between guerrilla units in various parts of the country disintegrated. Indonesian military efforts were concentrated on the capture of Nicolau Lobato, who had taken over from Amaral as President of Fretilin and commander of Falintil. To this end, General Yusuf whisked his 2,500 strong elite troops from place to place by helicopter. On 31 December, his tactics proved successful for a unit led by Lieutenant Prabowo (who later became Suharto's son-in-law) killed the Fretilin President in a battle in the Maubisse area, some 50 miles south of Dili. Prabowo was immediately promoted to the rank of captain, and General Yusuf flew to Dili to inspect the body of Fretilin's fallen leader; a photograph of him beside Lobato's body was widely published in the Indonesian press. In a press conference, General Yusuf announced that the 'rebel forces' in East Timor had ceased to exist. Although the Indonesian generals continued to make similar claims, subsequent events proved them wrong.

1979, the Year of Population Control

On 26 March 1979, the Operation Seroja Joint Command which had been established on 6 December 1975 to launch the invasion of Dili was disbanded. This symbolized the Indonesian generals' belief that they could consider East Timor pacified and the war at an end. In April, General Yusuf visited Dili 'for the twenty-first time' since his appointment as Armed Forces Commander-in-Chief the year before.[36] Such was the priority which General Yusuf attached to the war in East Timor and to his commanding role in that war. He went to Dili this time to attend a joint meeting between the Special Co-ordinating Committee for the Administration of East Timor and the military commanders of the Second Territorial Command (*Kowilhan II*) of Java, Madura and Nusatenggara which covers East Timor. The Special Co-ordinating Committee, set up in 1978 by the Department of Defence under the chairmanship of General Benny Murdani, has remained in charge of the administration of East Timor ever since. This top-level meeting laid the foundations for the colonization and control of East Timor. There were to be three major aspects to the Army's administration of East Timor: population control based on counter-insurgency techniques; the creation of an administrative structure under the close supervision of the military; and the appointment of Timorese personnel to occupy administrative posts such as village, sub-district and district heads but always shadowed by military officers holding equivalent posts to ensure strict adherence to Indonesian objectives.

During the dry season of 1979, no major military operations were launched by Indonesian troops although from March until July 1979 there were operations to round up people and herd them into the 'resettlements'. These operations, referred to as *Operasi Pembersihan* (Operation Cleanup), were characterized by the systematic intimidation and terrorization of the population. Professional killers, known as *nanggalas*, 'the knife-killers' as Xanana dubbed them, were employed extensively. Xanana summed up 1979:

> It was a year of great suffering for the Maubere people, living like captured animals, without agriculture, without clothes, without houses. The famished and diseased people who went to the bush for food were killed when they were seen by Indonesian soldiers on the pretext that they were contacting Fretilin guerrillas. The enemy used the difficult conditions of life that year to establish their system of collaboration.
>
> In some places, large numbers of people were massacred. Disease and famine in 1979 was worse than in the three previous years. In some *desas* (Indonesian-built villages) which had a population of 400 to 600 people, only five to eight families remained alive at the end of the year.[37]

By the middle of 1979, the surviving Fretilin forces were attempting to restore their lines of communications. Groups in the Eastern Sector took the initiative to establish contact with resistance fighters in other areas. Towards the end of the year, Fretilin was able to launch a number of ambushes in the east. The Indonesian military reacted swiftly. Ten fresh battalions were dispatched to Dili and pushed east, supported by bombing raids. Letters smuggled out of East Timor to refugees in Australia and Portugal brought information about these operations to the outside world. One such letter which reached Lisbon, dated 26 March 1980 described the situation:

The armed struggle continues to be intense, particularly in the eastern part of the island... despite the capture of thousands of rebel weapons G3s and Mausers, in the monsoon season of 1979... I don't know how it's possible for them to do it, but those in the bush are giving strong resistance to tens (sic) of Indonesian battalions which are fighting and pursuing them. The Indonesians are taking casualties. Helicopters arrive daily at Dili Hospital carrying soldiers from various fronts.[38]

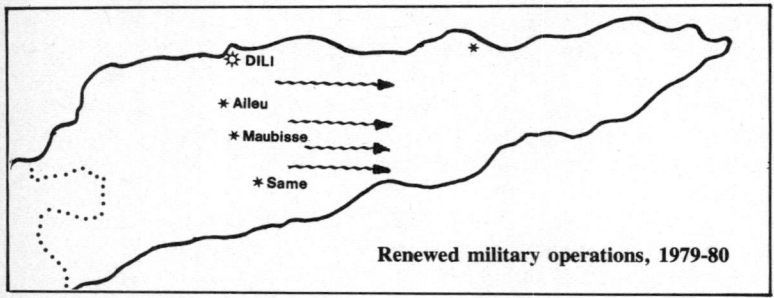

Renewed military operations, 1979-80

Following the destruction of the Fretilin support bases in the mountains and with most of the population held captive in the camps, Fretilin fighters began to set up a new clandestine organization network all over the country. 'The organization of the popular masses,' says Xanana, 'increased in breadth and depth,' for the actions of the Indonesians in 1978 and 1979 had only made the Maubere people transfer support bases from the mountains to the villages.

It is the people of East Timor who wage war for their own liberation and Fretilin is the blood that circulates in the veins of the children and elderly of East Timor. So, to exterminate Fretilin, it is first necessary to exterminate the Maubere people.[39]

By the middle of 1980, Fretilin units, scattered and still isolated from each other, were able to launch numerous counter attacks against the occupation forces. On 10 June, a Fretilin unit launched a daring attack on the outskirts of Dili. They inflicted serious damage on the television station (the very installation Suharto had come to Dili to inaugurate in July 1978) and carried out an assault against Indonesian military barracks in Dare, about two kilometres from Dili. The severe reprisals which quickly followed from the Indonesian troops have been described by an East Timorese who was staying near Dare at the time:

> Shooting began in the evening and continued till around 6am. Then the people around the place of the attack were rounded up and taken to the Koramil (Military Sub-district Command) for interrogation, one by one. They were all accused of sheltering Fretilin. All their houses were burnt down. Many people disappeared during this time, ordinary people living in the houses around where the army was

attacked. The people who were left were gathered around pla[ces] where the TNI (Indonesian Army) had a stronghold.[40]

This audacious attack infuriated the Indonesian military command. They must have already begun to realize that the tide was turning against them. Popular support for Fretilin was clearly undiminished, enabling the guerrilla fighters not only to ambush Indonesian troops in the countryside but even to attack Dili. This led the military to adopt a new policy of isolating the resistance movement from the population through mass arrests. Following the 10 June attack in Dili many people were executed and a further 600 people arrested, and sent to Atauro prison island, some 15 miles north of Dili. The military also arrested people in the settlement camps suspected of being in contact with the guerrillas or anyone related to members of the resistance movement. This policy was escalated in 1981.

By exiling people to Atauro and other islands, the Indonesian military hoped to achieve two objectives: to weaken or destroy the clandestine network that had developed in many of the camps linking the guerrilla fighters with the population under Indonesian military control, and to use the prisoners as hostages. Indonesian officials made no secret of the fact that detainees will not be released until relatives fighting in the bush have surrendered or been killed. Atauro is certainly not the only prison used for this purpose, but the Indonesians have allowed some public access using it as a showpiece for visiting foreigners or journalists. The island of Liran is also used as a prison camp but no outsiders have been allowed in. Indonesian islands used for the detention of Timorese prisoners include Bali and Sumba.

Timorization of the War

From the very early stages of the war, the Indonesian military have tried to recruit Timorese into their war machine. As a general policy, the Armed Forces insist that the population should be involved in 'their own' defence, a concept which is expressed in the militaristic catch-phrase, *Hankamrata* which stands for 'total people's defence and security'. Where a state of war exists as in East Timor, the need to use *putera daerah* or 'sons of the region' to fight the rebels is even more heavily emphasized. Xanana described the current extent of Timorization:

> Finally, the enemy has opted for Timorization of the army in order to end the war. Seven years ago, the enemy launched the war with the use of paratroopers and today they are giving the war to the sons of East Timor. They are arming the Timorese. They pay them to die instead of Indonesian soldiers and reward them with piles of inflationary rupiahs whenever they present the occupation forces with heads of resistance fighters. These heads are often taken from the bodies of defenceless people in the bush as well as from guerrilla fighters who have been killed.

To encourage these Timorese to commit such crimes, they have announced that the prize for the head of a Fretilin leader is a large sum of money, a good house, a trip to Indonesia, food and so on. As a result, we can see today in the East Timor bush the sons of the same country killing each other.[41]

Indonesian efforts to recruit Timorese in fact started early in the war. In 1976, two Timorese battalions, Battalions 744 and 745 were set up and a civil defence corps composed entirely of Timorese, known as *Hansip* (Pertahanan Sipil), was created. Although the Indonesian military authorities were able, as Xanana has pointed out, to make many Timorese recruits commit atrocities against their fellow-countrymen, the Army has gained little benefit from the armed Timorese units they have created. The brutal, senseless killing has shocked and disheartened many Timorese members of the Indonesian military machinery. An East Timorese interviewed in March 1982, identified as 'F', gave the following account:

> They (the Battalions 744 and 745) are composed of a mixture of East Timorese, Javanese and Indonesians from other parts, especially West Timor. When formed, about half of the battalion members were East Timorese but their numbers were being reduced because the Army does not trust the East Timorese. F agreed that being members of 744/5 would mean they would have to act against their own people. He said that once in the battalion, they would have to obey the Indonesian army orders. He believed the main reason for joining the battalions was economic. There are few jobs for Timorese; this is one. F thought that seeking revenge for alleged Fretilin actions against family members was not a significant factor in the reasons why East Timorese joined 744. Some people may have been forced to join.[42]

Indonesian attitudes towards the Timorese soldiers are in any case deplorable. They are treated as inferior beings and ordered around by Javanese soldiers who have an ingrained sense of superiority. On operational missions against Fretilin, the Timorese conscripts are expected to march in advance of the Indonesian soldiers.

Over the years, the number of Timorese in the two Timorese battalions had diminished significantly, and there are now reports that Battalion 744, which is based in Dili (Battalion 745 is based in Baucau) has been disbanded. Since 1980, a number of incidents have occurred in which members of Hansip have deserted, and fled to the bush to join Fretilin, taking modern weapons and ammunition with them. Shortly before the 10 June 1980 Fretilin attack in Dili there were reports that more than a hundred Timorese soldiers from the two battalions had deserted. In battle, these battalions have been extremely incompetent. During the 1981 Operation Security the battalions were withdrawn and dispatched to Central Java after they had surrounded the village of Lakluta at night and machine-gunned all the houses. Instead of finding a band of guerrillas, when morning came, they discovered that all their victims were women and children: there was not a single Fretilin soldier among them.

The *pagar betis* or fence-of-legs strategy is another type of Timorization used by the Indonesian armed forces in 1980-81. It involves the conscription of a large number of civilians who are required to move ahead of Indonesian troops, encircling an area in which guerrillas are thought to be hiding. As the encirclement tightens, the guerrillas are forced into the open and captured or shot.

Operation Security, May-September, 1981

Pagar betis operations first began during 1980, to combat the guerrilla resurgence of that year. Fretilin records that more guerrilla attacks were launched during 1980 than throughout the entire period of the 1977-78 Indonesian offensive. The intensity of guerrilla activity increased in 1981. According to one source quoted by ACFOA, an Indonesian plane and three helicopters were shot down by Fretilin forces in April 1981. The Indonesian armed forces were suffering heavy casualties, and fighting was taking place in places as far apart as Los Palos, Uatolari, Betano, Laklubar, Vemasse, Queliquai, Bobonaro and Bazartete.[43]

In May, the Indonesians launched a new operation code-named *Operasi Keamanan* or Security Operation. Some officers used the codename *Operasi Ganesha* invoking a legendary elephant figure from Javanese mythology. In Jakarta, Defence Department sources also called it the *perang terachir*, the 'final' or 'decisive' war. Its aim was to drive all Fretilin guerrillas and their families from the western and eastern sectors into the central sector, to Manatuto, where they would be rounded up and exterminated. The operation involved the recruitment of tens of thousands of Timorese men and boys; it was also intended to 'punish' the Timorese population for its persistent support of the resistance movement.

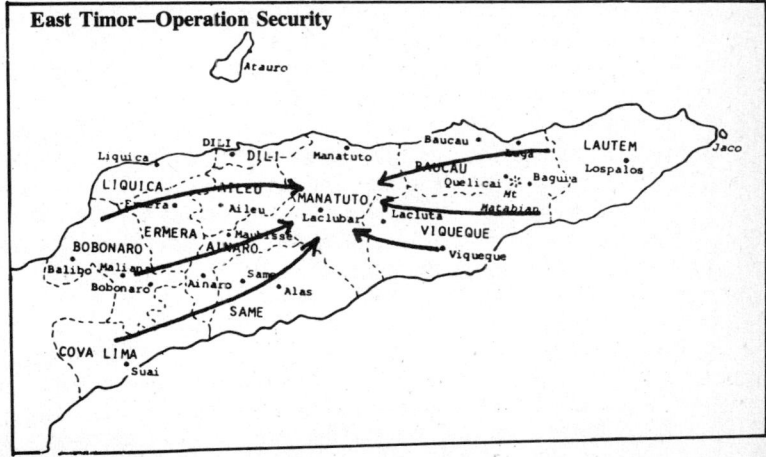

A news report in a Hongkong-based newsagency headed 'The worst situation in the world' described the operation.

> The Indonesian army is driving large groups of the male population in long sweeps through the mountains to eliminate the remaining guerrillas... (My) informants conservatively estimate the total (number of East Timorese involved) at 50,000. They march in groups of twelve ahead of Indonesian soldiers like African beaters for White hunters. They are ordered to look for guerrillas, shout when they see them and even engage them in struggle. (It is claimed) these human lures are not armed...[44]

Virtually the entire male population from the ages of 15 to 50 was pressed into service. In some places, boys as young as 9 and men as old as 60 were ordered to join. Some guerrillas were arrested during the operations though most managed to 'sneak through the fence of legs', often with the help of the frontline Timorese conscripts.

As in previous military operations, the civilian population were the ones to suffer most. An East Timorese living in Baucau at the time described its impact:

> The actual problem that the people in the centre-east are facing at present is extreme misery because of the campaign that is reigning in that region. Men and children are forced to the bush and that prevents them from growing food. People are suffering starvation, sickness, malnutrition and death. It is impossible for a man at war to go without food... Without food, even if you have planes, boats, cannons and all the war materials, they cannot move because the men are too weak.
>
> How can the people live when in their own houses there is no food and above that, they have to take food with them to the bush? In Laga, Queliquai, Seical, Vemasse and Laleia, it is the period of the rice and corn harvest. These crops are going to be wasted and eaten by rats and other animals as there are no men to harvest them. This year and last year, the people of Baguia went through terrible starvation because the *bapaks* (the term by which Timorese refer to Indonesian soldiers*) prohibited them from harvesting the rice and corn. The crops were destroyed and eaten by animals. This year 1981-1982, there is going to be starvation in all areas mentioned above because people are forced to go into the bush and there is no-one to prepare the land for cultivation. This time there will be another extermination of the people.[45]

---

* *bapak*, an Indonesian word, originally 'father' or 'uncle' was used deferentially to older men. It is now a deferential term for people of higher status or position. Used widely in East Timor, it is required as a mark of the respect Timorese must show toward Indonesian soldiers.

The writer refers to people being prevented from harvesting their crops. The inhabitants in the resettlement camps were ordered to quickly gather in crops because they were not allowed to leave camp perimeters while the operations were in preparation or in progress. The crops left standing were burnt by the troops or left to go to waste.

Operation Security was militarily a failure. Many guerrilla fighters escaped encirclement, often because they were forewarned of Indonesian battle plans. Some even succeeded in joining the fence-of-legs to conceal their identity. In numerous ways the use of Timorese was counterproductive for more often than not they effectively assisted the 'enemy'.

> ...the population gave one of the greatest examples of patriotism of conscious participation in the liberation struggle, by leading their resistance compatriots through the 'fence'. They hid small groups of guerrillas in their midst... They led the enemy far away from places where their brothers were... They led their sons through this huge human wall. In other regions, neither the resistance forces nor the population suffered defeat.[46]

But Operation Security was not only a military defeat. It boomeranged by intensifying the East Timorese hatred of the Indonesian troops. Forced to take part in operations to kill their fellow-countrymen and women, to leave their families without food, and abandon what few crops they had to the ravages of climate and pests, they lost their sense of fear. Only hatred remained for the alien troops who seem only intent on exterminating the Timorese.

The Indonesian military commander, Colonel Purwanto, admitted that Operation Security was a failure. When pressed by Indonesian journalists who visited Dili in January 1983 for an explanation of the length of time needed to round up 'a handful of rebels', he replied:

> It is indeed difficult. There are many risks when a village of, say, three hundred inhabitants is guarded by only two security troops, and even more so when these remnants merge with their relatives making it very difficult to identify the rebels. The troops don't know who they should be pursuing. 'They cannot be crushed in the way the PLO struggle was ended in Lebanon,' said Purwanto. 'Nor can they be rounded up in operations such as were launched during *Operation Ganesha*. From my childhood days, I have been known as a fierce person. But these Fretilin remnants cannot be crushed by fierce methods. They can only be dealt with by cajolement.'[47]

By this time Fretilin's new strategy was already in full swing, a situation described by Xanana in October 1982:

> The armed struggle has spread all over the country. The gunfire of liberation relights again in every part of the country and the actions of the glorious Falintil, from Tutuala to the border, is creating great

instability for the cruel, barbarous and bloody enemy. The cowardly occupier of our country is making propaganda, claiming we are only fifty in number or that we have only twenty guns and that we are only a hundred fugitives. We affirm that we are not many, but also that we are not just a few—we are an entire people at war![48]

The humiliating defeat of 1981 forced the Indonesian military command to realize that they had to counter the growing support for the resistance movement by means of psychological warfare, the so-called 'hearts and minds' policy. This is the strategy outlined in the secret Army documents that were captured by guerrillas on 31 December 1982. The documents were issued by Purwanto's predecessor, Colonel Sahala Rajagukguk who was later promoted to divisional commander in North and North East Sulawesi. Colonel Purwanto took command in East Timor at a time of great difficulty for the Indonesians. The policy of cajolement was part of a strategy which Purwanto described as

> a kind of *benteng stelsel* (fortification system) like during the Diponegoro War*, building up the settlements (ie the concentration camps) as forts to encircle the GPK (ie the guerrillas).[49]

The strategy failed mainly because the camps had themselves been penetrated by clandestine networks of guerrillas whose supporters had become so thoroughly absorbed by the inhabitants that, as Purwanto said, the Indonesian troops 'could not identify the rebels' and 'did not know who they should be pursuing'. The strategy failed too because of the poor discipline, inadequate training and low morale of the Indonesian troops. To have been workable, the strategy outlined in the documents needed highly-dedicated, well-trained personnel performing a complex combination of intelligence, operational and political activity. Their only success was in intelligence, much of it obtained from the brutally tortured victims of interrogators. The description of Fretilin's strategy in Document III[50] is reasonably accurate, as well as their summary of Falintil's structure.

By late 1982, with Fretilin's counter-offensive strategy well under way, Indonesian troops in many parts of the country were forced on the defensive. As a result many local commanders sought local ceasefires to reduce the pressures they faced; in some places, they even formed links with the guerrillas, stand-off agreements and agreements for the guerrillas to receive food, medicines and other supplies.

---

* The Diponegoro War, also called the Java War, was fought by the Dutch colonial army against the rebellion led by Diponegoro in Central Java, lasting from 1825-1830

Negotiations, March 1983

Dogged by the failure of Operation Security and of Purwanto's *benteng stelsel*, the military command decided to try a strategy of negotiation. Fretilin had, in its own words 'conquered the right to dialogue'.[51] This strategy was not without precedent in post-independence Indonesian military history. To understand the objectives the Army hoped to achieve during the extraordinary events of the first half of 1983, it is useful to examine briefly the Army's handling of regional rebellions in Indonesia in the 1950s and 1960s. These rebellions gave the Army experience in a number of strategies, all of which have been tried out in East Timor. The rebellions in West Sumatra and North Sulawesi were led by local Army commanders and were quelled when central government troops arrived from Java to undertake military operations against the rebel troops. The rebellions in Aceh (North Sumatra), West Java and South Sulawesi were inspired by Islamic ideals and presented the central government with far more complex problems. The Darul Islam rebellion in West Java, dangerously close to the seat of central government power, was eventually put down by the fence-of-legs tactic. Although the rebels had strong support in the area, the central government was able to call on pro-government mass organizations to participate in the operation, in defence of the principle of the unitary state. The Darul Islam movements in Aceh and South Sulawesi both situated in places remote from the central seat of power, were more difficult to handle. The leaders, Daud Beureuh in Aceh and Kahar Muzakar in South Sulawesi, not only had a strong religious appeal; they were also legendary heroes from the anticolonial struggle against the Dutch, giving them a wider appeal. They had both succeeded in establishing a degree of territorial control. Large-scale military operations were unsuccessful, while the fence-of-legs tactic was unworkable for lack of a popular basis locally in support of the central government. The negotiations tactic was therefore used in both cases, and successfully.

In Aceh, Daud Beureuh accepted the terms offered—special regional status, recognition of a greater role for Islamic teaching in the schools, and an honorific title and pension for himself. In South Sulawesi, the negotiations with Kahar Muzakar were initiated by Brigadier-General Yusuf, the divisional commander who two decades later as Defence Minister and commander-in-chief, was to attempt his 'Sulawesi solution' in East Timor. Although Kahar Muzakar refused to compromise, many of his followers were persuaded to give up the struggle. Negotiations took place at a time when local ceasefires were being agreed between local commanders and rebel groups, and special agreements were being reached to allow safe passage through rebel-held territory. These more relaxed conditions helped to soften the combat-readiness of the rebel forces and ultimately made the task of persuading them to surrender far easier.

In East Timor, the first moves towards negotiations were undertaken in late 1982; the first meeting taking place on 21 March 1983, when the Indonesian officer involved, Major Williem da Costa, actually referred to the offer as the 'Sulawesi solution'. The term was also used by *Radio Netherlands* in a report on 2 July 1983, after the negotiations had been made public. Crucial to this approach was an appeal to uphold the unitary state, to resolve a conflict 'between brothers'. 'They are our brothers,' Colonel Purwanto told a New Zealand television reporter in March 1983, 'We don't kill them because they are our brothers. We are just waiting for them to come down.' The Foreign Minister, Mochtar Kusumaatmaja later said, 'the problem of Fretilin is going to be solved in the Indonesian way, in other words by resolving it in a brotherly fashion.'[52] Simultaneously in an attempt to win popular feeling away from the guerrillas, the resistance fighters were depicted as bandits who burned down people's houses whereas Colonel Purwanto said 'we rebuild the houses in a better condition. The more they engage in terror, the more unpopular they become.'[53]

Such tactics could succeed in Aceh, West Java and South Sulawesi because in the end, an appeal to rally round the unitary state was effective; people in these regions could more or less identify with Indonesia's long history of anticolonial struggle against the Dutch. The lengths to which the military authorities went in East Timor in pursuance of Yusuf's 'Sulawesi solution' indicates the extent to which he believed his Sulawesi victory could be repeated in East Timor. The talks with Fretilin commander Xanana involved Indonesia in great risks. Even greater risks surrounded the acceptance of Xanana's insistence on negotiating with the military commander, not with the puppet governor of East Timor, particularly if news of the talks and their significance reached the outside world. Why should the commanding officer of East Timor agree to negotiate with a 'handful of bandits'?

The relaxed atmosphere which was allowed to develop during the ceasefire that followed the talks in the first half of 1983 was very much part of the same strategy. Armed guerrillas were allowed to go in and out of the camps and even into the towns. Some guerrillas were actually taken on trips to Jakarta, to impress them with the economic achievements of Suharto's Indonesia. A Timorese refugee in Lisbon told one of the present authors that the guerrillas returned home and told Indonesian officers: 'We are impressed but we intend to build up our country in our own way, according to our own ideals.'[54]

The 'Sulawesi solution' proved to be a complete flop in East Timor. Most fatal of all was the assumption that Fretilin could be handled like a regional revolt. There is no sense of common history to which the Indonesians can appeal. The 'unitary state' means nothing to the East Timorese. Offers of 'brotherly' affection are seen as being treacherous and hypocritical, and offers of amnesty which came fast and furious during the months of the ceasefire are regarded with contempt as a murderous trap. As for banditry and terrorism, these are the practices of the Indonesian troops and their commanders, not of Fretilin and the Falintil guerrillas.

The main talks between Fretilin and the Indonesian military command were held on 23 March 1983, with Xanana representing Fretilin and Colonel Purwanto representing the forces of occupation. The meeting took place in Lari Guto, a neutral area in the eastern sector. The meeting place was built by Fretilin who also provided all the facilities. Xanana displayed courtesy throughout the discussions, and spoke a lot about the need to stop hostilities and put an end to all the loss of life involved but he breathed not a word about compromise or surrender. He told Purwanto that Fretilin demands the complete withdrawal of Indonesian troops and free consultation with the people of East Timor. While agreeing to a general ceasefire, Xanana made it clear that further talks and the future of the ceasefire depended on the Indonesian side informing the United Nations about the talks. This the Indonesian failed to do for it would have given quite a different meaning to the talks than they had intended.

Just as the negotiations tactic was in progress, General Yusuf was replaced as commander-in-chief of the Armed Forces by General Benny Murdani who certainly had far less faith in the 'Sulawesi solution' than his predecessor. The tactic was allowed to proceed for several months during which time Murdani's patience must have reached breaking point. No surrenders occurred; on the contrary, Fretilin used the atmosphere of relaxation to consolidate its support networks in the camps and to send abroad a flood of information about conditions under Indonesian occupation. Then, when news of the talks broke in the international press, early in June, Murdani acted fast to switch to a strategy more in his line. Colonel Purwanto, whose role in the talks had been so embarrassingly exposed when Fretilin's representatives abroad published a photograph of his meeting with Xanana, was unceremoniously sacked as the scapegoat for Indonesia's strategic disasters during his brief term of office as commander in East Timor.

The Third Period of the War

The opening salvo of this new offensive was launched when General Murdani sent a message to Xanana on 26 June, news of which reached the outside world through church sources in July:

> Don't think that you can disentangle yourself. Do not think that you can receive assistance from other countries. There is no country on this globe that can help you. Our own army is prepared to destroy you if you are not willing to be co-operative with our republic. We are preparing an operation — *Operasi Persatuan* (Operation Unity) — which will come into force in August.

Other signs that preparations for an offensive were under way soon became apparent. Facilities that had been given to the International Red Cross to undertake relief activities were withdrawn in July making it impossible for the agency to continue the main aspects of their work in East Timor. The ICRC announced in September 1983[55] that it had decided to suspend food and medical assistance in mainland East Timor because the usual criteria were no longer being met. In mid-July, General Murdani made a visit to East Timor together with four top-level Defence Department generals, Major-General Gunarso, responsible for social and political affairs, Major-General Dading Kalbuadi, an old East Timor hand, now responsible for logistics at the Defence Department, Brigadier-General Edi Nalapraya, responsible for territorial affairs, and Colonel Ben Momongan, responsible for operational affairs. Colonel Rudjito was appointed as the new commander of East Timor in place of Colonel Purwanto.

On 16 August, Benny Murdani declared in Jakarta that Indonesia would show 'no mercy' to Fretilin forces in East Timor, and would employ all the equipment and weapons at its disposal to crush the resistance.[56]

The Death Toll

The people of East Timor have suffered enormous loss of life since the Indonesian invasion of 1975. The conditions of war, the tight control exerted by the Indonesians over the means of communication, the lack of unhampered access by independent observers and the suspect nature of Indonesian claims and statistics make it impossible to obtain an accurate and reliable figure of the present population of East Timor. Moreover, any figure would now include an unspecified number of 'spontaneous' Indonesian migrants in the towns, officially-sponsored migrants in some rural areas, as well as a large number of Indonesian military personnel and government officials.

The first public estimate of the death-toll came from Francisco Lopes da Cruz, a UDT leader who became deputy-governor of Indonesia's first post-invasion administration in East Timor. He said in February 1976 that sixty thousand people had died 'in six months of civil war'. Since estimates of the death-toll during the civil war (which in fact lasted only a couple of weeks from 11 August 1975) were between 1,500 and 3,000, the da Cruz figure meant that some 57,000 had died since the Indonesian invasion. Within days, he was forced to retract in an attempt to repair the damage caused by his statement; he claimed that he had been referring to 'casualties' not all of which were deaths and had also included Timorese who had taken refuge in West Timor.*

Later in 1976, Indonesian Catholic church circles produced a document which reported that church visitors to East Timor had questioned local priests about the estimated 60,000 death-toll in the conviction that it must be an exaggeration, only to be told that the figure was, if anything, an under-estimation. The figure was probably more like 100,000.

'50,000 or 80,000 people might have been killed during the war in East Timor... It was war....Then what is the big fuss?'
Adam Malik,
quoted by *Sydney Morning Herald,*
5 April, 1977

The above estimates were made before the encirclement and annihilation operations got under way in mid 1977. That was the military campaign which caused the most deaths of all.

---

* A close associate of da Cruz later told Jim Dunn that in his original statement, da Cruz had actually said 'massacred'.

Since the late 1970s, the figure most widely accepted as the death-toll is 200,000, a figure that has been confirmed by Mgr Martinhu da Costa Lopes, the former Bishop of Dili, who said recently:

'The population of East Timor has been reduced by 200,000 since the invasion. About 60,000 were killed and about 140,000 died as a result of starvation caused by economic disruption and inability to grow food.' (*The Irish Times*, 8 September 1983.)

This estimate from the former head of the Catholic church in East Timor must be taken very seriously indeed. The church has a well-established infrastructure everywhere and is better placed than any other institution to have an independent assessment of conditions, backed by facts and figures about the population.

What do official statistics show?

There are good reasons to question the accuracy of population statistics produced by the Portuguese colonial administration and now by the Indonesian colonial administration. The Portuguese figures, based on a regular census, are widely believed to have been too low as the census was related to tax assessment which encouraged people to evade registration. The Catholic church had its own population figures which tended to be higher than those produced by the census.

An Indonesian census was held in East Timor in 1980 as part of a nationwide census, though no information is available about the conditions under which it was conducted. The Catholic church has continued to compile its own population figures but by contrast with Portuguese days, these are now far below the official figure.

The following analysis compares Portuguese and Indonesian figures, for what they are worth, and incorporates church figures for purposes of comparison:

Pre-1975 figures
The last pre-invasion population figures:
    1. The Portuguese 1970 census 609,477
    2. The Catholic church 1974 figure 688,711

1975 projections, based on an annual growth rate of 1.7%
    1. 1975 projection of the official census 663,000
    2. 1975 projection of the church figure 700,000

Post-1980 figures
1980 projections of the above figures should take account of an estimated 3,000 people who died in the civil war (August

1975), and approximately 7,000 who have gone into exile since August 1975. The following projections make allowances for this decline of 10,000 people:
1. 1980 projection of the official census 713,000
2. 1980 projection of the church figure 754,000

Compare these with:

1. 1980 Indonesian census result for East Timor 555,000
2. The Catholic church estimate, published in UN Document A/AC.109/715, 13 August, 1982 425,000

A straight comparison between the official Indonesian and Portuguese figures produces a decline of 158,000. Using the 1980 church figure as the basis for comparison, the decline is anything between 199,000 and 329,000.

A Mounting Death Toll

The new offensive launched by Indonesia in August 1983 is bound to cause a new wave of killings, the consequences of which are difficult to predict. There can be no doubt that the 200,000 estimated death toll will soon have to be revised upwards.

Timor war casualties the second highest in world

In a report entitled *A World at War—1983*, the Centre for Defense Information based in Washington lists East Timor as the country that has suffered the second largest number of deaths in all wars then currently raging world-wide. The following table is reproduced from the report.

The Most Violent Conflicts

Conflicts	Number of Deaths	Year Began
1. Kampuchea Civil War	1-4,000,000	1970
2. East Timor Guerrilla War	100-250,000	1975
3. Afghanistan Civil War	100,000+	1978
4. Iraq-Iran War	80-100,000	1980
5. Lebanon Civil War	80,000+	1975
6. Philippine Guerrilla Wars	50-100,000	1972
7. China-Vietnam War	47,000+	1979
8. Guatemala Guerrilla War	30-40,000+	1967
9. El Salvador Civil War	30,000+	1977
10. Ethiopia-Eritrea Guerrilla War	30,000+	1962

The Center for Defense Information, whose Board of Advisors includes a number of retired US Armed Forces officers, businessmen and writers, including a former Deputy Director of the CIA, is headed by Rear Admiral Gene R. LaRocque (retired) of the US Navy.

3. Resistance and the Struggle for National Liberation

During the four years that followed the destruction of Fretilin's last support base in the east, and President Nicolau Lobato's killing, Indonesia's propaganda campaign was directed towards convincing the world that resistance in East Timor had ended. Then, suddenly came the news that Fretilin and the Indonesian military command had held ceasefire talks.

Although occasional reports had been received of the activities of the resistance movement through church and refugee sources, no one dreamt that Fretilin had been able to rebuild its position so dramatically that the Indonesian military were compelled to negotiate with them, in effect giving Fretilin *de facto* recognition and destroying the credibility of Indonesian claims that Fretilin was a 'spent force' and a 'gang of criminal remnants'. Fretilin's remarkable resurgence brought with it renewed international support and sympathy.

The Birth of the Liberation Movement

Fretilin—*Frente Revolucionaria de Timor Leste Independente*—was founded on 20 May 1974, immediately after the coup in Lisbon which toppled the Caetano dictatorship. Initially called the *Associacão Social Democratica de Timor*, it changed its name to Fretilin in September that year. Fretilin leaders still sometimes refer to the ASDT/Fretilin.

ASDT's first manifesto, issued two days after its inception, described its political aims as:

> The right to independence; the rejection of colonialism and the immediate participation of worthy Timorese elements in the administration and in the local government; no racial discrimination; fight against corruption and a policy of good neighbourliness and cooperation with the countries of the geographical area in which Timor is situated.

The other major political organization in East Timor, the *União Democratica Timorense* which accepted the ideology and values of Portuguese colonialism and wanted to retain East Timor's union with Portugal, enjoyed more popular support than Fretilin initially. This and the political confusion in Portugal hastened the decision to turn the ASDT into a revolutionary front. In September 1974, Fretilin's founding conference issued another manifesto which attacked the idea that fascism could be 'liberal' or colonialism could be 'democratic'. It rejected any form of dependence and denied that progress was possible within a colonial framework. National independence was the first prerequisite.

> The Social Democratic Party considers itself the interpreter of the profound ideals of the people of all East Timor and because of this reason, declares itself the only legitimate representative of the people, and will now be called, Revolutionary Front for an Independent East Timor.

By transforming itself into the only organization which clearly articulated Timorese aspirations for independence, Fretilin had distinguished itself from UDT and from the smaller group, *Apodeti* which advocated integration with Indonesia. Fretilin also identified itself with the liberation movements in the other Portuguese colonies, in particular the PAIGC in Guinea-Bissau and Frelimo in Mozambique.

Fretilin's social and political programme also clearly distinguished it from the other political forces in East Timor. It called for fundamental economic re-construction with production, distribution and consumption co-operatives becoming the basic units of economic life. Excessive dependence on imports should be ended, agrarian reforms implemented and the monoculture diversified. The programme called for the expropriation of large agricultural holdings and the inclusion of unused fertile land in the co-operative system. Fretilin also issued policy statements on education and culture, social justice, health, internal administration and national defence. In all these matters, it stressed the need for self-reliance, for a resolute struggle against colonial structures, and for the rapid development of Timorese participation in the affairs of society.[1]

All the Fretilin leaders were well-educated people living in Dili. Most of them had been born in the countryside, spent their childhood in the villages, but had received an education that estranged them from their origins.

> Educated by the Portuguese to regard themselves as *civilizados* and therefore superior to the people they left behind in the villages, it was not long however before the association came to reject this view and to argue that the future of the country lay in the hands of the peasants who made up over ninety per cent of the people.[2]

The founding leaders of Fretilin can be divided into four groups: The *anti-colonial group* was an informal clandestine group, formed in January 1970. They met regularly in Dili in a busy public park opposite the governor's office to escape the attention of the Portuguese secret police. Most of the members were high-school students or office workers who had been inspired by the African liberation movements. Among its ranks were men who were to become leading Fretilin figures: Nicolau Lobato who became the second president of the organization, Jose Ramos

Horta the movement's representative at the United Nations, and Mari Alkatiri, Minister for External Relations of the Democratic Republic of East Timor.

The *Casa dos Timores group* was composed of Timorese university students who lived at the hostel of that name in Lisbon and were politicized in the late 1960s and early 1970s. Leonel Andrade, one of the first Dili *Liceu* graduates to enter Lisbon university in 1969, recalls that

> The first among us who went to Lisbon immediately came into contact with revolutionary theories and developed joint actions with patriots from other colonies and with anti-fascist Portuguese patriots. From that moment on, we were no longer isolated. We could understand the just struggle of the peoples for national independence for we had assimilated the thinking of the great revolutionary leaders.[3]

It was members of this group who initiated Fretilin's social and political programmes. They included Francisco Borja da Costa, the poet and writer who became Fretilin's first information secretary; Abilio Araujo and Guilhermina dos Santos who maintained the link between Fretilin in East Timor and the Casa group in Lisbon, Mau Lear who introduced the first literacy campaign based on Paulo Freire's methods; and Bieki Sahe who initiated groups in the countrysde for the discussion of political affairs, and set up co-operatives, as well as youth and women's organizations. All these provided the nucleus for Fretilin activity during 1974-75.

The *group around Xavier do Amaral* who was older than the other Fretilin leaders and had not been involved in the political activities that led to the creation of Fretilin. He was invited to become president because he was a well-known and respected figure. Xavier do Amaral studied at the Jesuit seminary in Dare before becoming a teacher at a school for young people excluded from the Portuguese educational system. He was strongly influenced by populist aspects of Catholic social teaching and often publicly criticised Portuguese colonial rule. As a result he lost his job in 1967 and became a customs official in Dili.

The *group around Alarico Fernandes* who was also part of an older generation. When Fretilin was founded, he was working as a meteorologist in Baucau Airport, but he moved to Dili to become the first general secretary of the organization. He was a close friend of the radical Catholic priest, Father Roxa, a disciple of the well-known Colombian priest, Camillo Torres, who was expelled from East Timor in 1974.

All these groups were represented in Fretilin's first central committee. Although complete independence was the clearly stated aim of the organization, the 52-member central committee represented a diversity of ideological and political positions, a broad front of nationalist ideas and political perspectives encompassing social democracy, Marxism and populism. As an organization, it had a strong appeal and membership grew rapidly. According to Ramos Horta, by the end of 1974 it had a following of over 80,000 people. Anyone who sympathised with

Fretilin's aims could receive a membership card to identify them with the movement.

The social programmes implemented by Fretilin leaders, along the coastal areas and in the mountainous interior, were very successful. Abilio Araujo has described the programmes as serving a dual purpose, 'to mobilize in order to conscientise the people, to conscientise in order to mobilize the people'.[4] A number of these programmes have been described by foreign visitors; Grant Evans accompanied Nicolau Lobato to Bazartete in October 1974 to see a co-operative where people worked their private plots collectively and shared agricultural instruments.

> 'The people are still suspicious of the idea' says Lobato. 'They have been drawn into similar collective projects before by either the Portuguese or the Japanese only to find themselves dispossessed. We have started off with a small number so that we can work out the problems that arise easily, and when it has shown itself to be successful then others will follow quickly. It demands a great deal of trust amongst the members and that all decisions taken by the co-operative be taken democratically.' He was involved in what they call a 'production co-operative', and when things get off the ground they hope also to create 'consumer co-operatives' to market their goods and to break the present commercial stranglehold of the Chinese.[5]

Distribution co-operatives were also planned. After a visit in October 1974 to Bucoli, Denis Freney wrote that the people

> were planning a co-operative for next year's harvest. Villagers will pool their surplus crops (after deducting family needs) for sale in Dili for higher prices than they would get through Chinese middlemen. These receipts will be used as the villagers decide: to buy a truck perhaps or build a co-operative store, to buy wholesale basic necessities or to buy a small tractor.[6]

The dizzy pace of events during the eighteen months which led up to the Indonesian invasion in December 1975, had 'a profoundly maturing effect on the Fretilin leadership', as Jim Dunn has noted and gave it its first baptism of fire. It took Fretilin no longer than two weeks to defeat the UDT when it launched a coup in August 1975. This victory was achieved so quickly largely as a result of the support of the Timorese troops in the Portuguese colonial army. Among them were the troops at the Aileu military base south of Dili, the army unit in Maubisse a little farther south, and the Timorese troops stationed at the central barracks in Taibesse on the outskirts of the capital. This led to an influx of military men at all levels of the organization which in turn had a significant impact on Fretilin's internal structure and its political and ideological emphasis. The troops who sided with Fretilin had not been Fretilin members; soldiers in the Portuguese armed forces were prohibited from

from joining political parties, but because of their decisive role in UDT's defeat, they demanded a say in the affairs of the organization. Three professional soldiers were co-opted onto the Fretilin central committee and the armed forces were re-organized as the Falintil (*Forças Armadas de Libertacão National de Timor Leste*). This strengthened the more traditional or conservative elements at the expense of the radical wing influenced by the *Casa dos Timores* group.

UDT's decisive defeat and the withdrawal of the Portuguese colonial administration during the brief civil war left Fretilin with the formidable task of setting up central and regional administrations while concurrently dealing with the Indonesian border incursions which began immediately after the end of the civil war. A number of Australians who visited East Timor during the three short months prior to the Indonesian invasion were deeply impressed by Fretilin's performance and its strong popular support. Despite numerous social and economic problems, order was quickly restored and many people were able to return to their villages and resume food production.

Faced with the sudden and unexpected task of running the country's administration, Fretilin was compelled to devote more attention to these problems than to politization and mobilization activities to which it had devoted its energies prior to the civil war.

> Although its leaders were still aware of the need to mobilize people, the task was mainly handed over to the mass organisations whilst the Central Committee members concerned themselves with the day-to-day decision-making involved in running an administration.[7]

Much depended during this period therefore on the activities of the national union of students *Unetim* which had been set up early in 1975, the youth organization OPJT (*Organizacão Popular da Juventude Timor*) set up later in the year, and the women's organization OPMT (*Organizacão Popular de Mulher Timor*). The women's organization played a crucial role because of the deep-rooted traditions affecting women's lives.

Although the OPMT had been mentioned in Fretilin documents early in 1975 it did not begin to function until the end of August, but quickly developed as a major mobilizing force. Its founding secretary, Rosa Muki Bonaparte, had been a student in Lisbon and a member of the *Casa dos Timores* group. She described the OPMT as a mass organization of Fretilin

> which enables women to participate in the revolution ... The creation of OPMT has a double objective: firstly, to participate directly in the struggle against colonialism and second, to fight in every way the violent discrimination that Timorese women have suffered in colonial society.[8]

As well as running creches for needy children and launching health and welfare programmes, the organization set out to mobilize and organize 'the more active and conscious women and to awaken those who are passive and submissive under the exploitation which they suffer'.[9] The OPMT quickly mobilized many Timorese women in support of policies which would radically alter traditional ways of life. It also drew women into military service in defence of the country; by October 1975, reported an Australian relief team which visited East Timor, a women's army unit, a hundred strong, had been set up at the border under the command of a woman.[10]

By the time the invasion of the powerful Indonesian war machine began in December 1975, Fretilin enjoyed overwhelming popular support. It had a number of activist mass organizations which had, within months, made significant strides in mobilizing different sections of the people; and its political leadership encompassed a wide range of ideological and political viewpoints. It also had an army of some three thousand trained Timorese soldiers.

The People's War against Indonesia

In many senses, Fretilin was well prepared for the invasion. The numerous fierce battles fought along the border had destroyed any illusions there may have been about Indonesia's determination to pursue its military adventure against East Timor to the bitter end. In comparison with the invaders, Fretilin enjoyed several important advantages: its territorial control of the country was almost complete; it had secured possession of the entire arsenal abandoned by the Portuguese colonial army. Its armed forces and supporters had an intimate knowledge of the country's difficult terrain, an advantage that had markedly help the Timorese in their fight against the Japanese occupation forces during the second world war.

During the first phase of the war, from December 1975 to September 1977, Fretilin preserved its position of superiority. Although Indonesian troops, supported by tremendous air and sea firepower, captured Dili, Baucau and a few other administrative centres, Fretilin retained control of the countryside, where 90% of the people lived. With the support of its armed wing, Falintil, it was able to defend the liberated areas, and life continued as normal. Food production was quickly adapted to feed a larger population, as many people had fled the Indonesian-controlled centres swelling the population in the mountains.

A conference convened in Soibada from 20 May to 2 June 1976 proceeded without disturbance. This was proof of the effectiveness of Fretilin's territorial control. At this conference of the Fretilin Political Committee and the Supreme Council of Struggle, attended by delegates from all parts of the country, the character of the war and the strategy for fighting the invaders was discussed. It defined the invasion as a protracted war and agreed that preparations for a long, hard struggle were needed. Any compromise solution with the Indonesians was firmly rejected. Although these decisions were supported by the majority of the leadership, there were already elements that were wavering, for whom the prospect of a long-term people's war together with revolutionary changes in many aspects of daily life were unacceptable. As Denis Freney explained:

> Within a broad front for liberation such as Fretilin, there is naturally resistance to such a revolution. Members of the colonial elite who were nationalist and wanted an easy transition to independence in which they could replace the traditional colonial rulers also joined Fretilin. When the Indonesian fascists invaded, they also fled to the mountains and joined the resistance. For some it was possible to undergo a revolution in their own thinking and take part in the revolution in the liberated areas. But for others, it was impossible. Their own reactionary ideology was too strong to change. They imposed in the liberated areas they 'led' a new form of feudal relations, demanding (that) the masses give them the 'respect' they had experienced when they were Portuguese civil servants. For them, the overthrow of colonial and traditional relationships was 'communism'. For them, to live like Mauberes, to share their hunger, their nakedness and lack of 'civilised' facilities was impossible.[11]

Until mid-1977, life in the liberated areas proceeded with only occasional disturbances from Indonesian attacks. People were able to move freely from one area to another. Neobere, a Timorese resistance fighter who spent three years in the interior, described how he moved around organizing the medical services: he travelled along the coastal areas, north and south in 1976; in 1977 he travelled the length and breadth of the mountainous interior.

Food production was enhanced by a centrally organized system of seed distribution. In May 1977, Radio Maubere, the voice of Fretilin, announced that the previous year's harvest was an all time record. Production co-operatives were set up in many places and food was produced by collective labour. Neobere outlined the process:

> Much the same pattern developed everywhere. The main crops grown were maize, cassava, potatoes and rice. Where I was we couldn't grow much rice (as) we were too high up the mountains ... so we got rice by exchanging things with people in other regions. We developed a system of exchange in the interior. We could grow coffee and exchanged it for other things. We also transported it to areas occupied by the enemy.[12]

The 1976 conference decision to adopt the strategy of a people's war meant that urgent changes were needed in political, military and organizational affairs. On the military front, Falintil was reshaped into a regular army and small units called shock brigades were set up to launch short, sharp attacks on the Indonesian troops. The new style of political work in the liberated areas was described by Father Leoneto do Rego, a Catholic priest who lived with the resistance in the interior until December 1978.

There are political commissioners, and each commissioner has assistants. Many times they held meetings with the people for political clarifications on the evolution of the struggle. There is a political education school where they train political assistants.

There were also other types of meetings of the people, with the political assistants and sometimes without them, to programme the way of life and solve all the problems of the camps, from latrines to housing the pigs and other animals... They were conscious of what they were fighting for—independence. If they hadn't cared, then everything would have been finished. That meant that the population was able to organise things easily.[13]

Some essential goods were no longer available now that contact with the major towns was blocked. Sugar was grown and processed. Medicines including pills were produced at two centres, in Lakluta and in the Matabian region. Gunpowder was manufactured, and methods to recharge batteries were devised so that the radios could be kept operational. The school system was maintained and even developed; Fretilin built more schools in the first eighteen months of resistance than the Portuguese had built in five centuries of colonial rule.

This was also the period when a discernible shift began to occur within the Fretilin leadership. The influence of some leaders began to decline while new leaders emerged who had persevered in the face of formidable difficulties. Although Xavier do Amaral continued as president, his political support waned significantly. In mid-1976, at the time of the Soibada conference, he had been criticized for his feudalistic attitudes and insistence upon a comfortable life-style. Others like Mau Lear, Bieki Sahe, Mau Kruma, Mau Laka, Serakey and Hamis Basarewa took responsibility for the educational and political centres that were established in the liberated areas. They created the foundation for a new generation of leaders who would eventually carry the struggle into the 1980s.

Fretilin also waged a campaign against the remnants of feudalism and obscurantism in the liberated areas. This was a continuation of the campaign started earlier by the ASDT. Fretilin's political programme defended religious freedom and freedom of belief, it pledged protection for *uma lulics*—sacred houses—and traditional temples. At the same time it directed a campaign against tribalism, regionalism, arranged marriages and feudal servitude. Fretilin became the first Timorese political organization to develop cultural politics as part of its programme. It advocated the use of local languages at meetings and during literacy campaigns to enable people to read and write their own language first.

The introduction of the word Maubere to characterize the Timorese people was a successful example of Fretilin's decision to use Timorese cultural symbols politically. According to Helen Hill, 'In the decades before 1974, Mau-Bere was a term of contempt for poor, ignorant, supersticious peasants.'[14] Mau-Bere was originally a Mambai word. Elizabeth Traube, an anthropologist who conducted research among the Mambai people in the early 1970s, analysed the word's transformation under Fretilin. The Mambai people were regarded by their Tetum-speaking neighbours and the coastal peoples, particularly the more 'cosmopolitan' residents of Dili, as the most backward of the Timorese people. They were

> identified as a group of ignorant, taciturn, withdrawn highland hillbillies. At the same time, a certain sense of awe and mystery hangs over them. They are portrayed as suspicious, careful guardians of traditional Timorese wisdom. These multiple images of the Mambai intertwine in the usages of 'Mau Bere', a common Mambai personal name. During the colonial period, Mau Bere was a semi-derogatory tag for all the illiterate, ignorant impoverished hill people. Fretilin took up this Mambai name and made of it one of the central symbols of the liberation movement. The phrase, 'Mau Bere, my brother' became a pervasive refrain, a call for Timorese unity, for to be a Mau Bere was to be a 'son of Timor'.[15]

Contradictions around Three Central Issues

The first two periods in Fretilin's history, from the birth of the organization until the Indonesian invasion and from the invasion up till September 1977, were characterized by a spectacular growth of the organization: the leadership matured, its military capability improved enormously and the involvement of the population with Fretilin's policies had steadily risen. However, a number of weaknesses and contradictions had also emerged. These were revealed when pressure on the resistance movement intensified as a result of the three Indonesian attacks launched during their campaign of encirclement and annihilation. In an interview in December 1979, Abilio Araujo publicly announced the setbacks Fretilin suffered as a result of this Indonesian campaign:

> The situation has changed mainly due to the weaknesses in our organization. I say weaknesses, because of the historical development of Fretilin as a front. In a very short time, it had to develop very quickly. We were also forced—in a very short time—to face tremendous offensives from the imperialist forces represented by Indonesia. But (it) lacked in many respects a sound ideological basis. I refer mainly to the leadership of the Fretilin Central Committee; I refer to our army.[16]

Major differences developed in the central committee over three issues: compromise with the enemy, the nature of the war and the implementation of Fretilin's social and political programmes.

Compromise with the Enemy

The majority of central committee members had always rejected the idea of negotiation with the enemy. The debate carried on at the time was centred on whether Fretilin should accept a compromise with the Indonesians and agree to become its client state or stand by its policy of opposition to neo-colonialism and persevere in the struggle for total independence. In early 1977, the leadership split over the question and as a result Xavier do Amaral was removed as president in September.

According to an interview he gave many years later, Amaral had favoured a compromise solution right from the start. He told the *Far Eastern Economic Review* in 1983, that even prior to the Indonesian invasion, he recognized that armed struggle against the Indonesian military was doomed to failure: 'Since the beginning, since 1975, I told the other Fretilin leaders to set up a committee,' he said. 'Let us try to contact the Indonesians.'[17] These remarks may have been coloured by the fact that he was speaking as a man in captivity. The argument he put forward during the controversy in 1977 was the terrible price in terms of loss of life among the women, children and elderly people that the constant fighting exacted. To suggest that compromise would save lives was false and even dangerous as it would only drive the population into the hands of troops whose last concern was the preservation of Timorese lives. Realizing during 1977 that only a small minority on the central committee supported his views, Amaral attempted with force to take over the Fretilin leadership. The attempt failed and he was arrested. A year later after his guards were captured, he surrendered to the Indonesians.

A policy of negotiating with the Indonesian occupying forces from a position of weakness is not only futile, but also extremely costly. Numerous surrenders by guerrilla fighters, as a result of the policy of compromise pursued by Alarico Fernandes, were met by the merciless slaughter of almost all those involved. The ideological transformation that led to the defection and surrender of Alarico Fernandes was different to that of Amaral. Fernandes, who became minister of information and was responsible for Radio Maubere's broadcasts to the outside world, represented a group within the early Fretilin leadership that genuinely supported the goal of independence. However, a difference developed between him and others in the leadership over the question of self-reliance. The majority on the committee stood by the principle of independence through self-reliance. Fernandes and his group held to the conviction that sooner or later assistance would come from the socialist countries. As the war intensified and this expected source of external aid failed to materialize, Fernandes began to waver and slowly shifted towards Amaral's position of compromise.

Because of the influence Fernandes wielded within Fretilin, his betrayal had a far deeper impact on the resistance than that of Amaral. He succeeded in persuading several Falintil commanders as well as some regional political commissars that it was futile to continue the war. He collaborated with the Indonesian intelligence operation called Skylight, the aim of which was to provoke defections within the leadership and ranks of Fretilin. He sent messages to the enemy and even revealed the location of resistance units to the Indonesians. As a result of Operation Skylight some Falintil commanders and their troops left their hideouts and surrendered, in the belief that a solution to the struggle was near. The Indonesians mercilessly dealt with those who surrendered; they were all killed except Fernandes. Details of these atrocities were contained in a report of the Revolutionary Council of National Resistance, in July 1983. The present Fretilin leaders have learnt from these disastrous events and harbour no illusions about compromise or surrender.

The Nature of the War

The 1976 conference in Soibada had adopted the strategy of people's war and this was reaffirmed at a Fretilin's Political Committee meeting in Lalini in 1977, which also stressed the principle of self-reliance. However, the implementation of these decisions proved far from easy. Another national conference held in March 1981—the first to be held following the severe setback suffered by the movement in 1978 and 1979—discussed the weaknesses that had arisen during the armed struggle and arrived at the following conclusions:

1. There had been a failure to define the stages of the war.
2. There had been a failure to define and characterize the real nature of the war.
3. There had been an inability to assemble and draw lessons from the many combat experiences in the different regions, as a result of which it was not possible to make a general or global plan.
4. The national command had failed to take initiatives on the battlefield.

This overall analysis was in fact the culmination of discussions that had been ongoing within the Fretilin leadership since the establishment of Falintil in September 1975. The influx of so many soldiers from the Portuguese colonial army into Fretilin and its organizational structure was both beneficial and disadvantageous. Fretilin undoubtedly benefitted from the support and participation of so many professional soldiers, but the central committee was aware that this could create ideological and political problems. It was Fretilin's policy from the beginning to keep the army under control, to insist that politics were in command, and to uphold the slogan of 'the political line prevailing over the military line'. For their part, the professional soldiers from the Portuguese colonial army had been trained in the spirit of *apartidarismo*, which meant keeping the army out of politics. Fretilin's insistence upon the primacy of politics was in sharp contradiction with that tradition.

The democratic character of a political organization like Fretilin also created difficulties for soldiers accustomed to a hierarchical structure. They had to adapt to a new system Falintil introduced, abolishing ranks and requiring commanders to be elected. Moreover, the military men often assumed an air of superiority because of the role they played in armed confrontations with the Indonesians, and refused to obey orders from the Fretilin Supreme Command to give weapons to the peasants and train them as a militia. Whereas 'politics in command' required the troops to acknowledge the people as the source of strength for the resistance, former professional soldiers tended to look upon the population as a burden.

In spite of the many efforts made by members of the leadership like Mau Lear, Bieki Sahe and Hamis to politicize Falintil, the fact remained that in many instances it was the military line that dominated, not the political line. Such problems were exacerbated as the war progressed; at the beginning Falintil was well equipped with the weapons and ammunition acquired from the colonial army depots, but with the start of the Indonesian offensive in September 1977, supplies became scarce and the feeling that these should be concentrated in the hands of the professionals tended to be reinforced.

The national conference held from 1-8 March 1981 took a number of decisions for the national reorganization of the resistance forces; Falintil was rebuilt on the basis of the lessons learnt during the previous years. The many weaknesses that emerged during the course of the 1977-78 Indonesian offensive were thoroughly analysed. Some of the salient points which emerged during the conference were:

> Falintil had not been able to exploit the specific features of the war dynamically or to good effect. The many advantages which Falintil enjoyed over the enemy troops were not effectively used to defeat the enemy. These advantages included a superior knowledge of the territory, a much higher level of enthusiasm by comparison with the low morale of the enemy troops, and the support of the population. The conference came to the conclusion that the enemy had won so many battles not because of its own strength but because of Falintil's weaknesses. Such a conclusion placed the onus firmly on the resistance movement to improve its own organizational structure and policy implementation, in conformity with the principle of self-reliance.
> - Many Falintil commanders entered the force after having been sergeants in the Portuguese colonial army. These origins made it difficult for them to understand and implement the people's war strategy.
> - There was a lack of co-ordination and participation between commands in the various regions. Regionalism still played an important part in the minds of the commanders. When one region was attacked, the forces in other regions failed to launch attacks in order to distract and disperse the enemy's forces. By focussing their operations on one region at a time, the Indonesian military were able to gain control of the population. Falintil commanders in the regions concentrated mainly on defending their own sectors with the result that they were ultimately defeated by the enemy. Exchange of experience was very limited. Thus, although the Indonesians repeated the same strategy time and again, Falintil forces were taken by surprise every time.

- Co-ordination and contact between the regional commands and the headquarters were ineffective. The betrayal of Alarico Fernandes worsened this situation. The flow of information from headquarters to the regions and back which was so essential to the struggle failed to work. As a result, there was no general or global plan, and strategy, and it was not possible to mount a general counter-offensive.
- The shock brigades set up to launch short, sharp attacks on enemy troops never really functioned in the way intended, and they became a defensive force.
- The white zones (the territory under enemy control) were totally neglected. As the Indonesian offensive progressed, more and more people came under the control of the Indonesian military, and Fretilin lost contact with the vast majority of the population.
- Falintil failed to develop its confidence in the strength of the population.

In 1982, proclaimed the year of the strategic counter-offensive by Fretilin, the reorganized Falintil successfully launched many offensives throughout the country, particularly in the latter months of the year. A new Falintil had been born.

Implementation of the Social and Political Programme of Fretilin

From the outset, most Fretilin leaders had taken the social and political programmes very seriously. Around the middle of 1975 when Fretilin realized that an Indonesian invasion on East Timor was inevitable, these programmes became even more crucial. The leaders anticipated that their strength would be most severely tested in the mountains where the majority of the population lived. Ramos Horta described their plans in a letter to the journalist Jill Jolliffe, written in May 1975.

> Every Fretilin militant in Dili (is) to give up their job; Dili (is to) become a branch with just a few members. Students and teachers will be mobilized for this campaign... they will go out in groups to the villages, stay there for a programme of 'political conscientization'. They will grow their own crops, work and live like villagers. They will also teach the villagers about hygiene, (to) read and write, agricultural systems, etc. Once a month, a member of each group will come to Dili to report on activities in each area.[18]

These programmes should have continued but were cut short by the August UDT coup and later by the Indonesian invasion. The aim, to become one with the population, to mobilize them and to involve them in the people's war, was also obstructed by internal rifts within Fretilin. While leaders like Sahe, Mau Lear and others continued, in the first months after the invasion, to set up and consolidate political education centres and people's libraries, others like Xavier do Amaral did their utmost to reinforce feudal customs in the liberated areas.

In a speech on 14 September 1977, Nicolau Lobato dealt at length with the behaviour of Amaral and his group. They had not only boycotted Fretilin's programmes but started setting up a feudal-type administration, encouraged regionalism and so disrupted life in the central sector that it became particularly vulnerable to Indonesian attacks.

The programme also encountered difficulties from 'the class of sergeants', many of whom could not grasp the connection between these political programmes and the task of fighting a people's war. The 1981 Fretilin national conference devoted serious attention to this problem. In an interview Abilio Araujo said:

> The indiscipline of several commanders resulted in many casualties among the population, the dismantling of the organization and the deportation of many people to Atauro.[19]

These commanders lacked confidence in the people and did not understand why they should be drawn into the struggle. This led to passivity in encounters with the enemy. Falintil's struggle during the Indonesian campaign of encirclement and annihilation became a defensive one. Instead of launching counter-attacks, they were driven to withdrawal and retreat. In terms of mobility, the unarmed peasants became more and more of a burden on Falintil. In the end, the Indonesians attained their goal of annihilating Falintil and encircling the population.

The period 1979 to 1981 gave the surviving Fretilin leaders a new range of experience. As a result a major reappraisal took place at the March 1981 conference. The political work and the pattern of thinking introduced by the generation of fallen leaders, Sahe, Mau Lear and Nicolau Lobato, is now being carried on by the present leaders: Mau Hodu, Lere Timur, Kilik Wae Gae and many others. Learning from the mistakes of the past, they are convinced that without the participation of the people, the struggle is doomed to failure. Even if some military actions are occasionally successful, these can be nothing more than isolated victories. The liberation of the country can only be achieved as the result of mobilizing the entire population to participate in the political and military resistance.

The Period from September 1978 to March 1981

The downfall and the resurgence of Fretilin occurred during the period September 1978 to March 1980. When the Indonesians launched their third and final massive attack, moving eastwards from Baucau and Viqueque, supported by heavy bombardment from air and sea, Fretilin resistance was already at a low ebb. The scorched-earth tactic was used savagely by Indonesian troops to destroy the food-production areas of the population. The two previous Indonesian attacks, in the western and central sectors, had forced Fretilin onto the defensive. These earlier attacks were characterized by the continuous retreat of Falintil troops.

Initially, they retreated with the population, but as the situation deteriorated, the Fretilin leadership had to take the difficult decision of telling the people to surrender to the Indonesians. They were forced to explain that they could no longer continue the old strategy of establishing frontlines and waging semi-positional warfare. It would now be a matter for them to uphold their ideals and build resistance organizations inside the Indonesian concentration camps, in the villages and towns including in Dili.

Even during this period of extreme hardship, the people's determination to continue the struggle remained high. By late 1978, defence was concentrated in the Mount Matabian region, the last support base of the resistance. Realizing that further retreat would be synonymous with committing suicide, the leadership had no option but to defend this last bastion of resistance. The Matabian base was indeed a good place from which to mount a defence. The food situation was good; care had been taken in the previous years to bring all fertile areas into production so there was no immediate danger of a food shortage. From a military and strategic point of view Matabian was ideal for a defensive operation. Enemy troops penetrating the mountainous region could be attacked from at least three directions. Nevertheless, the defence of Matabian proved to be a serious and costly mistake.

Although the people fought with great courage, the overwhelming strength of the enemy was too great. The Indonesian military employed two devastatingly brutal methods to attack Mount Matabian. Realizing that the area was inhabited by tens of thousands of people, the Indonesians first launched a scorched-earth policy to destroy the agricultural system of Matabian. Then, in October they tightened their encirclement and launched a campaign of intensive air and sea bombardment. On 22 November 1978, the last base of the resistance fell to the enemy. Fretilin leaders and Falintil troops fought their way out of the encirclement both westwards and eastwards. Twelve battalions of Indonesian troops in pursuit managed to capture or kill many of them, but many others escaped. In his message to the United Nations, Xanana described this situation and the brutalities perpetrated by Indonesian troops during the months that followed the fall of Matabian:

> Not satisfied with their successes, they increased their criminal bestiality. But thousands of patriots continued to reject enemy control and were aggressively massacred when captured. Throughout the territory the most inhuman spectacles were witnessed, such as the cutting off of sexual organs, tongues, lips, ears, fingers, arms or legs, or victims screaming horribly after their abdomens were ripped open and who were then either burnt alive or tied to tree trunks where they were left to rot in the sun or rain. Women were stripped and sadistically violated then beaten until they died in an orgy of blood and crime. All this because they were identified as Fretilin and didn't want to surrender!

These spectacles aimed to impose an acceptance of control and avoidance of the possibility of desertion. But nevertheless, the badly-treated population, violated and oppressed, once more began to rush back to the bush.

With the control of the population established, the enemy then concentrated, first of all, on the extermination of the wise, intrepid and heroic Fretilin central committee, the clear-sighted vanguard of the Maubere people, then to annihilate the heroic combatants of Falintil. These operations continued until March 1979 when they achieved success by concentrating all their effective troops available at that time in the central region of the country.[20]

Although losses suffered by Fretilin in the eastern sector were enormous, the resistance movement there was in better shape than in the border and central regions. The surviving members of the central committee, along with dozens of staff members, troops and ordinary people, immediately began to reorganize Fretilin and resume the struggle. Things were far worse in the central and border sectors. Following the death or capture of the leaders of the Supreme Command, most of the resistance forces were forced to surrender by their own commanders who had lost all confidence in the struggle. At its conference in March 1981, the first after the fall of Matabian, the Fretilin leadership gave an account of the losses sustained during the Indonesian campaign from September 1977 to March 1979. These losses were crippling:

- 79% of the members of the Supreme Command had been killed, and only three members of the Fretilin central committee had survived, Serakey, Mau Hunu and Xanana, all of them in the eastern zone.
- 80% of Falintil troops had been lost, and more than 90% of its weapons.
- All the support bases had been destroyed and the Indonesian troops now had the population under their control.
- All lines of communications between the remaining resistance fighters had been severed.
- Communication with the outside world was cut off, making it extremely difficult to channel information to supporters abroad.

In the eastern sector, the surviving Fretilin leaders and Falintil troops immediately set to work to reorganize their forces. Agricultural production was resumed as quickly as possible. It was decided to send out search parties to find surviving resistance fighters in other parts of the country and to begin the task of restoring the lines of communications. At the end of March 1979 the first search mission left the eastern sector for the central sector but never returned; it was captured. In April, a second group departed, led by a political commissar, Serakey, but it too was captured by the enemy. In July, determined to reestablish contact, the surviving groups in the east sent out yet another search party. This one returned, but only to report that they had found no one. In December 1979 a company of Falintil troops embarked along the south coast, then northwards towards Alas and Turiscai. It encountered Indonesian troops near Laklubar and a battle ensued. The company returned to base in the east, again reporting that they had discovered no surviving resistance.

In May 1980 a unit, consisting of half a company under the command of Xanana, travelled along the north coast to the western border. On their way back, at Remexio, south-east of Dili, they engaged in battle with Indonesian troops and succeeded in breaking through enemy lines, retreating into the central sector. In August, they managed to reach Kablake, in the border sector, before finally returning to the eastern sector.

During this time, independent Fretilin units that were active near Bazartete and the Comoro river launched a series of attacks on Indonesian positions in and around the capital, Dili. The prestigious television transmitter on the outskirts of town was attacked as well as Indonesian garrisons in Railaco, Bazartete and Tibar. These attacks were evidence that Fretilin was still very much alive.* In October that year, another mission from the east, led this time by Mau Hunu, travelled again through the central sector and succeeded in establishing contact with two isolated units in Kablake and Maumela. By the end of the year, communications between a number of surviving units had been well enough established to convene a national conference, the one held in March 1981.

The Year of National Reorganization: 1981

Although in 1980 Fretilin units had already shown themselves capable of mounting attacks on Indonesian positions, it was in 1981 that the resurgence of Fretilin really occurred. The March 1981 conference proved that, with the lines of communication restored, the resistance movement was again functioning as a nation-wide organization with a developing strategy. The conference discussed the new methods of organization and struggle that had been implemented since 1979, and on the basis of these experiences endorsed a new strategy and programme. Fretilin for the first time became an organization with unity of principles, unity of action and unity of command.

The new strategy consisted of two main features which sharply distinguished the post-1979 period from the earlier three years. The strategy of maintaining permanent bases was abandoned; Falintil units would now function as mobile units, continually moving from place to place. A network of clandestine organizations was created, behind enemy lines, inside the concentration camps and in population centres under the control of the occupation forces. Although most of the population was now physically in the hands of the enemy, the policy of relying

---

* The Indonesian counter-insurgency documents reproduced in Part II mention other Fretilin attacks in 1980: Mulia village on 20 June, Baguia on 21 August and Baucau on 25 December.

on the people would be implemented far more effectively than it had been in the earlier phase of the struggle. The link between the resistance movement in the bush and the clandestine network was to be established and maintained by the *nucleos de resistencia popular* (nucleus of popular resistance).*

On the basis of this two-pronged strategy, many errors committed in the first three years of resistance were corrected. Regionalism was stamped out and replaced by a global view of activities. The shock brigades, originally intended to mount lightning attacks on enemy positions, would now be able to function properly, often with the benefit of intelligence supplied by the support network behind enemy lines. In fact, during 1980, Falintil forces launched more attacks on the enemy than during the eighteen months of the Indonesian offensive up to the end of 1978. Not all these guerrilla attacks were successful but the switch from defensive to offensive action, combined with the principle of mobility and linkage with the population, created a style of warfare that has constantly threatened the Indonesian military.

Reliance on weaponry strength was replaced by reliance on the strength of the people. But to ensure that this did not mean being a burden on the people, guerrilla units were responsible for securing their own supplies of weapons and ammunition. By maintaining a high degree of mobility, combat units would not need to rely on the people for their food supplies. Wherever units have found themselves stationary for a few days, they can undertake food production. New forms of rationing and stockpiling of food and ammunition have been developed. Roaming in the interior so much of which has been forcibly abandoned by the population has given the guerrillas the free run of many fertile areas and village gardens. Indonesia's population policy has placed the resistance in a much better position vis-a-vis food supplies than the people cooped up in the camps. Through the support networks in the camps and towns, guerrilla forces have been able to obtain equipment such as radios and tape-recorders, which has enabled them to improve their lines of communication and to keep in touch with the outside world.

The Present Fretilin Leadership

The 1981 national conference elected a new leadership: Kay Rala Xanana was elected National Political Commissar, President of the Revolutionary Council of National Resistance and Commander-in-Chief of Falintil. Past experience had shown Fretilin the need to build its structure and appoint people to positions of responsibility in accordance with the requirements of the struggle. Those who now occupy senior positions in the leadership include Kilik Wae Gae, who is Chief-of-Staff; Mau Hunu,

---

* This unit is referred to in the secret Indonesian military documents by the acronym *nurep*. The attention devoted to *nurep* in these documents is testimony to the spectacular success achieved by the strategy adopted in 1981.

who is Deputy Chief-of-Staff; Mauk Moruk Teky Timor, who is First Commander of the Red Brigades; and Bere Malay Laka, who is Secretary of Information, Agitation and Propaganda.

Xanana, who now leads both Fretilin and Falintil, was a construction worker under the Portuguese. He became a militant member of ASDT/Fretilin. During the brief period of the Fretilin *de facto* administration in the last quarter of 1975, he worked at the Department of Information and as an elected member of the Fretilin central committee. After the Indonesian invasion, he became Deputy-Secretary of the regional command of the central-east sector and was put in charge of a Falintil platoon. He was later given charge of the Hacsolok support base in the eastern sector before becoming the principal man in the Ponte Leste (eastern tip) sector at the time of the 1977-78 Indonesian offensive. After the collapse of the resistance, he took provisional control of Falintil, as Commander-in-Chief, during which time he wrote two theoretical works: *Country and Revolution* and *Themes on the War*. These describe the revolutionary process of a people's war based on the specific experience of East Timor. He is considered the main architect of the post-1979 reorganization of Fretilin and Falintil.

The other person in the new leadership with such long-standing experience is Mau Hunu Bulerek Karataianu. He was also a founder member of ASDT/Fretilin, who became a central committee member before the invasion. In the early period, he worked at Fretilin's Department of Internal Affairs. After the invasion, he became Commander of the central zone, and was later transferred to the Ponte Leste sector to become the Deputy Secretary of the regional command and Commander of his sector. He was instrumental in the development of the new strategy and tactics of the new born resistance movement.

After the adoption of the new strategy, the organizational structure of the military command was changed. The country was divided into three military regions:

1) The eastern sector, stretching from Baucau and Viqueque to the eastern tip of the island, is called *Funu Sei Nafatin*, which means 'the war never ended' or 'the struggle continued'. It symbolizes the fact that resistance never ceased in this part of the country despite all the defeats in 1978. The reorganization started in this region, which still continues to be Fretilin's main base. Many of the present leaders, including both Xanana and Mau Hunu had their base there during the earlier period of resistance.

2) The central sector, called *Nakroma*, covers the area from Baucau and Viqueque in the east to Dili and Betano in the west. Nakroma means 'light', to recall that it was here that the founders of Fretilin first began their clandestine meetings and held their founding conference; it was here that the ground was laid for the long and bitter struggle of the East Timorese people for independence.

3) The western or border sector is called *Hacsolok*, which is the Tetum word for 'joy'. This sector stretches from Dili and Betano

to the border with West Timor. This name was chosen to commemorate the feelings which greeted the contacts made in 1980 with isolated, roaming Fretilin units, making it possible to begin to rebuild and reorganize the nationwide resistance.

The political administrative structure was also reshaped. At the national level, the resistance is now led by the Revolutionary Council of National Resistance (CRRN). This includes the members of the Fretilin central committee, commanders of Falintil units and representatives of people living in the Indonesian-controlled concentration camps and population centres. Below the CRRN there are Regional Committees for the Resistance at the district level and Centres of National Resistance at the sub-district level. At the lowest level of the structure are the nuclei of popular resistance.

Fretilin since 1981

The new strategy adopted in early 1981 has been enormously successful. In 1982, proclaimed 'the year of the strategic counter-offensive'. Falintil forces launched many small attacks on Indonesian posts particularly in the latter half of the year. The Indonesian military were rattled by the new upsurge in the fighting. Indonesian casualties mounted and troop morale declined. Although equipped with superior weapons the Indonesian soldiers were ill-prepared psychologically and inadequately trained to handle guerrilla warfare. There are reports from the resistance that during this period, Indonesian soldiers surrendered with their weapons, or refused to do battle and fled, leaving their weapons behind. It was during this period, in December 1982, that guerrillas managed to capture the secret military documents published at the end of this book.

Fretilin's new strategy has developed four political and military objectives:
1. *All-out mobilization of the population*, politically as well as militarily. People, inside the camps as well as in the towns, are involved in many aspects of the resistance struggle, from information-gathering to helping supply the guerrillas with goods—clothing, medicines, equipment—that are unobtainable in the bush.
2. *To dissipate the forces of the enemy* by carrying out political work among Timorese who have been won over to fight for the Indonesians or to help run their local bureaucracy. The objective of Indonesia's policy of Timorization is to make Timorese fight Timorese. Instead of falling into the trap of adopting an attitude of hostility towards these Timorese or even taking up arms against them, Fretilin's policy is one of persuasion. The clandestine groups have a particularly important role to play in this respect and make effective use of literature as well as discussions to convince Timorese collaborators of the justice and favourable prospects of the liberation struggle. Such activities have certainly contributed to the many defections that have occurred among Hansip troops and Timorese soldiers in the 744 and 745 Battalions. The policy of persuasion is also

used towards Indonesian soldiers who are captured, to inform them of East Timor's strong desire for independence and then allow them to return to their own base. It is not in any case Falintil's policy to keep prisoners of war because of logistical and other problems.

3. *Building a broad front.* In the pre-1979 period, this was frequently neglected because of the diversity of viewpoints within the leadership which was by its very nature a front. Today, a strongly united leadership that enjoys wide popular support makes it far easier for Fretilin to build a front. The slogan of the CRRN is: 'Open wide the doors of the front to serve the struggle.' The fact that Fretilin is the only political force defending the aspirations of the population greatly enhances its appeal and attraction even to people who carry their own burden of traditionalist and backward feudal ideas. These include the *rajas* and *liurai* many of whom have been appointed by Indonesia to the figurehead positions of *bupati* and *camat*, district and subdistrict heads. Fretilin is in a good position to appeal to the frustrations and patriotic sentiments of people who are often misused and humiliated by Indonesian officials.

4. *Annihilation of the enemy.* The central objective of the strategy is to destroy enemy troops, by waging continual attacks and mobilizing the people as far as possible. Although the Indonesian military command has never made public any figures about Indonesian casualties—the figures are a tightly guarded secret—there is no doubt that many thousands of Indonesian troops have been killed in East Timor.

By late 1982, the morale of Indonesian troops was very low and it was becoming alarmingly apparent to the military command that the new strategy of the resistance movement had placed them in a position of defensiveness. It was during this period that a whole series of local ceasefires came into effect, on the initiative of local Indonesian military commanders unwilling to cope with continual combat. This led ultimately to the talks in March 1983 which were held on the initiative of the Indonesian military command and which resulted in a general ceasefire that was to hold for several months. For Fretilin, the talks were an opportunity to force the Indonesian military command to acknowledge the movement's strength and, because of this, to score an outstanding international political victory. During the months of the ceasefire, Falintil guerrillas and Fretilin militants entered the Indonesian-controlled camps where they carried out propaganda work and consolidated the position of the clandestine network.

Fretilin leaders rejected an Indonesian proposal that the puppet governor Mario Carrascalao should represent the Indonesian side at the talks. The Indonesians were therefore compelled to agree that Xanana, the Falintil Commander-in-Chief, would negotiate with Colonel Purwanto, Commander of the military command in East Timor. The demands set forth by Fretilin involved no element of compromise. They were:

- the unconditional withdrawal of Indonesian occupying troops;
- the presence in East Timor of a United Nations peace-keeping force;
- the holding of free consultations with the population on the country's future;

- the maintenance of Falintil forces in the mountains in order to protect the population from any pressures.

The objectives Indonesia had hoped to secure by means of these talks were completely frustrated. In fact, the talks boomeranged and became a source of humiliation for the Armed Forces. Despite efforts to keep the talks secret, the news broke internationally, forcing the Indonesian high command to abandon the negotiations policy and try to repair the damage done to its image. The ceasefire was halted as the Indonesian Armed Forces Commander-in-Chief, General Murdani began preparations for the third offensive against East Timor's struggle for liberation. This time however, the movement is in a vastly better position to cope than in 1977. The resurgence of Fretilin and its counter-offensive strategy has made the world of difference to the conditions in which war is now being waged in East Timor. The four main objectives defined in 1981 have to a considerable extent been achieved. In his 1983 New Year's message, Xanana proclaimed 1983 'the year of national unity'.

4. The Population Uprooted

Indonesia's successful encirclement and annihilation campaign in 1977 and 1978 forced hundreds of thousands of Timorese to leave the mountainous interior and enter Indonesian-held territory. Their objective had been secured: the vast majority of people were now resettled in heavily guarded camps, isolating the resistance from its broad popular support. However even when the resistance was at its lowest, Fretilin leaders never lost sight of the need to preserve close ties with the population. Under the changed circumstances, this meant transforming the concentrations of people firmly behind enemy lines into centres of opposition to Indonesian rule. With the growth of the camps, a new form of resistance emerged from 1979 onwards.

Before the Indonesian invasion, the population of East Timor was widely dispersed. Most people lived in hamlets (*povoacão*) which were no more than five or six houses clustered together. These were scattered throughout the country, but particularly in the mountainous regions. The densely populous areas of the country were: the central region, south of Dili; the eastern central region, from Baucau on the north coast to Viqueque in the south; Baguia in the east; and in several regions near the West Timor border. The Portuguese colonial administration had divided the country into thirteen *concelhos* (councils or districts), each of which was subdivided into *postos* which incorporated a number of *sucos*. The *postos* were run by administrators operating from centres which were also known as *postos*. These administrative centres as a rule consisted of little more than an administration office in charge of tax collection and conducting the regular population census, a church, a few Chinese shops, occasionally a school, sometimes a health centre and a market-place in those regions where neighbouring peasants produced marketable crops.

There are numerous accounts of the social and economic conditions in East Timor in the early 1970s. Two American anthropologists researching in different parts of the country in the early 1970s have both testified before US congressional hearings and UN committees since the invasion. Shepard Forman spent more than a year among the Makassae people, who live along the north coast around Baucau and in the high mountain valleys of east central East Timor.

They live primarily by the cultivation of corn and root crops in patrilineally-inherited ancestral gardens; grow rice in elaborately sculpted and irrigated mountain terraces; herd water buffalo, goats and pigs; raise chickens and fighting cocks; and weave *ikat* cloths which, along with their crops and livestock, ancient swords, glass beads and a few gold amulets, comprise the totality of their exchangeable wealth. Socially, the Makassae are organised in patrilineages, resident in small and scattered family compounds of thatched houses built up on stilts in highly defensive positions on mountain abutments.[1]

Elizabeth Traube, who lived among the Mambai people in the district of Aileu, south of Dili, explained the pre-invasion relationship between the *postos* and the surrounding hamlets. The Aileu *posto*, she said, was the weekly market place for the people of the whole district.

> ...most of native social life transpires on the surrounding hills and high valleys of Timor's rugged interior. There the Mambai eke out a subsistence existence based on the swidden (dry land) cultivation of rice, corn and root crops. Gardens are individually held and co-operatively worked by kin groups. Mambai also herd water buffalo, goats and pigs, which are primarily used in formal ceremonial exchanges. Most families own small coffee holdings which are the major source of cash income. Like other Timorese peoples, the Mambai live in tiny, highly dispersed hamlets of two to five houses.[2]

A German agronomist, Joachim K. Metzner spent over a year in the Baucau-Viqueque district studying the methods of food production evolved by Timorese peasants in face of a rigorous climate and unfavourable soil conditions. Population dispersal, he wrote was prompted by

> a desire to settle in localities where the soil is more fertile... and was also stimulated by the persistence of shifting cultivation as the main form of Timorese agriculture (which) required much more land than the area actually under cultivation in any one year. Furthermore, the spread of people was often influenced by the scatter of more fertile land and good water supplies through the mountainous terrain in the central part of (East) Timor.[3]

The method of shifting cultivation developed in East Timor, which he calls 'bush fallowing', generally meant that the cultivator did not actually move but cleared and cultivated several plots of land in succession, planting a variety of crops over a wide area accessible from the family homestead. Maize was the main crop. It was grown both by the 'bush-fallowers' and the peasants who grew wet rice where climatic conditions allowed double-cropping. Rice cultivation was expanding at the time of his research, both on rainfed and irrigated fields. A specific feature of rice cultivation in East Timor was the use of buffaloes to trample the soil in preparation for sowing. A large number of animals were needed to trample a field which accounted for the large number of buffaloes; they were an integral part of food production. In addition to 'bush fallowing' and rice cultivation, permanent gardening on plots adjacent to their homes 'is practised by every Timorese (and) plays an important part as a source of food supply'. These home gardens were planted with a profusion of fruit trees, bamboos and bananas interwoven with climbing and winding plants, vegetables, tubers and so on.[4]

A Captive Population

> What I must stress is that villages (*povoacão*) as we knew them before the Indonesian invasion simply don't exist any more. All village life has stopped. Everyone has been brought together in the settlements, around the *postos*.[5]

Indonesia's population control policy became apparent in 1976 when Radio Maubere reported on several occasions that thousands of people were being herded into guarded camps. In March 1977, the radio broadcast an account by someone who had escaped from a camp in Laga; there was widespread starvation in the camp, he said, and the inhabitants were being severely maltreated.[6]

In September 1978, when the second phase of the encirclement and annihilation campaign in the central sector had just been completed and the third phase in the eastern sector was being launched, a group of ambassadors and foreign journalists were taken to East Timor. The reports that appeared in the press following their visit to Remexio some fifteen kilometres south-east of Dili allowed the outside world the first glimpse of the catastrophe that had befallen the Timorese people during the 1977-78 Indonesian offensive.

> 'These people are totally stunned by what has happened,' a senior Timorese official told the *Review*. 'Thousands died in this *Kabupaten*. The people are shocked both by the severity of the killing and by the recent political changes.[7]

Church aid workers told the journalist of a camp where people were dying at the rate of 500 a month. Conditions in Remexio, which had only been in Indonesian hands for two months, were by no means the worst. 'This is nothing,' one official told the *Review*, 'At Suai things are much worse and there are many more people. There is an urgent need for humanitarian aid.' The *Melbourne Herald* reported that the diplomats and newsmen who visited Remexio were convinced that 'a major international relief effort is necessary'.[8] Yet is was another thirteen months before the military authorities allowed a relief programme to begin: not until the encirclement and annihilation campaign had thoroughly accomplished its objectives and Seroja Joint Command disbanded. The International Red Cross (ICRC) was allowed in for its first, brief on-the-spot assessment, in April 1979, only a few weeks after *Seroja* was dissolved. The ICRC had been kept out of the territory by the Indonesians ever since the invasion began. Its relief operations did not commence till October.

An indication of the death rate in the Indonesian-controlled camps during the first year after population control had been completed is given in *East Timor: Some Experiences and Reflections* by a Catholic priest. He described conditions in Maubisse, south of Dili in one of the Indonesian controlled corridors and in Ermera, formerly the centre of the relatively prosperous coffee-growing region, east of Dili. By 1979, both centres had far greater populations than before 1975 when they were *postos*.

> 'During the first week of March, 26 people were buried in this area' the Catechist said, who then opened his prayerbook in which was noted: February 1979—101 dead; January—74. Since 1976 this village which had a population of 9,607 has lost 5,021 people...
>
> (Refugees) hope that they can obtain help with food, clothing and medicine in the towns. They are greatly disappointed in this hope. Aid, if available, often comes too late and in total is very small so that it is almost without meaning. For example, the Maubisse health centre, for the month of February, received from the Regent's office a total of 300 chloroquine pills and five metres of bandage cloth. Each day on average, 150 people come here for treatment. In one or two Chinese shops in the village there is much more medicine than in the Government Health Centre. But the people cannot afford to buy it.
>
> In the same village in the middle of March 1979, there came about 2½ tons of corn aid. About 6,000 people were waiting for this aid for five weeks... The volume of aid, which is so small or so late, is sometimes felt more as an irony. It is not surprising if the complaint is heard: We are being allowed to die slowly by the Government...
>
> (According to the *Camat* in) Turiscai, the population of the village at the beginning of March was as much as 7,314. In 1977 6 people died, in 1978—164 and in 1979, up to 13 March, 120 died. The figure of deaths climbed in 1978 and 1979. Apparently this happened in many places where there were 'refugees'.
>
> In Ermera, someone said that this was the least safe (area); until Easter 1979 almost every day ten people died... 'Many more refugees, many more dead' became a kind of formula.[9]

He also described conditions in Laga, a few miles east of Baucau. Rice supplied by the authorities for distribution had been commandeered by officials and was only available for sale in a house in the town. Six months later, the Australian journalist Peter Rodgers was to take photographs in Laga of emaciated children on the verge of death. The Rodgers report, with photographs, smuggled out of Jakarta after the authorities denied him the use of press facilities to transmit them to Sydney, created a major international stir when his material was reproduced by newspapers in many countries. He had visited East Timor to report on the relief programmes just being launched by the ICRC and the Catholic Relief Services (CRS). He quoted the CRS regional director, Frank Carlin as saying that the problem of starvation in East Timor was 'greater than anything I have seen in fourteen years of relief work in Asia'. David Delaprez, head of the ICRC relief operations told him it was

> as bad as Biafra and potentially as serious as Kampuchea... Look at our figures. One third of the 60,000 people under the ICRC programme need medical care. The same cannot be said of the Vietnamese refugees.[10]

The strategic purpose of the camps which the Indonesians call *daerah pemukiman* (resettlement areas) was first examined in an Australian Council for Overseas Aid (ACFOA) report. The camps, it said, were variously being referred to as 'relief centres', 'concentration camps', 'prisons' and 'strategic hamlets'. People had been ordered to move from their own village or district into one or other of these centres.

> The strategy, which resembles counter-insurgency techniques employed against guerrillas in such places as Rhodesia, Malaysia and Vietnam has increased the Indonesian army's control over the local population and allowed it, in the words of an Indonesian parliamentarian, 'to separate the people from the terrorists'.[11]

ACFOA also reported that the military had identified three aspects of the policy of population control: *keamanan* (security), *pemeriksaan* (investigation) and *instruksi* (instruction or command). Already in 1979, the military were aware of the danger of resistance developing inside the camps. The 1982 secret army documents describe the army's counter-insurgency operations against what was by then a well-organized resistance support-network in the camps.

Initially 150 camps were to be set up with an average population of 2,000 each. However it is impossible to say how many camps are currently in existence. In December 1979, the US ambassador to Indonesia, Edward Masters submitted an official map of East Timor to a US congressional hearing which indicated the locations of the 'resettlement camps'. The map shows 145 camp locations[12] but certainly underestimates the actual number. A Fretilin report compiled in 1983 names several camps in locations identified on the map: eight in Ainaro as compared with the three on the map; eleven in the district of Same instead of six.

Masters told the hearing that:

grouping these people in these settlement areas is the only way under the present circumstances to provide them with food, with the medications and with the essential services that they have to have.[13]

This fabrication clearly shows that Washington justifies Indonesian policies in East Timor, whenever they come under public scrutiny. Masters' crude cover-up for the Indonesians was exposed in a stinging attack two months later by Professor Benedict Anderson, a scholar in Indonesian affairs at Cornell University. Ambassador Masters had personally witnessed conditions in Remexio in September 1978, Anderson told a congressional committee in February 1980, yet it was not until June 1979 that the State Department determined 'that a disaster of such magnitude as to warrant US Government assistance existed in East Timor'.[14]

> In other words, for *nine long months*, from September 1978 to June 1979, while 'in ever increasing numbers the starving and the ailing, wearing rags at best, drifted onto the coastal plain'[15], Ambassador Masters *deliberately* refrained, even within the walls of the State Department, from proposing humanitarian aid to East Timor. Until the generals in Jakarta gave him the green light, Mr Masters did nothing to help the East Timorese... Adding further distortions to the record, Mr Masters made no mention whatever of Indonesian counter-insurgency operations or their effects when he testified before this Committee last December 4. In fact he had the effrontery to suggest that the appalling plight of the East Timorese was primarily their own fault. It was a consequence, he said, of 'the extreme backwardness of the East Timorese economy'. (*Emphasis from the original*)[16]

The Camps and the Food Situation

By forcing the people of East Timor to abandon the homesteads in their widely dispersed hamlets in the mountains, the Indonesians have fundamentally disrupted the East Timorese economy. As the former Bishop of Dili said, 'If the people of East Timor could live where they like, there would be no food shortage.'[17]

Famine has followed the Indonesian bombing raids which ravaged great stretches of productive mountain regions and rice-growing areas on the hill slopes. Starvation reached endemic proportions in 1978 and 1979 during the latter stages of the encirclement and annihilation campaign and the clean-up operation that followed. These operations forced hundreds of thousands of people, stricken by starvation and disease, to enter Indonesian-controlled territory. In the lowland areas, food production had virtually ceased due to the Indonesian invasion; there were no provisions—food or medicine—to cope with the huge influx of people. The death-rate soared. By 1979, it was widely accepted that over 200,000 deaths had occurred. It was not until after international relief operations began in late October 1979, that the horrendous death rate fell.

The food situation was dominated by Indonesia's policy of population control. After a visit in 1980, the pro-integrationist academic, Donald Weatherbee warned that 'the agricultural foundation of these large resettlement centres is inadequate to provide for the (inhabitants). The restrictions imposed on access to land away from the centres means that larger populations have to be supported on less land.' Around Queliquai, he wrote, people

> are only able to work fields that can be reached and returned from in a single day. There is no fertiliser. Rodents destroy a substantial percentage of the crops in the fields. There is no regular water supply, and they are wholly dependent on rainfall. The land they are working cannot supply the population, but they are not permitted to move out or open up other land...
>
> Flying over East Timor by helicopter, one is impressed by thousands of acres of field—for corn, dry rice, wet rice and pasture—now going back to waste, *land whose utilisation was essential to support the population at a minimal subsistence level of existence. (Emphasis added)*[18]

The location of the camps and their security remain the most critical obstacles to current food production in East Timor. Agricultural activities in the camps are also interrupted when military operations are launched, in the interests of Indonesian security objectives. The five-month long Operation Security (May—September 1981) had a particularly devastating effect. On a visit in May 1982, the American journalist, Rod Nordland checked the Biship of Dili's warning the previous year that the Operation would increase famine in the country. Nordland described East Timor as 'beset by widespread malnutrition and hunger'.

> The greatest casualty of Operation Security, in fact, was the 1981-82 corn and rice harvest, much of which was not planted before the rainy season began in September because the men of East Timor were with the army in the mountains. ...According to the clergy here, the result has been a famine or near famine in many parts of the province.[19]

One of the worst-hit areas, Nordland reported, was in and around Baucau and Viqueque, where continuing fighting between government troops and the guerrillas was severest. His conversation with a Catholic nun at a concentration camp in Baucau highlighted the impact the Operation had on food production. The nun described conditions in the camps:

> In Baucau, district administrative staff member Sinago, an Indonesian, introduced Sister Osario Saurez (*sic*), a Timorese nun who is principal of the Catholic primary school there.
>
> She listened as Sinago described what a success Opertion Security had been. 'Every time we go to a village now,' he said, 'they are happy to see us.'
>
> 'Because of the political situation,' Sister Saurez said quietly,

'because the people had to help the military for the Operation Security, they were not able to plant the fields.'

'There is plenty of food here,' Sinago said insistently, and a little nervously.

The nun continued to contradict him with a soft-spoken resolve that clearly astonished some of the officials present. 'We are very short of food, namely in Baguia, Queliquai and Laga. But even here, the food is not sufficient, the health care is not sufficient. Last year it is (sic) better, this year it is worse because of Operation Security'.

The problem had been complicated, she explained, because much of the population had been resettled in the lowlands, far from the mountainside fields. In Baucau District, for instance, 61,000 of the 74,000 people in the district now live clustered around the town of Baucau proper.

'They can grow enough food there,' said Sinago. 'More than fifty per cent of the people are short of food,' Sister Saurez said.[20]

Nordland also measured children at a resettlement camp in Lahane he visited secretly on the outskirts of Dili; eighteen of the twenty-two children he checked before police appeared and told him to stop were 'chronically malnourished' according to World Health Organization criteria. There were several hundred people living in the Lahane camp. most had been moved from their mountain farms by government order in 1980. 'In Lahane, they cannot farm, and most have no steady work in Dili.'

> Although their resettlement area, unlike many of the more than one hundred in the province is not remote, several residents said no aid had been brought to Lahane this year. Each family has a card recording visits of the Indonesian Red Cross with food and medical aid. On each of a dozen cards examined, the last visit noted was in September 1981.[21]

Another journalist later reported on the serious food situation of the camps along the north coast. David Jenkins wrote that, 'the trouble with many settlements is that they are not productive' and are located where the soil 'is often white with salt'.

> The bald, dry hills are difficult to cultivate, and there is in any case a continuing restriction on movement of the people.[22]

He was told about plans to 'regroup' some villages back to the highlands 'in the interests of higher production'.

> However, the families which return to these areas... will not be allowed to disperse once again into tiny scattered units but must stay within the villages and neighbourhoods, the lowest level of the Indonesian military structure (and will still) yearn for the freedom

to move about and freedom from administrative control.[23]

Security and Resistance in the Camps

In his message to the UN General Assembly on 14 October 1982, the Fretilin leader, Xanana said that Indonesia's encirclement and annihilation campaign 'made the Maubere people transfer their support bases from the mountains to the villages'. The secret army documents confirm this when they say of Fretilin that

> (their) system of communications is linked to the settlements system, so that facilities from the Goverment and ABRI units can be harnessed both to supply information and to give logistical support as well as to draw people into action.[24]

Another document admits that GPK* support networks exists in all the settlements and villages as well as in the towns.[25]

The link between the armed resistance in the bush and people living in the camps is maintained by the *nucleos de resistencia popular*, the lowest rung in the structure of the resistance movement. This link, which is identified in the army documents as the *nurep*, is one of the main targets of Indonesia's counter-insurgency campaign. Resistance inside the camps had become so powerful by 1982 that the Army was compelled to 'make the village the focal point of attention' for military personnel at all levels of command.[26] This was a new departure, a shift away from the earlier policy of leaving camp or village security largely to the *babinsa* (*bintara pembina desa*), the officer in charge of village guidance. Now all Koramil (district) and Kodim (subdistrict) officers would have to familiarize themselves with 'the inner workings' of the camps, the layout and security of the camps, and the biographical data on all its formal and informal leaders.

When the Australian parliamentary mission was in East Timor in August 1983, it was offered the chance to meet a support network operating inside the Saelari concentration camp. The invitation was conveyed to the leader of the mission, Bill Morrison, by a group of armed Fretilin fighters who managed to wave down the last two vehicles of the mission's convoy on its way back to Baucau from Los Palos. The spokesman for the group, Cancio de Sousa Gama told Morrison that forty men and women from the bush had been living in Saelari for two months, preparing for this opportunity to meet the parliamentarians. In Gama's words, 'even in this camp controlled by the Indonesians, everyone has made up his/her mind that they have their goal which is total independence'.[27] The Mission turned the invitation down; indeed, the dialogue between

---

* GPK stands for *Gerombolan Pengacau Keamanan* (gangs of security disruptors), the term by which Fretilin is always referred in official Indonesian documents.

Morrison and Gama reveals that Morrison had no idea of how Fretilin supporters could be organizing themselves right inside enemy territory. Morrison's Report claimed that '(t)he administration in East Timor appears to be in effective control of all settled areas'[28] yet his own encounter on the roadside with Gama and his group contradicts this view.

The Indonesian Army's counter-insurgency documents which were captured by Fretilin deal at great length with the 'troublesome' camps. The criteria for such a classification include such things as:

- discontent among the inhabitants because of the misdeeds of Indonesian troops;
- the inability to produce enough food for the inhabitants;
- lack of 'homogeneity' among the inhabitants;
- having a camp leader whose offspring are fighting in the bush;
- having inhabitants who only recently surrendered to the authorities.

Even when none of the many 'causes of trouble' are present, a camp can still be 'troublesome'. No camp, warned the documents, should be regarded as 'clean of a support network. Every possibility exists...'[29]

The documents show that counter-insurgency is directed as much against the population inside Indonesian-controlled camps as it is against the armed fighters in the bush. Military personnel are under orders to operate a comprehensive system of spying and surveillance on all camp inhabitants. This includes keeping watch on 'every single activity' of the population, appointing 'reliable' people to control and spy on their friends and neighbours, organizing house-to-house searches and check-ups to discover whether people have left without permission or entered without reporting to the authorities. No-one may leave camp territory without a travel pass, even to go and cultivate food on nearby fields or tend livestock. Territory immediately beyond the camps must be regularly patrolled to prevent contact with the guerrillas, and surprise raids must be made on gardens or plots suspected of being used as meeting places with people in the bush.

On paper, a civil administration exists in the camps, and the military authorities use Timorese personnel to become village-heads and districts or sub-district chiefs. In fact the soldiers are in control. Colonel Purwanto made no secret of the fact that government administration at the village level is non-existent; 'zero effectiveness' is the way he described it.[30] This has nothing to do with lack of people to run the administration. Control of the camps is a matter of security, not of administration. The main purpose is to stamp out resistance, not to encourage food production or care for the living conditions of the inhabitants.

Fretilin Report on Conditions in the Camps

In mid-1983, Fretilin produced a detailed report on conditions in the camps compiled by the *nucleos de resistencia popular*. It was drawn up soon after reports had appeared in the Australian press based on material gathered during Indonesian-sponsored tours of the country. Occasional references to these distorted reports, in particular the series of articles published in April that year by John Hamilton in the *West Australian* , leave no doubt that its purpose was to give a first-hand account of conditions behind the facade shown to foreign visitors. The Fretilin report covers 61 camps or groups of camps in eight districts covering well over half the country: Viqueque, Baucau, Dili, Ainaro, Same, Manatuto, Aileu and Lautem.*

Western Viqueque
[This is an area where armed guerrilla activity is widespread. It was here that Fretilin hosted the negotiations with the Indonesian military command in March 1983, and the first military clashes occurred in August 1983 ending the 1983 ceasefire.]

With the population confined to the camps, huge tracts of land formerly used to grow rice and corn have been abandoned. The camps are located in places well away from the most important food-growing area and the inhabitants are prohibited from going beyond the immediate vicinity of the camps. The fertile valley of the river Uai Mori (the upper reaches of the river Laleia) has been abandoned as well as the region of Bibileu farther to the south. A number of places near the town of Viqueque have been abandoned: Fatu Lessu, Nae Bosuk, Kai Uailale and Ue Suli Manas. Food-growing areas around the town of Ossu, twenty kilometres north of Viqueque have also been left uncultivated: Tali Modo, Uatu Mada, Uatu Kira, Ka Katanan, Dambua Tula, Ueru Eaka and Lakota, as well as Liaruka which is situated on the southern slopes of Mount Perdido.

There are four concentration camps in the town of Viqueque—Monumento, Mercado, Be Obe and Belay. The inhabitants are restricted to growing corn and cannot supplement this with any other means of earning a living. There is a shortage of agricultural implements and no way to replace worn-out ones. On average, the families in these camps produce only thirty to forty *lata* (tin) of corn a year.** With no other source of food supply, shortages occur regularly from December to February, when the inhabitants gather sago or yams to make up for the lack of food. Occasionally they manage to gather *betel* leaves or *camin* nuts to sell for cash to purchase other basic necessities like clothes.

A few privileged Timorese own large cornfields on which other camp inhabitants have to work without pay. Apart from these landowners, hardly anyone owns buffaloes any more; most of the livestock has been killed or requisitioned by the Indonesians. The use of forced labour—so-called

---

* Except for any text exclosed in square brackets or in boxes, everything from here to the asterisks on page 95 is taken from the Fretilin report.
**A *lata* or tin, the customary bulk measure in East Timor, is a 20-litre oil can which holds 12.8 kgs of unmilled rice, 16.3 kg of milled rice, or 18 kgs of beans. The weight of corn held by a *lata* is not known.

'gotong-royong'*—is widespread for road-building and timber-logging, as well as on a state-owned sugar plantation in Ue Tice. As a rule, forced labour gangs work on Saturdays but sometimes they have to go out for several days running.

> ### Destruction of Livestock
>
> There has been a calamitous fall in the number of livestock in East Timor since the Indonesian invasion. This has not only affected the availability of meat and other proteins, it has also severely hit crop cultivation which depends so heavily on buffaloes to trample the soil before planting a crop. In the following table, prewar figures are compared with figures for 1983.
>
> | | *1973*** | *1983**** |
> |---|---|---|
> | Buffaloes | 141,006 | 26,183 |
> | Beef cattle | 82,473 | 29,157 |
> | Horses | 139,490 | 13,000 |
> | Pigs | 304,565 | 88,620 |
>
> ** *These figures are taken from the Report of the Australian Parliamentary Delegation, 1983, page 49, and are based on data from the East Timor provincial authorities.*
> *** *East Timor After Integration*, (published by the Indonesian Government) p. 118.

The tin-roof houses often mentioned in foreign reports as an important part of Indonesia's development contribution are all occupied by people working for the Indonesian administration. Most camp dwellers live in tiny hovels, in conditions of famine, poverty and disease. When foreign visitors come, people are ordered to turn out in any decent clothes they have.

In the camps at *Krakas*, *Bikary* and *Luka* most people grow nothing but corn. The few who have access to land for rice-growing have no buffaloes for trampling, so preparing the soil for planting is back-breaking work and yields are low. Families growing rice produce no more than two tins in Kraras and five or six tins in Bikary and Luka. The privileged families make use of forced labour and live better. Food shortages are critical from December to February every year when people can only survive by gathering wild leaves and sago. The regular thud of people pounding the sago loose from tree-trunks can be heard late into the night, and sometimes up to morning.

People in camps along the coast from Viqueque westward to Betano

---

* *Gotong-royong* is a Javanese term for the traditional practice of mutual help in the villages. It is widely misused to coerce people to work on government 'development' projects without pay.

live in similarly dreadful conditions. This is where journalists like John Hamilton (*West Australian*) should go if they really want to know how Timorese people live today.

The camp at *Dilor* (Rade Uma) is where people from Lakluta have been resettled. Corn is about all they can produce. Conditions are, if anything, worse than in the other camps in Western Viqueque.

[Dilor camp was visited by the Australian Parliamentary Mission in 1983. They found Dilor

> uncannily empty... The few people to be found, mostly the old, appeared reserved, if not afraid. Only the schools were bustling with life. Dilor... created an uncomfortable first impression. The model resettlement village, it is apparently shown off regularly to visitors.[31]

Dilor was 'impressive for its cleanness, neatness and layout', the Parliamentians reported, 'with one section containing the more modern style of house that we were to see in most places which have been built for Indonesian officials'. Their Report noted that Dilor was 'the new Lakluta'[32]. The 'old Lakluta' was in fact the site of the worst massacres perpetrated during the Operation Security in 1981.]

Western Baucau
[The region of Baucau which extends from Vemasse in the west to the river Laivai in the east, and south to the slopes of Mount Perdido, is an area of intense guerrilla activity. The encounter between the Fretilin group of Sousa Gama and the Australian parliamentary mission took place here. Baucau airport is the Indonesian air-base and an important centre of military operations. Foreigners often travel through by road, so some camps enjoyed better conditions, to contradict reports about food shortages. This is the region inhabited by the Makassae people among whom Shepard Forman did his research in the early 1970s.]

Vemasse camp accommodates people from five *sucos* (sub-districts), Kay, Kua, Uaigae, Ossoala and Taci. Huge areas of productive land have been deserted because the people are now concentrated in the town. Many people were killed in these *sucos* during the second phase of the encirclement and annihilation campaign. Fertile lands all the way down the river Vemasse valley from the upper reaches at Ossoala now lie empty.

More livestock are to be seen here than elsewhere in East Timor. Some privileged families have as many as a hundred head while others possess a dozen or so, but the majority of people have none. Rice land around Vemasse is being cultivated by local government officials, *liurais* or civil guard commanders, but non-privileged families can at best produce three or four tins of corn and five or six tins of rice a year; the main reason is the heavy demand for forced labour to build new roads or clear existing ones and to work on other projects of military value. When people want to leave the camp boundary to forage for camin nuts as a means of earning some cash, they must pay a tax of Rp 50 a day.

Many zinc-roof houses have been built along roads to impress passing visitors.

Conditions at *Ostiku* camp, some miles inland, are far worse than in Vemasse. A number of Fretilin fighters who surrendered in the late seventies were resettled here. Inhabitants may not travel more than two or three kilometres beyond the camp boundary to cultivate food or forage for wild plants. A lot of rice- and corn-growing land has been abandoned. The inhabitants of Ostiku grow no rice, only corn and few can produce more than five or six tins a year which lasts about three months. For the rest, they must rely on gathering yams, wild coconuts, betel leaves and camin. The camp chief, Armando, owns a large plot of land and ten buffaloes. He and other privileged families benefit from the unpaid labour of camp inhabitants. Some people cut sandalwood for sale.

[Ostiku is occasionally visited by foreign journalists. During his visit in April 1983, John Hamilton met a former Fretilin fighter, now a contractor and lorry-driver. Hamilton's impression of the man was that:

> (He) seems rather resigned to his fate—being put on show as a reformed Fretilin leader is the price he has to pay for now being allowed to drive a truck for a living.[33]]

Conditions at *Loilubo camp* are much the same as in Ostiku. A herd of livestock intended for all camp inhabitants is in fact used by a few privileged families who therefore enjoy a better standard of living. Many people living in Loilubo only entered Indonesian-controlled territory in 1979 after the final destruction of Fretilin bases in late 1978.*

Most of the two or three thousand people living in *West Venilale camp* come from the *sucos* of Fatulia and Builale about a quarter of whose population was killed during the war. Much rice-growing land has now been abandoned, especially on the northern slopes of Mount Perdido; the camp inhabitants can only grow corn but even if they had access to riceland, they could not plant rice as they have no buffaloes or implements.

Early in 1981, when Operation Security was in preparation, the inhabitants were ordered to harvest their corn by April, whether ripe or not. [The Operation commenced in May.] All corn left standing in the fields was then burnt. The ceasefire from March to August 1983 improved the conditions for growing corn, but in June people were again ordered to harvest their crops by the beginning of August [which is when Indonesia's 1983 offensive was launched.]

During the critical hunger months from December to February, people gather wild plants but must do this in great secrecy. Medical facilities are almost non-existent. Medicines intended for the clinic end up in shops and are sold at prices few people can afford. Between 40 and 60 people

---

* People in the camps who surrendered in 1978 or 1979 are always treated more harshly than those who surrendered earlier.

go to the clinic daily for treatment, but medical supplies each month amount to only five small bottles of penicillin, five vials of streptomycin, twelve quinine injections and not more than fifty tablets of other drugs. Whatever illness they have, most people are sent away with nothing more than B-complex pills.

Eastern Baucau

Camp conditions in this district are amongst the worst of all. Former inhabitants of the *suco* of Laivai were first resettled in Moro, but not long ago they were hastily ordered to move back to Laivai for resettlement in a concentration camp in the *town of Laivai*. The new accommodation was intended to be a showplace for foreign visitors but conditions did not improve. This was formerly good rice-growing country but now large tracts of riceland have been abandoned. Much of the district is in guerrilla hands. [Sousa Gama who met a member of the Australian Parliamentary Mission on the roadside in August 1983 invited the parliamentarians to visit Saelari camp.]

The *Laga-Saelari-Atelari* corridor is dotted with camps. People living near the coast at the Laga end of the corridor who gave themselves up in 1976 are better provided with land for the cultivation of food. Those who surrendered in 1979 have a much harder time. Formerly this was rice-growing country; corn and cassava were only supplementary foods. Today even these are in short supply and people rely largely on wild roots. About 70% of the territory is in guerrilla hands and is not therefore available for food production to those living in the camps. With so much land held by Falintil, restrictions on movement for those in the camps is even tighter than elsewhere.

Conditions in the camps in *Baguia town* and along the road across the mountain to Lavateri to the north rank among the very worst throughout East Timor. Tin-roof houses have been build along the road and are clearly visible from the air. Security is very tight because much of the territory is guerrilla-controlled. Hardly any crops can be grown and there are few wild roots to be foraged. The climate is too cold to grown corn or cassava in the uplands, and much land has been abandoned—in Defavasi, Uacala, Samalari, Ossu Una, Alawa and Afaloikkai. Some inhabitants grow potatoes or eke out a living from keeping poultry. Restrictions on movement are extremely tight; disease and starvation are widespread and the people are reduced to extreme poverty.

[Rod Nordland's information tallies with this report:

> Although visits were permitted to the districts of Los Palos and Baucau, reportedly the past and present sites of the heaviest fighting with Fretilin, they were confined to the district capitals. No visits at all were permitted to places like Lufa in Los Palos, and Batumacela, Baguia, Queliquai and Laga in Baucau, where clergymen say widespread starvation exists.[34]]

In *Queliquai*, south of Laga, the level of food production is extremely low. Things improved during the 1983 ceasefire, but even so it was not expected that output would last longer than three months. Previously people were reduced to living almost entirely on wild roots. Had it not been for the ceasefire, some one thousand people would almost certainly have died from starvation. Although security is very strict, people take the risk of violating the many restrictions imposed by the military. Disease is rife especially among children and the old. The health centre provides little more than a few pills.

[The Australian Parliamentary Mission described Queliquai as 'the poorest place visited' and estimated that among the five hundred or so people who turned out to see the visitors, one in eight of the children had distended bellies. The mission's report described the camp as consisting of 'an old section and a new section, the latter obviously dominated by people from elsewhere in Indonesia'.[35]]

Viqueque District
People living in *Uatocarabau camp* who surrendered in 1977 are allowed to till land down near the south coast and are not too badly off. But those who surrendered at the end of 1978 are much worse off and subjected to tighter security control; they have access to much less land and can grow less food. For them, the food-crisis months last from December to March and are very severe.

The camps in *Uatolari* and along the road to Viqueque are intended as showpieces; the tin-roof houses are very much in evidence. This is good rice-growing territory and was well-cultivated before the war; now much has been left to waste—Iratokar, Naedala, Narekisa, Mae Buti, Tae Tun, Fae Debun and Laliu, plus Sana, Bui Tau and Taru Nira in the fertile Be Bui valley. What little land is now available for cultivation is mostly owned by Timorese who collaborate with the Indonesian administration; they also own the cattle that survived the war.

Most people possess no buffaloes or agricultural implements and are reduced to digging the soil with sticks. This is back-breaking, time-consuming work with poor yields. The inhabitants can only grow corn or cassava, and try to supplement this by foraging for wild leaves and gathering sago. Many are nothing more than skin and bones, particularly the very old and very young. Hardly any wild roots are to be found. Disease is rampant but medical treatment is only available to those who can pay. Many are on the verge of death from starvation.

The authorities trust no one. Even during the ceasefire, people were prevented from going out in search of roots and coconuts. With an important rice-growing area like this reduced to such straits, how can anyone believe Mario Carrascalao's claim, reported by John Hamilton, that rice production in East Timor will reach 65,000 tons this year? Most of Uatolari up to Matabian Mountain is now guerrilla territory.

The Children of Uatolari

When a party of officials descended on Uatolari by helicopter, the grassy public square was crowded with scores of children, standing just at the edge of the rotar wash. Many of them appeared to be severely malnourished with the classic distended bellies and stick-like limbs that denote longterm serious hunger. Or so the reporter thought.

Hans Meier-Eybers, the project director for a Catholic Relief Services agricultural recovery project, a $5 million, US-funded programme, thought otherwise. Meier-Eybers, a Swiss, surveyed the children critically and said, 'They look like healthy kids to me. Sure, they're a little dirty but that's all.'

An Indonesian doctor, S.C. Kurniati approached and was asked if he thought the children appeared to be malnourished. 'You can see for yourself,' he said, seeming a little taken aback by the question. 'These children are all malnourished.'

The Philadelphia Inquirer, 28 May 1982

District of Dili

The people who have been resettled on the outskirts of the capital live on only corn and cassava. In the camps of *Balibar*, *Dare*, *Madubeno*, *Aito Hospital* and *Mota Alun*, food production is very low and the inhabitants rely mainly on foraging for wild plants. During the fruit season, they pick mangoes, citrus fruit, bananas and papayas to sell for a bit of cash.

Farther south in the *region of Railaco*, conditions at the camps in *Daileu*, *Samaletan* and *Fatisse* are very bad and the people are always hungry. When guerrillas visited Fatisse in May 1983, people had only three months stock of cassava in their huts. Things are far worse than before the encirclement and annihilation operation began in 1977. No medical facilities are available, and parents refuse to allow their children to learn Indonesian. Conditions in the camps at *Mau Toba* and *Remexio* are much the same.

At the camps in *Likor* and *Laclo* on the river Laclo, the only food people had in their huts when guerrillas visited in February 1983 was *aidak* fruit (*Schleichera oleosa*). About half the inhabitants were ill or severely under-nourished. Many huts were flooded at the time and people had little clothing. This was formerly rice-growing territory but no rice is grown here any more.

The *region of Bazartete* is a major coffee-growing region. People in the camps here still have coffee bushes as well as coconut and betel trees. There are restrictions on taking coffee to Dili for sale, and when sold locally, the price fixed by Denok, the monopoly trading company, is very low indeed. Some people manage to take coffee to Dili for sale by bribing officials. In March 1983, the colonial authorities started taxing sales of these cash-crops; in addition, people are required to contribute to the army's 'clean-up' operations.

District of Ainaro

There are eight concentration camps in and around the district capital (*posto*) of Ainaro. The camps of *Ainaro town*, *Builiku*, *Fatuk Maria*, *Manotuci*, *Suru Craic*, *Soro*, *Mau Ulu* and *Nau Nuno* are all within a radius of five kilometres from the town of Ainaro. People can grow corn, cassava and potatoes as well as rice but only on a limited scale. Growing rice is more a privilege for the better-off families who also have livestock to trample the soil. Others manage to grow rice if they hire livestock but the price is high and few can afford to pay. Families manage to grow about 20 to 25 tins of corn which lasts about five months; they also grow cassava and gather it wild because what they grow is not enough. December to February are food-crisis months. The people recruited into the Civil Guard and other auxiliary forces are paid Rp. 10,000 a month but this is not enough to live on, so they try to grow food to make ends meet.

Forced labour is widespread in this region, for road-building, house-construction and road repairs and clearance,* and to till privately-owned land for those employed by the administration. On the former projects, forced labour sometimes lasts for three days a week. In addition, people are often required to carry loads for the army. At times of extreme hardship, the inhabitants try to get work from those employed by the state.

[Ainaro is a region mentioned in the Indonesian government's *East Timor After Integration* as being where irrigation canals were built by 'voluntary' labour.[36]]

The camps at *Hatubiliku* and *Maubisse* farther to the south are in more mountainous terrain. In the colder climate, corn takes longer to grow. Output is low and the only way the people survive the food-crisis months is by working for better-off people. The tin-roof houses are for officials only but even these dwellings are poor. The people's huts are much worse.

District of Same

There are a number of camps in and around the town of Same: *Sipantiga*, *Holarua*, *Bahula*, *Grota*, *Dutuluro* and *Letefoho*. Conditions here are far worse than before the war. The only ones who still own some property—land and livestock—are government employees, policemen, school-heads and traditional chiefs. Most people produce only cassava and potatoes, plus a little corn which they sell for cash to buy other things. The crops they grow last no more than six months.

'Gotong-royong' demands are made by the colonial authorities, particularly at planting time and for road-building. Some people work at a privately-owned coffee plantation. Some better-quality land is owned by privileged people who have livestock, but a lot of land has been abandoned—in Gonlau, Saturas, Leolima, Sumul, Butas and elsewhere.

---

* Many dirt roads are affected by landslides and erosion during the rainy season, and need to be repaired when the rains have stopped.

The *Betano camp* is situated about ten kilometres from the town. The inhabitants grow rice and corn but although the soil is good, they have only primitive implements so output is low. Most riceland belongs to landowners who have livestock which they also hire to others who must then work on their land free of charge. The poorer people tend to sell what little rice and corn they produce to get cash for basic needs. Forced labour demands by the authorities are high especially during food-crisis months. When agricultural activity is the most intense, camp inhabitants often have to work for one or two weeks on other people's land.

The *Alas camp*, a few kilometres inland on the hill slopes, is situated in a region where two crops of corn can be grown annually, but this is a malaria-infested area and illness is widespread. With nothing in the way of medical treatment, the many stricken people do not have the energy to work on the fields, so they rely on gathering sago and *ukitrik*, an edible root. The *We Susu camp* nearer the coast is better off because malaria is less of a problem. People grow corn and cassava but rely on sago during the food-crisis months.

There are two concentration camps in *Fatuberliu* where people produce corn but not enough for more than five months. Then they rely on sago. There are a few tin-roof houses for officials, but everyone else lives in dark, unhealthy and badly-built hovels.

District of Manatuto

[Manatuto is situated on the north coastal road from Dili to Baucau. Foreign visitors often pass along this road, so the district, like Baucau district, has some camps where conditions are better, to impress outsiders. Elsewhere though, conditions are generally very bad.]

There was formerly a lot of fertile riceland around the town of Manatuto, but much is now abandoned; most people at the camp in the *town of Manatuto*, have also lost their livestock. People who work for the government get regular incomes and own land and livestock. Other families in some of the camps in this district can grow up to 20 or 25 tins of rice; some supplement this with fishing or salt-production. Even so, cash surpluses are limited and people gather sago during food-crisis months. Forced labour requirements are considerable. *Kaelilo camp* about two kilometres from Manatuto town enjoys reasonably good food-growing conditions but still, they cannot grow enough to last the year. Most people live in poor hovels; the tin-roof houses along the road are there to impress passing visitors.

Laleia camp lies on the road to Baucau, about 27 kilometres from Manatuto. Living conditions are far worse than in the district capital. The inhabitants grow rice and corn but output is low because of the lack of livestock. The population is concentrated around the town and many important rice-growing regions are lying wasted—Mau Ra Rain, Rotuna, Segat, We Tiran, We Noreni, Seram Boek, Hok Hoio, Tisaek Um, Boko, Lian Aen, Todos and Cairui. Implements are lacking so output is not more than five or six tins a family. Only two families have livestock which were actually donated by the Catholic mission to the whole camp.

People here are in a constant state of hunger and rely on foraging for yams. Local sago supplies have been virtually exhausted and the inhabitants must go farther afield to Vemasse, if they can get permission, to find sago trees. Some do fishing and salt-production but hunger is widespread.

At *Laklubar camp*, 34 kilometres inland from Manatuto, conditions are extremely bad; almost no crops are grown. Both climate and soil are unfavourable for corn production so people rely mainly on foraging for cassava and other roots, and sometimes have to survive only on palm-wine from the palm-tree. The food crisis lasts virtually the whole year and disease is rampant.

Laclo camp, by the coast, is better off and families can grow up to 40 or 50 tins of rice a year; corn production is also better than in places nearer Manatuto. Some people still need to gather sago. The dwellings are poor, except for the ones built for the administration officials. Major ricelands have been abandoned in this region, in We Koi, Lisore, Lor, Keli and elsewhere.

District of Lautem
[This is a major region of guerrilla activity, the basis from which Fretilin's resurgence was launched after the collapse of the Matabian support base in November 1978. Much of the territory is guerrilla-controlled which has the effect of reducing the amount of land available to people living in the camps and also intensifying the security precautions imposed by the army. The Fretilin report reflects both these aspects of camp conditions, but its ability to describe the circumstances in so many of the camps means that it has an extensive support network in the camps.]

In *Tutuala*, on the eastern tip, conditions are appalling; many people die of hunger. Little land is available for food production by people in the camps who can produce only small quantities of corn. They rely mainly on cassava and some fishing. There is a cooperative (KUD) which is run by the subdistrict chief and the Koramil officer, and is used to extract money from the people.

People living at the camp in *Meara (Mehara)* may not go more than 200 to 500 metres beyond the camp boundary. Only two or three families can grow rice. Camps on the road from *Poros to Assalaino* live in much the same conditions because security control is so strict. Before the war, there was a lot of arable land nearby but it has now all been abandoned; much of the livestock was confiscated by the army just before the people surrendered to the enemy.

In the camp at *Kon*, 20 kilometres from Moro, things are much the same as in Tutuala though the inhabitants can do a bit of fishing and salt-production for cash. Death from starvation is a common occurrence. People in camps along the *Moro-Raca corridor* live in somewhat better conditions thought they too face food-crisis months from December to March every year. The only person able to grow rice is the subdistrict chief, Edmundo who owns riceland and some livestock and runs the local co-operative.

In camps along the *Titilari-Los Palos corridor*, people who surrendered earlier to the enemy live in much the same conditions as those in the Moro-Raco region. But for those who surrendered in 1978, conditions are harsh; security control is strict, land is limited and people are physically so weak that they often lack the energy even to forage for wild plants. People are frequently forced to leave their camp for security reasons, but sometimes these evacuation plans are cancelled at the last minute because of operations in the area. When people living in Leuro were driven from their homes and told to move to Souro, Indonesian troops demolished the huts with their weapons and burnt everything. But then, the move did not take place and people had no alternative but to live out in the open until new homes had been built. This kind of thing happened most recently in Leuro early in 1983; the inhabitants were left completely without food supplies and had to live on wild coconuts and leaves.

Conditions in camps along the *Ililapa-Lore corridor* are quite atrocious because of the sharp fall in the amount of land available for growing food. People live almost entirely from foraging for coconuts and wild plants, and many die of hunger.

The inhabitants of the *suco* of Mapitine were told to move to *Vailoro (Fuiloro)* in mid-1982. In the new place, they can grow almost nothing at all, and survive on leaves and roots foraged from the forests. The people now living in *Laleno camp*, a mountainous region, were moved here from three low-lying sucos—Maina, Serelau and Badura. Security control is very tight indeed and hardly any land is available for the production of food. People survive thanks only to a reasonably good supply of coconuts and wild plants.

Before the war and during the years of Fretilin control from 1976 to 1978, people living in *Luro* were able to grow a lot of rice but since 1979 when they were forced to move into the concentration camp, the food shortage has been acute. They may only travel short distances from the camp to grow food and manage to grow a little corn, cassava and potatoes but no rice. Along the roads, there are tin-roofed houses which outsiders see when they come to the area; what they do not see are the hovels where most of the inhabitants live. Almost every day, the inhabitants go out in search of coconuts, sometimes over to the western slopes of the Laleno hills when they are allowed to, or to places around the town of Luro. Starvation is the constant companion of people here who often have no staple food at all and pick unripe mangoes which they consume without waiting for them to ripen.

All that can be said of conditions in *Iliomar camp* is that they are just as bad as in Luro.

[Iliomar camp was under International Red Cross care until its relief programme was abandoned in July 1983, just before the 1983 Indonesian offensive started. An Australian embassy official who visited East Timor in September 1982 was told by the ICRC that all 5,554 inhabitants of Iliomar were dependent on its food aid programme; they were receiving 300 grams of corn a day with extra amounts for children and nursing mothers.[37] The ICRC said that when its delegates visited Iliomar on 27 March 1983, they 'noticed a deterioration of the situation in comparison with November 1982', which was due mainly to 'distribution problems caused by logistical difficulties.'][38]

* * *

Fretilin's report on conditions in the camps was compiled during the ceasefire, shortly before Indonesia launched its new offensive in August 1983. Five months after the offensive began, AFP quoted church sources in Jakarta as saying that the military move had completely disrupted already precarious food supplies in East Timor.

The circumstances in which East Timor's uprooted population now lives are indeed so precarious that the renewed military operations can only recreate the famine conditions which killed so many people in 1978 and 1979.

Contrasts

The character of the Portuguese occupation, which unfolded gradually and involved relatively little use of military force, contrasts sharply with the sudden and violent imposition of Indonesian rule. The Portuguese initially confronted and dealt with isolated, individual local groups to whom an alliance with the Portuguese often seemed economically and politically advantageous. The Indonesians, in contrast, confront a population bound by a common past, a past which includes the recent, aborted experience of self-determination. Here we come to the third and critical factor which differentiates Indonesian from Portuguese intervention: the presence of Fretilin , a well-organised, dedicated, energetic national independence movement actively involved in cultivating a new national consciousness and in mobilizing national resistance.

Elizabeth Traube at the Fourth Committee of the UN General Assembly, 17 October 1980.

5. The Indonesianization of East Timor

> All the state organizations in Timor are just like a curtain to block from the eyes of the world. In reality, they are there for the exploitation and extinction of the people of East Timor. This reality might be unknown to the world; everybody thinks everything is going marvellously in East Timor.
>
> An East Timor refugee

'Integrasi'

East Timor was formally incorporated as Indonesia's '27th province' on 17 July 1976 when President Suharto signed the Bill of Integration, which had been unanimously adopted two days earlier by the Indonesian Parliament. This was based on the fiction that an act of self-determination had taken place through the unanimous decision of a People's Assembly which represented no one. This Assembly was a creation of the puppet Provisional Government of East Timor established immediately after Indonesian troops took control of Dili in December 1975. The puppet government was formed from: collaborationist Timorese from the UDT, which was by that time deeply split over its response to Indonesian intervention, intrigue and invasion; the Apodeti, created by Indonesian intelligence; and two 'groups' called KOTA and Trabalhista, both without following but which made the collaborationist 'parties' sound more numerous and therefore 'representative'.

The puppet government's first act was to proclaim 'integrasi'. It notified the United Nations of its decision and announced that a regional body would be convened to ratify integration.[1] The puppet government then passed a law creating a 'People's Assembly', and notified the UN of this.[2] The Assembly typically embodied Indonesian-style 'democracy'; the principle of direct universal suffrage was supplanted with a 'representative system by means of consensus and consent'. 'Representatives' for twelve out of thirteen *concelhos* were to be selected, while in Dili 'one man, one vote' was to be applied. However, terror reigned in Dili and Indonesian troops controlled very little territory beyond a few coastal towns and the border area. Elections of any kind, or indeed any form of political activity, were completely ruled out. According to Dunn,

> What really happened was that Indonesian intelligence officers, usually accompanied by Apodeti officials, summoned local rulers and, in some cases, simply directed them to become members of the Assembly.[3]

When the 'duly elected' Assembly met in Dili on 31 May 1976 to ratify 'integrasi' a small group of ambassadors in Jakarta attended, to give it an air of legitimacy. The UN was invited but refused to attend. Indonesian and foreign journalists were taken to Dili to witness the meeting but were tightly controlled. The Jakarta weekly, *Tempo* made no secret of the fact that journalists were prevented from speaking to any of the Assembly members:

> As soon as we took a step down the stairs, officials in civilian clothing told us to get back. We were not allowed to approach Assembly members who wandered into the vicinity where we were.[4]

Nor did they speak to any Timorese in the streets when they were taken on a tour of Dili, as the town was 'quiet and deserted'.

After the Assembly's 'integrasi' petition had been formally delivered to the generals in Jakarta, the Indonesian government staged an 'on-the-spot assessment' of Timorese attitudes. This consisted of a one-day visit to East Timor by the Home Affairs Minister, General Amir Machmud who never left Dili and who proclaimed on his return to Jakarta that 'the wish for integration with Indonesia was decided by the whole people of this territory.'[5]

The State Organs

Unlike any other region administered by Indonesia, East Timor administration is run not by the Department of Home Affairs but by the Department of Defence and Security. The Defence Department set up a Special Co-ordinating Committee for the Administration of East Timor in 1978, the year the Armed Forces succeeded in bringing most of the territory under their control. The Chairman of the Committee was, and still is, General Benny Murdahi, the present Commander-in-Chief of Armed Forces. All the critical areas of administration—security and order, political affairs, information, communications, population control and settlement, manpower, family reunions and religion—are under the direct supervision of the Committee in Jakarta. Local government bears responsibility for only five areas of activity: primary education, health, public works, agriculture and social welfare.[6]

As a province, East Timor is by far the smallest both in size and population. Were it to have been treated normally, it would, like West Timor, have become part of the sixteenth province of Nusa Tenggara

Timur, which also includes the islands of Sumba, Flores, Solor and Alor. Security considerations and the continuing state of war forced the military to handle East Timor as a separate unit where both military and non-military activities are geared to the needs of war.

> ## Civilizing Mission
>
> It is the new Indonesian civilization we are bringing. And it is not easy to civilize backward people.
>
> *Colonel Kalangi*, Provincial Secretary of East Timor, formerly Military Commander of the region, quoted in *Far Eastern Economic Review*, 6 August 1982.

Militarization is part of Indonesian life. The Armed Forces run the country with a doctrine known as *dwi-fungsi*, the dual function. This establishes the Armed Forces as both a military and a political and social force. The *dwi-fungsi*, doctrine is taken to its extreme in East Timor, where power in effect is wielded by two men: the Military Commander in charge of military operations; and the Regional Area Secretary or *Sekwilda (Sekretaris Wilayah Daerah)*, in charge of local government. Indonesianization of East Timor in political, social and economic affairs is the responsibility of the Sekwilda. So far every Sekwilda has been an Army man, appointed after first serving as military commander of the territory. The present Sekwilda, Colonel Kalangi has held the position since 1980 and appears to be on the way to making East Timor a lifelong interest. He has privately invested in local ventures such as a bar and restaurant in Dili, his involvement in the profitable coffee trade is widely acknowledged and he picks up sizable commissions from his powers to grant licences.

The position of governor, held in almost every Indonesian province by Army generals, is occupied in East Timor by a Timorese and this is bound to continue as long as self-determination remains an international issue. This explains why, unlike elsewhere, the governor is largely a figurehead and the military wield control over the administration through the post of Sekwilda.

The choice of governor for East Timor is made in accordance with Indonesia's current political and economic requirements. The first two men to occupy the post were both from the pro-integrationist Apodeti party, which was regarded at the time as the most reliable group to serve Indonesian needs. UDT, the party which went through several phases before assuming a pro-Indonesian posture, had to be satisfied with the position of vice-governor. Arnaldo dos Reis Araujo, the president of Apodeti from the time of its inception, was the first governor. Not long after the Army took control of Dili, however, he began to voice, privately, criticism of the brutal practices of the troops and the widespread looting of Timorese property. But his downfall finally came as a result of an embarrassing remark he made while at the UN General Assembly, when he boasted about his collaborationist role during the Japanese occupation of East Timor in the 1940s.

Araujo was succeeded by Guilherme Goncalves, the *liurai*, or 'king' of Atsabe who, according to Jim Dunn, is 'one of Timor's most despotic rulers'. He served Indonesian intelligence well in 1975 by forcing many of his followers to go to a special Indonesian intelligence base near Kupang for training as Indonesian agents.[7] The rise and fall of Gonvalves was closely linked with coffee. East Timor's second governor was appointed when the military establishment in East Timor was pressing ahead to restore coffee as a profitable export from the territory. Atsabe is a major coffee-growing region and with Goncalves as governor, it was hoped that pacification of the region would be enhanced and the people would willingly acquiesce to the systematic extortion of their valuable cash crop. His short reign ended when he became embroiled in a bitter conflict with the Sekwilda, Colonel Kalangi over the share-out of coffee levies paid to the provincial government. Each man wanted to use the funds as patronage payouts and for personal gain. The Sekwilda had the power and Goncalves was sacked in 1982.

By this time, Apodeti had lost its relevance to the military rulers of East Timor and they turned their attention to the UDT. Mario Carrascalao, one of the three brothers in the most prominent coffee plantation family in the country, was chosen as the next governor. The Carrascalao family is a typical product of the Portuguese *assimilado* policy, the co-opted Timorese elite who enjoyed the privilege of a first-class Portuguese education so as to promote the assimilation of Portuguese social and cultural attitudes in East Timor. Like many other members of this well-educated elite, Mario Carrascalao has long harboured feelings of contempt for Indonesians, regarding them as racially inferior. During the time he spent abroad after 1975, promoting the idea of 'integrasi' as a member of Indonesia's permanent mission to the UN, he seriously considered defecting and discussed this with his brother-in-law, Jose Ramos Horta, Fretilin's permanent representative to the UN, but in May 1980, the family's extensive land-holdings were restored to his brother Manuel, which must have made defection far less attractive.

Mario Carrascalao's appointment in October 1982 represented a shift in Indonesian perceptions of the image they needed to project in East Timor. His long experience of dealing with UN diplomats was an important asset in a period when Indonesia needed above all else to win international opinion to its side. Moreover, it was a time when the development image had become an important part of international strategy and when security in East Timor was directed towards a 'hearts and minds' policy. This required a Timorese figurehead of a superior calibre than the previous governors; a man with bureaucratic and technocratic training who could speak with conviction to foreign visitors about Indonesia's development plans, and who could, when the time came, negotiate with the resistance movement.* Thus it was hoped that he could

---

* During the March 1983 talks, the Army wanted Carrascalao to represent Indonesia but the Fretilin leader refused to deal with him.

stand in for both Colonel Purwanto, the military commander, and Colonel Kalangi, the Sekwilda. Certainly, since his appointment as governor, Kalangi has tended to take a back seat when foreign visitors come to the territory. Carrascalao's deal with the regime hinges on his family's profitable landed interests which have been well served by special pricing arrangements for the family's coffee output, in exchange for which he provides the military establishment in East Timor with an acceptable Timorese image, concealing the truth of Indonesian brutality and exploitation.

Although Mario Carrascalao has thus been given a higher profile as governor, the administrative apparatus is still completely dominated by the military. All the leading positions are occupied by Armed Forces personnel. The Sekwilda runs the administration with the help of some thirty army officers.[8] All the deputy secretaries are army officers and the eleven provincial bureaus are also headed by Indonesians. Mario Carrascalao wanted some of these top positions to go to Timorese loyal to him as this would strengthen his own position in the administration. To reinforce his claim he has sometimes expressed resentment at the high-handed attitude of Indonesian officials towards Timorese, their air of superiority and lack of regard for Timorese customs and habits. Kalangi's primary concern on the other hand is to create a bureaucracy that will consolidate military control and conform to the needs of a difficult and unstable security situation.

Besides setting up a military-dominated administration, the Indonesians have also encouraged the creation of a typically colonial social structure, based on the principle of divide and rule, involving a system of privileges for those Timorese willing to collaborate with the Indonesians. The 'playboy' of Dili, Mr Brito, is an example of this new privileged elite. Formerly the manager of the Portuguese Banco Nacional Ultramarino, he now manages seven coffee plantations for the military. The Portuguese television journalist, Rui Araujo described Mr Brito as

> a privileged person. He works, and works hard for the Indonesians. There are few others like him. To encourage the Timorese, Jakarta pays the collaborators generously. They want them to set an example by (creating a) contrast between plenty and generalized penury. Inequality serves, on top of it all, to create or emphasise the abyss that is beginning to separate the Timorese from each other. (By) creating first-class and second-class citizens, Indonesia is applying the old axiom of dividing to dominate.[9]

People who have become civil servants in the provincial administration or have been appointed as district and subdistrict heads enjoy certain privileges but are of a lower station than the Carrascalaos and the Britos. They enjoy the security of a regular cash income and hold positions that give them the chance to engage in extortion, petty corruption and exploitation at the expence of other Timorese. The vast majority of Timorese are deprived of the most basic rights even the right to decide where to live, and are subjected to all kinds of forced labour 'for the cause of development'.

Most civil servants got their jobs as a reward for past loyalty to the cause of 'integrasi'. They were appointed when Apodeti men held the post of governor and were regarded as a reliable source of support for their Apodeti patrons. Carrascalao would gladly be rid of most of them and has been quoted as saying that a third of their number—altogether 6,500—would be more than enough to run an efficient administration.[10]

No one conceals the fact that the provincial administration is in a parlous state. Colonel-Kalangi told *Tempo* that 'the wheels of government at the provincial level are only 30 per cent effective'.[11] This, he argued, and 'the process of integration' is why members of the Armed Forces have become the 'pioneers of development' in East Timor. 'We had to start from scratch here and function with untrained personnel of minimum quality'. However it would be wrong to conclude, as Kalangi implies, that the Portuguese colonialists had no working administration structure. The fact is that most people who worked in the Portuguese civil service are unacceptable to the Indonesians, particularly if they refuse to renounce Portuguese citizenship and adopt Indonesian citizenship. This reflects the assumption that people who decline the 'superior' status of Indonesian nationality must be a threat to Indonesian interests. But many Timorese have rejected Indonesian citizenship above all because it would ruin their chances of leaving a country that has become a hell on earth for them. This has turned them into non-persons, people who are denied the right to hold an identity card, without which they simply cease to exist as far as the authorities are concerned. One Timorese has explained how a Colonel Ngudiono warned of the consequences of rejecting Indonesian citizenship:

> See, I am your friend, I just advise you, People who don't want to be Indonesian citizens voluntarily will be subject to hard manual work. They will be sent to build roads in the country. They will be considered strangers. They will have no freedom.[12]

When in 1980, the International Red Cross invited those wishing to leave the country to register, the response was so overwhelming—more than 17,000—that it had to suspend registration, thus arousing much anger and disappointment.

The men who run East Timor are overwhelmingly Indonesians in uniform. For non-military personnel from Indonesia, working in East Timor has few attractions to offer. Apart from the language barrier and lack of social contacts, the risky security situation and the hostile environment can hardly be inviting. A high percentage of Indonesian teachers, upon whom the school system depends, leave the country after a one-year assignment. According to Susumu Awanohara, civil servants from Indonesia are paid a premium rate. 'The province is considered a hardship post and most Jakarta officials come out for a short stay without their families'.[13] A report on the construction workers sent to build the irrigation project in Maliana complained that within a few months, most had returned to Java because of illness or other difficulties.

Within the province, the Indonesians have created the same local government structure as exists elsewhere. East Timor is divided into thirteen *kabupatens* (districts) each headed by a *bupati*. Under the kabupatens come the *kecamatans* (subdistricts) of which there are 64 altogether, each headed by a *camat*. Then there are the 'villages' or 'resettlement areas' with their heads, and at the bottom of the structure, the *rukun tetangga* or residential administration and the *rukun warga* or clan association. East Timor's military rulers have made a point of filling all these posts with Timorese hoping, as some observers have said, 'to avoid the mistakes made in Irian Jaya (West Papua)' where many such posts are filled by non-Papuans. This local government administrative structure is accompanied at every level by a military command structure. Each district has a matching *Kodim* (Komando Distrik Militer), each subdistrict has its matching *Koramil* (Komando Rayon Militer), and the 'villages' and 'resettlement areas' all have their *Babinsa* (village guidance officer) or *Team Pembina Desa* (village guidance team). The existence of parallel civilian and military stuctures is identical with that which exists throughout Indonesia, but the overriding power of the military and the shadowy role of the Timorese apparatus underscores the special character of military rule in East Timor. One pro-integrationist academic has observed:

> The paper identity between civil and military units in East Timor and their counterparts in other Indonesian provincial settings does not include functional reality. In meaningful, substantive terms, civil administration does not exist below the governor's office in other than a clerical sense. It is at the Kodims and the Koramils that local policy and programme implementation takes place.[14]

The civilian apparatus in some parts, 'exists only in name; in others, even where district or subdistrict heads exist, the provincial government does not seem to trust their loyalty or integrity.'[15]

East Timorese, including those in positions of trust, are treated as suspects and constantly 'screened' to prove their worth as Indonesian citizens and loyal adherents to Indonesia's Pancasila doctrine. This 'screening' is conducted by a special branch of the Armed Forces known as *kotis* (komando taktis). *Kotis* officers are to be found at all levels of the command structure and are responsible for day-to-day intelligence and control of the inhabitants. Anyone wishing to obtain a work permit, a travel pass, an identity card, or even a marriage licence, must first complete a fifteen-page questionnaire in the presence of the *kotis* officer. The questionnaire not only covers all imaginable aspects of a person's private life, going back several generations. It also includes numerous questions about political attitudes: a person's behaviour and response on 11 August 1975 (the day of the UDT coup) and activities before and after that date, on 7 December 1975 (the Indonesian invasion) and before and after that date. 'How would you behave towards people who oppose 'integrasi'?' and 'what would you do if you met a Fretilin guerrilla in the bush?' Answers are 'legally binding' with penalties for 'false statements'. This follows the pattern of 'screening' political prisoners in Indonesia who were held for years without charge or trial; in East Timor, 'screening' is inflicted on all inhabitants who require anything from the administration.

Travel passes are required for any journey; passage to and from East Timor is tightly controlled by the intelligence. All mail and phone calls are censored. Timorese travelling from one place to another are halted at military checkpoints where they are required to answer questions about the Pancasila, to name the president, the vice-president, the governor, and so on.

The Development of a Plantation Economy

From the moment Indonesian troops landed in East Timor, interests closely linked with the military began to engage in business. The company that took charge of exploiting the country's economic resources was P.T. Denok Hernandes International which Colonel Kalangi has described as 'the only company which landed with the marines. They came together.'[16] Within six months of the capture of Dili, Denok's first cargo of coffee had been shipped to Singapore, a shipment of 500 tonnes which was unloaded there in June 1976. This was followed five months later by a second shipment of 800 tonnes, earning Denok no less than $3.1 million from the first year of 'integrasi'.[17]

Preparations for Denok's operations had in fact begun well before the marines landed. Two companies were ready to handle the import and transshipment of coffee to Singapore. One of these companies, P.T. Timorlaut International, was incorporated in Singapore on 1 September 1975, even as Suharto and his general staff were directing their first military operations against East Timor, across the border from West Timor.

Denok typifies businesses which flourish under military rule, serving the interests of a coterie of generals and providing them with the framework for economic control and exploitation. The company is run by a group of Indonesian Chinese businessmen well connected with trading and finance houses in Singapore and Australia. From the start Denok took charge of keeping the Armed Forces supplied both with military equipment as well as consumer goods for the troops. The proceeds from those first shipments in 1976 were used to purchase trucks and other vehicles, tyres, spare parts, generators, boots and clothing for the Army in East Timor and to supply consumer goods to the shops in the occupied towns. As Michael Richardson pointed out, East Timor 'was paying for its invasion in coffee'.[18]

For a company just beginning to operate, the time could hardly have been more propitious. Coffee prices on the world market doubled in 1976 and rocketed even higher in the following twelve months; by 1977 they were four times the 1975 level. Denok also enjoyed the benefit of running its export and import operations beyond the control of government departments in Jakarta, having beaten off attempts by the Ministry of Trade to regulate it through licensing and the payment of duties. Conditions could hardly have been more conducive for a company to speerhead the systematic colonial exploitation of East Timor.

Indonesian propaganda claims that Jakarta subsidises East Timor to a greater extent than any other province. According to official figures, the central government allocated Rp. 52 billion for East Timor in 1982-83, in return for Rp. 150 million in revenue from the 'province'. A high percentage of the expenditure is allocated to building the roads and bridges which provide the infrastructure for Denok operations and for the military activities of the occupation forces. The roads under construction in 1984 ran from Dili through Aileu to Same in the southwest, from Ermera to Maliana and from Dili to Baucau, the chief military and air base.[19] The Dili-Aileu-Same road will serve the needs of expanded coffee planting which has taken place, according to official sources, in Ermera, Aileu, Ainaro and Same.[20] One of the earliest roads to be asphalted was from Dili to Ermera in the heartland of coffee-growing country. Much of the remaining funds are ploughed into education, a high priority for the indoctrination of the younger generation, to be analysed at greater length below.

Denok's shareholders are unknown; the company is not listed in official corporation records in Jakarta, but it is an open secret that it is the 'front for Indonesian military interests in East Timor'[21] The two Dili directors, Hendro Samanpouw and Hartantosutejo, both Indonesian Chinese and part owners, run the company from headquarters located in Java. Denok has offices throughout East Timor, according to a Timorese who once worked for it as a driver, and its undisputed monopoly powers have assured it spectacular growth; coffee which was the blockbuster now accounts for only 30 per cent of Denok operations:

> After starting in coffee and other cash crops, it has branched into sandalwood processing, the entertainment and hotel business and general trading. It now has 2,200 employees. Even more impressive than Denok's expansion and diversification is its market position in East Timor. It has a monopoly of the purchase and export of coffee. It alone is allowed in the sandalwood trade. It operates the only movie theatre in town.
>
> Denok also has clout in other fields. One Timorese says he needed its authorisation to import a cow from West Timor. If Denok sometimes seems to exercise the authority of government, locals figure that's just about the size of it.[22]

East Timor produces both arabica and robusta coffee. Its arabica is reputed to be top quality and sells at a premium on the world market. In Portuguese times, the coffee was produced on plantations, some of which were owned by the government and some by private interests; there were also many smallholdings. Following the Indonesian takeover, all land including the coffee plantations and smallholdings were commandeered by the State. The confiscated plantation land including huge estates owned by SAPT, a Portuguese state enterprise, is now controlled by Denok which also operates East Timor's two main coffee processing plants in Dili and Fatubessi, near Ermera. The only large privately-owned coffee plantation land to have been returned to its pre-1975 owners belongs to Manuel Carrascalao, the present governor's brother. The family's 521 hectares of coffee plantation plus 179 hectares of other land was restored in May 1980. Coffee smallholders continue to work land which they regard as their private property, but in the view of the provincial government, this land is state property and they are, say government officials, 'labourers picking coffee that doesn't belong to them'. The Carrascalao estate gets nearly twice as much as the smallholders for the coffee it sells to Denok because it is paid a price whereas the others are considered as being only entitled to a wage for their labour. In 1982, Carrascalao was getting 92 cents a kilo for arabica and 84 cents for robusta while other producers were paid only 58 and 38 cents respectively. When asked about this outrageous discrimination, the Sekwilda Colonel Kalangi barked back: 'They aren't the owners. Why should they protest?'[23]

Denok's monopoly over the purchase of coffee as well as other cash crops produced in East Timor is enforced by the military. During coffee harvest time, military check-points carry out intensive searches along the roads to prevent growers from taking their coffee to town for sale, while company agents, working on a commission basis, roam the coffee areas and purchase the coffee at prices fixed by Denok.

> Anyone who is caught transporting crops to other districts, even in small amounts for private distribution among family... will be punished. If the amounts are small, 2 or 3 kilos, (it) will be confiscated either by Denok or by the military for Denok. If the amounts are large, (it) will be confiscated and the people carrying it will be put in jail.[24]

The *Asian Wall Street Journal* was told in mid-1982 that growers got only a quarter of the price paid in real terms before Indonesia took over. Then a kilo of coffee was worth four kilos of rice, now it is worth less than one kilo. ACFOA's sources, referring to 1981, said growers received at most Rp. 350 a kilo and sometimes as little as Rp. 150; Denok then resold it to Chinese merchants in Dili for the local market with a 100-150 per cent mark-up. In 1983, the Australian Parliamentary delegation was told that Denok was paying Rp. 500 a kilo (roughly $0.50) a kilo when the world market coffee price was around $3.00 a kilo.

It is impossible to calculate the dollar earnings netted by Denok in the years since 1976 from coffee export. Under the Portuguese, average annual exports were 5,000 tonnes. According to Indonesian official statistics, this level was exceeded in 1980. At 1975 prices, East Timor was earning about $5.5 million a year from coffee. Mario Carrascolao predicted that 1984 would be the year of the 'highest coffee production ever' reaching 10,000 tonnes as compared with 4,000 tonnes in 1983.[25]

At 1983 prices, which were roughly three times as high as 1975, Denok probably raked in well over $16 million from coffee alone. Earnings in 1984 when prices again rose are certain to be much higher. These huge earnings have made it possible for Denok to set up several other companies. PT Batara Indra is in charge of the entertainment business; it runs the Dili cinema as well as the New Resende Inn, the Dili hotel where foreign visitors are accommodated. Denok paid no compensation to the former owners for the property involved. Another company, Toko Marina, runs the Dili supermarket, while the sole importer of a wide variety of food products and consumer goods is PT Nadiake. A fourth company, PT Scent Indonesia, was set up by Denok to process sandalwood for export.

Sandalwood was the product that first attracted Portuguese traders to the country several centuries ago. After Indonesian troops invaded, Denok imposed a monopoly on the collection and sale of sandalwood and encouraged the rapacious felling of trees without regard for the longterm consequences. By 1980, reports in the Indonesian press were warning that sandalwood could face extinction. Trees were being felled well below the traditionally accepted minimum age of 50 years and saplings were even being uprooted. The same complaint was contained in a statement of the East Timor regional assembly, issued in June 1981, which said that 'certain individuals' were forcing Timorese to cut down sandalwood trees, including saplings, then selling the timber to Denok at well below the market price. The first sandalwood processing factory was set up in 1979, symbolically on 5 October 'Armed Forces Day', and had within a year already 'done away with' a thousand tons of sandalwood.[26] In 1982, PT Scent Indonesia was producing 240 tons of perfumed sandalwood and exporting a considerable quantity of aromatic oil.[27]

The occupation forces are building a plantation economy in East Timor like the Portuguese colonialists did before them, but they are doing it far more systematically, helped by the surplus extracted by Denok. An additional 10,000 hectares of land have been turned over to coffee plantations; by 1980, a million coffee seedlings had already been planted.[28] These investments have already begun to bear fruit with 1984's 'highest production ever'. A million clove seedlings have also been planted, heralding the development of a new cash crop that enjoys a vast market in Indonesia where clove-scented cigarettes are immensely popular. The domestic clove trade also happens to be monopolized by the brother of President Suharto. Ten thousand hectares have been converted to sugar cane, some of it in Ue Tice, West Viqueque and some farther east, to supply a sugar mill that is now being built in the vicinity of Los Palos.

In March 1984, the East Timor Plantation Service announced that the area of land given over to plantation crops had almost doubled, from 78,004.9 hectares in 1977 to 144,234.6 hectares in 1983, and cash crop production had risen in the same period from 18,584 tons to 30,766.05 tons. The most striking acreage increases were for coconut which had risen from 19,009.5 to 48,203.1 hectares and for areca nut which had risen more than sixfold, from 4,485 to 34,690.14 hectares over the same period. The Plantation Service spoke of the 'enormous potential' of East Timor as a producer of cash crops. But since much of the expansion has gone into new crops which are not yet productive, coffee still accounts for 90% of the foreign exchange earnings from the territory. Other new cash crops which have been introduced since 1977 are cinnamon (2,512.5 hectares), candlenut (3,470.1 hectares) and kapok (8,569.75 hectares) as well as rubber (832.25 hectares), cocoa (50 hectares), pepper (12.50 hectares), tea (4 hectares) and cloves (590 hectares), none of which has yet come into production.[29] Once all these new crops begin to produce, the Army's business interests will enjoy a huge boost to the profits they have already made from East Timor's rapid conversion to cash-crop cultivation.

As for food production, Indonesia's policy is to leave Timorese agriculture to wither, and concentrate on introducing new techniques. These are being promoted on the one hand by bringing in peasant farmers from Indonesia as the nucleus for rice production schemes while also launching a large-scale 'integrated rural development' programme financed largely by the US Agency for International Development (US-AID).

The critical reason for the precarious food situation in East Timor is the fact that hundreds of thousands of Timorese are forcibly confined to concentration camps, denied access to fertile land, and are required to subordinate their food-growing activities to the security criteria of the occupation forces. But the Indonesian colonial authorities constantly pour scorn on the 'backwardness' of Timorese food production methods, thus creating the impression that the Timorese are themselves to blame for the current food shortages. The 'superiority' of Indonesian agriculture is a constant theme. The Jakarta weekly, *Tempo* reported on a special course for Timorese farmers held in Jogjakarta, Central Java; Indonesian officials were quoted as saying that the Timorese were being taught 'to use their brains'.[30] After a visit to Dili and an intensive briefing from Indonesian officials, a journalist claimed that Timorese farmers had no idea about how to clear the soil, they just 'stick corn seeds into the ground, then leave them untended without caring whether they live or die'.[31] By contrast, a German agronomist, Joachim Metzner who undertook a lengthy and detailed investigation of agricultural production in the central region of East Timor in the early 1970s, showed how Timorese farmers have skillfully adjusted to difficult soil and climate conditions, always seeking out ways to produce as much food as possible despite the numerous obstacles. So much so, he wrote, that 'the visitor is bewildered by the ingenuity the Timorese display in the construction of their rice terraces'.[32]

In keeping with the theme of 'superiority', the Balinese farmers who have been resettled in the region of Maliana as part of Indonesia's transmigration programme are always referred to in official literature as 'exemplary' farmers. The Maliana transmigration scheme, as yet in its early stages, is part of a general Indonesian population programme for the resettlement of people from the densely-populated islands of Java and Bali to the less populated islands in the archipelago. But in West Papua where Indonesian control is strongly challenged by the native inhabitants, transmigration also performs a distinctive security role by populating the countryside with communities loyal to the Indonesian Republic, thus watering down resistance to Indonesian rule. Transmigration is bound to play a similar role in East Timor, though at present it would appear to be directed more specifically at Indonesianizing the methods of agricultural production. According to figures given by Indonesian officials, fifty Balinese families (the former Bishop of Dili estimates two hundred families) have so far been transmigrated to the Maliana area, with another 250 families due to be resettled in 1984, in the region of Kovalima, south of Maliana.[33] This influx has already disrupted land ownership patterns, as the former Bishop explained in an interview with TAPOL. The military authorities had told him that

> it would be good to bring some farmers from other parts to teach the Timorese about agricultural techniques. So, about 200 families were brought to Maliana from Bali. But... they settled these families on land that belongs to Timorese who were driven off the land. The Timorese were very angry but, being powerless, they kept silent. They came and told me about it. There is plenty of other land they could occupy. Why don't they go there, these people said to me.
> ... And another problem is that these newcomers not only occupy the land of the Timorese. They also take over their jobs. These Balinese farmers are not familiar with the soil and didn't have much experience in agriculture so they have taken other jobs, house-building, carpenting and other crafts. They are favoured against the Timorese who have thus not only lost their land but have also lost various jobs they used to do. This has caused conflicts between the Indonesian peasants and the Timorese who have been thrust aside—the ones who have lost their land as well as the ones who have lost work.[34]

Apart from the disruptive effects described by Monsignor da Costa Lopes, Timorese people in the vicinity of these projects are being required to do forced labour to reclaim land for rice-growing. In the language of Indonesia's 'White Book', ten thousand hectares of rice-fields in Bobonaro were constructed with 'voluntary' labour, while the local inhabitants near Ainaro 'collectively' dug canals to irrigate about 90 hectares of rice-fields.[35] 'Voluntary', 'collective' labour are the euphemisms used in official translations for 'gotong-royong', an Indonesian term that has become all too familiar to Timorese people. 'Gotong-royong', an old village tradition in Java of mutually benefitial community work, has today become the cover for requiring people to work on development projects without pay.

The 'integrated rural development' project is situated farther north, centred in the Lois River Basin, south-west of Maubara. US Government funding is involved in this project to the tune of $5 million from US-AID. Additional funds from the Indonesian Government will pay for building the irrigation system and the construction of a 30km road linking the project with Dili (no doubt, with more 'voluntary' labour being used). The huge investment involved suggests that this is intended to be a high-profile project to establish a new rice-producing area for Indonesia. Construction of the project is being managed by Catholic Relief Services. Unlike other Catholic agencies the CRS has never collaborated with the local church network in East Timor. It functions in effect as an arm of the US State Department and prefers to work in partnership with the occupation authorities in East Timor.

The style of development being promoted in the Lois River area has been strongly criticized by Australian Catholic Relief, an organization that has been closely involved with the problems of East Timor ever since the Indonesian invasion. An ACR representative told the Australian Senate Inquiry:

> They have a lot of Massey Fergusson tractors sitting up there in this programme... Of course any agricultural programme will not be successful unless the local people want that sort of thing to happen. I would worry that the CRS programme is in the same mould as others that have been dumped on the community. From what I was told, I understand that the people have been told to go and work in that area, and whether the Timorese want it and will be part of it when they get there is a very big question in my mind.[36]

Indeed, the Timorese people now cooped up in the camps have nothing to gain from such development programmes. It will mean nothing to them if East Timor sooner or later becomes a surplus producer of rice while at the same time the Timorese people themselves are prevented from returning to their former lands and from engaging in their former agricultural pursuits. Rice surpluses in Indonesia's '27th province' are an insult to people who have been reduced to extreme levels of poverty, dependent on handouts from international relief agencies and left to forage for wild roots and leaves when Indonesia's security conditions permit.

Education

Indonesia's 'basic commitment... to the next generation rather than the present'[37] underlies the authorities' concentration on education. The Australian journalist, Peter Hastings, clearly outlined the Indonesian assumptions:

> I think it will be a long time before Indonesia is accepted in East Timor in the same way as I believe it will be a long time before it is accepted in Irian Jaya. It will, in fact, take the time needed until a new generation arrives speaking Indonesian, accepting Indonesian social and political institutions and sharing Indonesian cultural attitudes.[38]

The apologists for 'integrasi' see nothing wrong with the intense indoctrination of Timorese children and they confirm without any doubt that older Timorese will never accept the Indonesian takeover.

There is no way of checking Indonesian claims that in 1982-1983 there were 90,437 children in 376 primary schools, 5,622 children in 28 junior high schools and 1,047 children in 5 senior high schools.[39] The figures seem high and may even exceed the number of school-age children in the country, but there is no doubt that it is in Indonesia's interests to have as many children as possible in school. The available evidence indicates that great efforts have been made to reorganize the education system. A Timorese refugee who worked as a sub-district head in East Timor until 1979 reported that these efforts intensified in 1978 'when there was a major attempt to set up their education system and staff it with Javanese'.[40]

The Catholic church played a leading role in education prior to 1975. The first schools established were the mission schools founded in the nineteenth century. The best-known primary schools were the seminaries in Soibada and Dare. The teachers training college, Canto Rescendi, was run by Catholic priests although it was a state institution. Elementary schools existed in many of the administrative *postos*, and there were about 30,000 children at school by the early 1970s. There were also a number of Chinese schools run by a special commission and funded by the Taiwan government. The curriculum has been discribed by one Timorese refugee;

> Secondary school was strict, academic, and contained no Timorese culture. Instruction was in Portuguese; we studied Portuguese history and geography but not Timorese. We only knew Timor from our experience and what our parents told us.[41]

The Indonesians have set out quickly to smash the Portuguese colonial system of education and erect a new colonial system serving Indonesian integrationist interests in its place. That they have set up more schools in five years than the Portuguese were able to do in the hundred years or so since the first mission schools were founded, only testifies to the top priority given to Indonesianizing the younger generation.

Among the many people who testified before the Australian Senate Inquiry was an activist from Tasmania, David Freeman, who spent several months collecting evidence from Timorese refugees with first-hand experience of Indonesia's policy and practice in education and culture. By presenting their evidence for them, he was able to protect their anonymity while ensuring that their testimony was put on public record. The testimony of Timorese refugees who testified *in camera* is unfortunately unavailable to the public. His submission provides a comprehensive account of the school system now functioning in East Timor, and of the concerted efforts being made to force East Timorese to accept Indonesian ideological, social and cultural values. The principal modes used in schools—language, ideology and curriculum—are:

- Insistence upon Bahasa Indonesia as the sole language used in schools.
- Relentless indoctrination of Pancasila, Indonesia's state dogma.
- A school curriculum which is thoroughly Indonesian—and devoid of information about East Timor.
- A strong emphasis on physical education and on membership of Pramuka, the state-controlled scout movement dedicated to training youngsters in parading, long marches, saluting the flag and singing nationalist Indonesian songs.

The use of Indonesian throughout the entire school as the medium of instruction, and the only language that may be spoken in the school precincts, is strictly enforced. Children are punished for speaking Tetum, Portuguese or Chinese. Courses in these prohibited languages are secretly run outside the school system. Indonesian is also compulsory in government offices. As most adults cannot speak the language, they often discover that paying bribes is the only way to deal with the bureaucracy.

The use of Indonesian in the schools automatically disqualifies Timorese teachers. The teachers come from Indonesia and remain in the country for short periods only. Soldiers sometimes take classes, provide physical instruction and train school children in marching. Some of the refugees explained that in the early days schools were often run almost entirely by soldiers. It is likely that troops are still used in schools in more remote areas where Indonesian teaching staff would be less likely to go. Troops certainly play a particularly active role in the Pramuka sessions which take up much of the school timetable.

One recurring theme in all the testimony submitted was the heavy emphasis on forcing children to learn the Pancasila by rote.

> We also did a subject on Pancasila principles. You must know it by heart. We had two months to learn the Pancasila. If you didn't know it, you had to run round the block or stand in a big wooden box for three hours. And tomorrow, you must know it. Every morning before school started, we sang 'Garuda Pancasila'.[42]

Pancasila is the set of five principles that have been officially decreed as Indonesia's only ideology and belief, the articles of faith for every citizen. The five principles are: belief in one God, nationalism or Indonesian unity, democracy by means of consultation and consensus, humanitarianism, and social justice. Under military rule, all parties and organizations must, by decree, adhere only to the Pancasila; opposition to these articles of faith is regarded as an act of subversion punishable under Indonesia's draconian Anti-Subversion Law.

The constant harping on the principle of nationalism and Indonesian unity must be particularly offensive to Timorese people whose own patriotic sentiments are strictly denied any expression. Inculcating people with the idea of consultation and consensus is a deliberate attempt to destroy the will to resist, to create a set of values that rejects conflict and opposition. Saturating children with this set of values is central to the whole process of Indonesianization. The principle of belief in one God not only makes religious belief compulsory, it excludes traditional beliefs which have always had a wide following in East Timor.

Naturally, all this Pancasila indoctrination is often counter-productive. The Timorese who testified gave numerous examples of jokes that circulate: 'Pancasila sounds good but it kicks you in the bottom!' Indonesia's five principles, say the Timorese, are: 'Ask, borrow, take, grab, and in any case, everything belongs to the Indonesians!' One refugee said that when children are told to sing 'Garuda Pancasila' for foreign visitors, 'the first three rows sing it properly, and the rows behind sing their own version.'[43] Nevertheless, joking about the Pancasila can incur serious trouble; children are constantly being warned about the need to conform with Indonesia's particular brand of patriotism.

Schoolbooks in Indonesia are standardized, and all schools are required to use textbooks compiled by a State commission in 1975. In a country with a wide diversity of ethnic origin and cultural heritage, these textbooks set out to create stereotypes, models of perfection, primarily constructed around the Javanese set of values. These models are no less alien to the children of East Timor than the stereotypes forced upon their parents and grandparents by the Portuguese colonialists. Geography and history concentrates only on Indonesia, with 'the 27 provinces, their features and maps' as one refugee said. History deals only with Indonesia's past and its struggle against the Dutch, its leaders and presidents. 'The teachers do not talk about Indonesia's reasons for coming to East Timor in 1975, and the children dare not ask.'

Physical education and singing nationalist Indonesian songs are emphasised. 'There is much physical education, less academic work and much learning of songs: the Indonesian (national) anthem, the Pancasila set to music which you must memorize, school songs, songs patriotic to Indonesia... They also (teach) Indonesian folklore, no Timorese.'[44] Another refugee who attended a technical college in Dili explained how even there, in grade one, the timetable was much the same. 'At first, we just learnt songs and Pancasila. The only day that was different was Monday when we studied music from 8 to 10am. On Saturdays we did Pramuka. On Thursday we trained for gymnastics.'[45] 'Studying music' was in fact the inescapable singing of patriotic songs.

Pramuka sessions have become an extension of the curriculum. Pupils are under pressure to join, and most refugees described membership as being compulsory. The degree of pressure varies, but as most witnesses explained that every afternoon and the whole of Saturday were devoted to Pramuka, pupils have no choice but to join in. One witness succinctly expressed the views of most when he said:

> We have Pramuka every afternoon Monday to Friday and all day Saturday. We must stand at attention, put the flag up and down, and some just faint. You have to be in Pramuka. If you miss a day at school, they will accept a note from your parents. If you miss Pramuka, they come to your house to see if you are really sick. Some

students say: 'Why do we have to stand out in the sun to march? I could be at home helping my parents instead.' Others say: 'We can get a free trip to Jakarta.'[46]

According to all the available accounts, physical education consists largely of marching and other military pursuits. Children are trained to march for all occasions, but the training becomes particularly intense when foreign visitors come and need to be impressed by the vigour and seeming enthusiasm of children for the new Indonesian culture.

> The students of our school had a marching band. We had uniforms of an Indonesian style. The marching was led by a policeman who was also in the army. We marched to Indonesian tunes. We marched passed Suharto when he came to Timor... We practised marching to different tunes before his visit. We practised every school day for two months before his visit... The students borrowed some of the uniforms from the Pramuka for the marching.[47]

An example of how children are used to impress foreigners is given in the Australian parliamentary delegation report. Dilor, the concentration camp near Lakluta, was almost deserted when the mission came. 'Only the schoolrooms were bustling with life and excitement at the visit, the children singing loyal Indonesian songs lustily'[48]

The hundreds of schools now being run by the Indonesian authorities are dedicated to crushing the Timorese identity and creating in its place a militaristic, patriotic fervour with which to seal East Timor irreversibly as Indonesia's 27th province. The total disregard for Timorese traditions and values reinforces the essential aspect of Indonesian tutelage, the idea that Indonesia's way is superior and that Timorese people are backward, ignorant, dirty and uncivilized and need to be 'upgraded'.

Political Life

Political activity has ceased to exist in the Indonesian-occupied parts of East Timor, apart from the clandestine political activity of the liberation struggle. In January 1976, the puppet provisional government disbanded all Timorese political parties as was required the moment they declared 'integrasi' with Indonesia. State regulations in Indonesia permit the existence of only three parties—the 'Muslim' PPP, the 'nationalist' and 'Christian' PDI and the Army's party, GOLKAR. The first two are now mere shadows of their former selves in Indonesia since no party may advocate any beliefs other than the Pancasila. These Indonesian parties are totally alien to the East Timorese. The 1982 Indonesian general election was used in an attempt to prove that the people of East Timor fully back 'integrasi'. The official returns for East Timor claimed a turnout of more than a hundred per cent of registered voters; 99% of the votes were said to be for GOLKAR. Both claims are uncorroborated by any other evidence. The fullest account of the elections was given by Neobere, a Timorese refugee who left Dili for Lisbon at the beginning of 1983:

> Long before polling day, the government sent military officers out to all areas to tell people that they had to take part in the election, and that they must vote for GOLKAR, not for either of the other parties. I myself attended such a meeting where a soldier told us how we must vote. We were told that if we didn't vote, we would be branded as Fretilin. This meant that voting was compulsory. So our people thought: well, if we have to vote, we shall try to do it not in the way they want, so as not to give the impression that they have the support of the Timorese. But the point is that people felt they had to vote, otherwise they could be killed.
>
> At the polling stations, there were three ballot boxes, one for each of the parties. The GOLKAR box was in the middle (No.2) and the PPP and PDI boxes were on each side. In front of where the polling booth was there was a small hall with military police on guard. The three boxes were concealed behind a curtain but the curtain didn't come down to the floor, only to knee height, so the guard could see by watching people's feet which box they went to. People knew what was happening, so they tried to keep their feet in front of the middle box but put their voting slip into one of the other boxes.[49]

Some voting booths did not even have curtains. A photograph of an election booth published in Indonesia's 'White Book' shows two sets of three ballot boxes standing unconcealed on the floor, one set for the parliamentary election and one for the local assembly election. The booth is crowded with people; the election is in progress and three election officials are seated at a table less than a metre from the six boxes. The captions reads: 'The casting of votes were made free, direct, universal and secret.'[50]

Public Health: Myth and Reality

The level of health in East Timor has deteriorated drastically as a result of the Indonesian takeover. Not only did the trauma of famine and disease from 1977 to 1979 leave deep and lasting scars on the community; the conditions of the people now living in the camps, most of whom survive on the brink of starvation, has continued to have a deleterious effect on people of all ages. The forced resettlement of people in the lowlands and coastal plains has also brought them into contact with physical conditions conducive to disorders that have created new hazards to health. It is widely acknowledged that one of the main reasons Timorese peasants settled by choice in the hills was that the coastal plains, particularly in the south, are malaria infested. Not even the attraction of more fertile soil could induce them to descend unless major anti-malaria campaigns were mounted. Living on the coast, says one observer, means that 'former hill people have been hard hit by malaria, skin and eye disorders and influenza.'[51]

The Indonesian authorities claim that the medical services are working well, that a new hospital has been built in Dili with two others under construction in Maliana and Baucau, and that 34 *puskesmas* (community health centres) are now operating. An account of the reality of these services has been given by Neobere, a trained nurse who was with the resistance until 1978. He spent the subsequent five years in Indonesian-occupied East Timor, and worked for the Catholic Relief Services. The *puskesmas*, he said, have hardly any medicines and people going there for treatment are lucky to come away with a few pills. Hospital treatment for serious cases is only available at a very high cost, up to Rp. 100,000. Anyone who cannot afford that is denied hospital care.

> Outside Dili, in the *postos*, there's little to be had in the way of medical treatment, but people are not allowed to go to Dili for treatment. The result is that people often die for lack of treatment. In any case, treatment in the hospitals and clinics is very unsatisfactory, given without care or attention... Some of the Indonesian doctors are poorly qualified. Others are well qualified but they only want to treat people properly in their private practices, and for high fees.[52]

D.J. Richardson of the Australian embassy made an extensive tour of East Timor in September 1982 during which he concluded that 'overall health facilities in the province were sparce'. The district hospital in Maliana was 'devoid of any worthwhile medical equipment'. He visited a hospital in Iliomar, in the east, which treats patients with serious illnesses but which received visits from a doctor only once or twice a month.[53]

East Timorese now living abroad recall that without the aid of the International Red Cross (ICRC) and the programmes of the Catholic church, conditions in the late 1970s would have been even more catastrophic than they were. The ICRC's food and medical programme on Atauro island inaugurated in April 1982 has been instrumental in saving many lives. ICRC operations have however been short-lived and are subject to curtailment at the whim of the military authorities. The first programme launched in late 1979 lasted only eighteen months. Then followed a one-year gap, the period when Operation Security was launched, until ICRC was allowed to resume operations in April 1982. Their operations were again suspended in July 1983 when the preparations for the 1983 offensive began. In May 1982, ICRC's programmes in a few camps were taken over by UNICEF, but these too had to be suspended for several months in mid-1983.

Several Timorese who have commented on the hospital facilities stress that they are used almost entirely for the treatment of Indonesian troops. Colonel Purwanto said as much himself in a remark to the Australian parliamentary delegation when he was trying to impress upon the visitors that there were no security hazards in East Timor, only the danger of 'road accidents'. He told the visitors: 'The hospital here is full of my men who are there because they have had road accidents and not because they have been shot.'[54]

There is an acute shortage of doctors. The Army doctors who are sent to East Timor only treat the troops. Most of the civilian doctors who go there comply with a government regulation which requires medical graduates to do a period of bonded service. The length of service varies in an attempt to attract doctors away from the big cities. In a 'hardship' post like East Timor, the service is cut to the minimum of only one year but, as the *Asian Wall Street Journal* has pointed out, 'many doctors assigned to villages for a year find excuses to spend most of their time in Dili.'[55]

People in East Timor in any case lack confidence in Indonesian doctors and in particular are very suspicious of injections administered by them. The reason is not hard to find: stories abound about people being injected with poison or with lethal doses of water.

Birth control is being actively promoted despite the fact that people totally reject the idea that the growth of population needs to be checked. This is, as Neobere has said, 'part of a strategem'. Even before the heavy loss of life during the past few years, East Timor was not over-populated.

> Now, after at least 200,000 people have been killed off... any talk of over-population is even more ludicrous. There's absolutely no need for family planning, but it's quite clear that the reason why the Indonesians are resorting to this kind of thing is because they want to kill off the Timorese and re-populate our country with their own people.[56]

The former Bishop of Dili has disclosed that another way of forcing birth control on an unwilling population is by sterilizing women without their knowledge or consent. Women were being sterilized while under anaesthetic for a quite different operation. Officials try to browbeat people, warning that the government will 'withdraw facilities' from people with big families. But, said Mgr da Costa Lopes,

> the Timorese say: 'Never mind! We don't need or want to rely on help from the government. In any case, so many people have been killed since the invasion, we need more children, not less.[57]

The birth control programme in East Timor includes the use of the Depo Provera contraceptive injection. Administered on a large scale against a population that is unfamiliar with its harmful consequences, this form of contraceptive could have a particularly disastrous effect on the level of population growth and the health standards of women and children.

The Catholic Church of East Timor

The only institution in East Timor to have escaped severe persecution by the Indonesians is the Catholic Church. The Church has played a central role ever since the beginning of Portuguese colonialism. Over the centuries, Dominican, Franciscan, Salesian and Jesuit missionaries worked there as an integral part of the colonial system. The notorious Concordat concluded between Portugal and the Vatican in 1941 guaranteed the Portuguese Catholic Church special privileges in return for which the Church agreed to serve the interests of the corporate state.

Already in the first year of its existence, Fretilin faced problems in its relations with the Church. Although the majority of Fretilin leaders were practising Catholics, they became the target of criticism from the Portuguese Bishop of Dili, Jose Ribero. In a Pastoral Letter on 'The new situation in East Timor', issued in January 1975, the Bishop reaffirmed the role of the Church as 'the traditional religion of the Portuguese nation' and stressed the need for the rights of property to be respected. He also warned against 'materialistic and atheistic communism and socialistic Marxism which is seeking to extinguish the positive values of the Timorese people.'[58] Notwithstanding such an attack, Fretilin avoided conflict with the church while standing by the principle that in a democracy, there would be no place for special privileges for the church and there would have to be separation between church and state.

At the time of the UDT coup in August 1975, Fretilin leaders had reason to become more disappointed with the Church. During the civil war that followed the coup, more than 90% of all priests and nuns, many of them Timorese, left for Portugal. Xavier do Amaral who was then Fretilin president, himself a seminarist commented:

> As a Catholic I am concerned and a little bit angry with the position of the Church in East Timor. In times of peace, they say the shepherd will always stay with his flock, but this is the second time that these words have been empty for the people of East Timor. During the Japanese war, most nuns and priests ran away to Australia, leaving the Catholic people here alone.[59]

The response of Bishop Jose Ribero to the Indonesian invasion symbolizes the disintegration of the Portugese Catholic Church in East Timor. Mgr da Costa Lopes, the man who later succeeded Bishop Ribero, said of his predecessor during the first days of the invasion:

> Oh, poor man, he could not cope at all. The whole situation was more than he could bear. All he did was cry—cry every time he heard about what the Indonesians were doing. He just cried and cried. Also, you must not forget, he is Portuguese, and it wounded his feelings very deeply to see the Indonesians pull down Portuguese flags and trample on everything Portuguese. So he asked the Vatican to allow him to resign. He retired in 1977. He is now living in

Portugal and he is a very sick man.[60]

The withdrawal of the religious and the retreat of the Portuguese colonial administration shattered the old system into which the church had so snugly fitted. The disintegration of the Portugese Catholic Church in East Timor accelerated the transformation of the Church into a national church. The majority of priests now working in the country are East Timorese, most of them opposed to both political and ecclesiastical integration with Indonesia.

The appointment of a Timorese, Mgr Martinhu da Costa Lopes to replace Bishop Ribero as head of the Church in East Timor in 1977, and the Timorization of the clergy, which was already in progress, was a turning point for Catholicism in East Timor. But even though Mgr da Costa Lopes was now the Apostolic Administrator, he was not made a bishop, an indication that the Vatican was waiting to see how things would develop. For people in East Timor however, Mgr da Costa Lopes came to be regarded as 'the Bishop of Dili'. As the tragic sufferings of the population intensified, the understaffed Church with its overworked personnel were thrust into a new social role. A new generation of Timorese clergy now had to shoulder the responsibility of running the Church as virtually all the older ones had left. It is worth noting that this new group of priests is of the same generation as the leaders of Fretilin, and in many cases they had attended school or seminary together.

From 1977 onwards, as the Indonesian military took control of the population, the Church came more and more to assume the role of a church of the people, a 'Maubere church'. Four years later, this deep-rooted commitment was revealed in a statement, 'Reflection in Faith', issued on 31 July 1981 by the religious of East Timor:

> The people of East Timor are suffering. They feel themselves misunderstood, although knowing what is happening and aware that they are being humiliated. But they remain in a position which is very clear concerning their ideals. In the midst of all of this, their faith stands firm and is strengthened although it is not always able to be expressed in words, but is seen with the eyes of faith by the religious who accompany the people.
>
> The East Timorese religious feel solidarity with the people and because of that feel obliged to express the people's experience of faith. This is even more so because they are in the midst of the people, in a position which helps to understand and formulate better the faith of the people, particularly because they know the language, standards and heart of the people.

The attitude adopted by the Bishop and many of the Timorese religious during the years of overwhelming tragedy led to a dramatic growth in the Church's following:

> Though there has been an overall decline in the population well in

excess of 100,000, the proportion of Catholics has risen from thirty per cent before 1975 to well over fifty per cent. The search for security has led many who have come down from the mountains to actually build their huts on Church grounds.[61]

The Attitude of the Military and 'Integrasi' of the Church

At first the Army had little time to devote to civilian affairs; their aim was to defeat the resistance militarily. But after the encirclement and annihilation campaign had been completed and Operation Seroja disbanded in March 1979, military officers devoted more attention to social and political control, and therefore also to the role of the Church. The Church in East Timor maintains a position of neutrality between the occupation forces and the resistance under Fretilin leadership, but its stand on the side of the suffering population has brought it into conflict with the military.

Having ceased to be part of the Portuguese Church in 1975, the Church in East Timor is administered direct from Rome: it has not become part of the Indonesian Church. Although the Indonesian government would like to see 'integrasi' of the Catholics in East Timor with the Indonesian Church, this goal has thus far eluded them. This however is a matter for the Vatican, and there are several reasons why it does not favour 'integrasi' at the ecclesiastical level. The Vatican has always been in a good position to monitor the situation in East Timor with the help of reports from the local church and because of the many visits of Vatican officials to the island. When Pat Walsh, an Australian Catholic who has closely followed church affairs in East Timor since 1975, visited the Vatican in 1980, he was told by officials of the Vatican Secretariat of State that they regard East Timor as an 'occupied country' where no genuine act of self-determination has taken place. He was also given to understand that the Catholic hierarchy regarded the East Timorese Church as being as mature as the Indonesian Church and that 'incorporation' would create difficulties.[62]

The delicate relations between the Church and the forces of occupation is the result of caution on both sides, each trying to avoid open conflict. For several years, Church leaders helped channel important information about conditions to the outside world while at the same time engaging in silent diplomacy against the brutality of the Indonesian troops. It was not until 1981, the year of Operation Security which had such a catastrophic effect on economic and social conditions, that some of them felt the time had come to speak out openly. Mgr da Costa Lopes has since recalled the circumstances of this decision:

> At first I agreed with those who say we should keep quiet and until 1981 I was silent. I complained privately to General Dading about human rights abuses, and to the local commander. But nothing changed. In 1981, after 6 years, I decided that because there were no other means I should speak openly in accordance with the Church's

prophetic mission. At a rally of 12,000 people in honour of Our Lady I condemned the abuses, without naming Indonesia. That was the first time I spoke out publicly.[63]

From this point on, relations between the Church and the military deteriorated rapidly. In their handling of Catholicism, the occupation forces clearly face a dilemma. On the one hand, they nurture a deep distrust of the clergy as is evident from a remark made in one of the secret counter-insurgency documents. Yet in the very same breath, they are compelled to admit that the Church is in very close touch with the population, so much so that 'ideas that are conveyed through Church channels... reach the community fast and are obeyed'.[64]

It was the latter point that must have prompted General Yusuf, Commander-in-Chief of the Indonesian Armed Forces, to summon Mgr da Costa Lopes for a talk at the time Operation Security was in progress. The Bishop was summoned to Baucau for the meeting, and went, dressed in his ceremonial clothes for the occasion. The General asked the Bishop to make a public statement in support of 'integrasi', fully convinced this would bring the population round to participating energetically in the Operation. The Bishop refused to do so, and used the occasion to complain to Yusuf about brutalities committed by his troops and about the deplorable lack of sustenance supplied to the tens of thousands of Timorese who were being forced to join the operations.

Later that year, the Bishop sent a letter to the Australian Catholic Relief warning that famine could strike again in parts of East Timor because of the harmful effect of Operation Security on food production. The letter was released to the Australian press, much to the embarrassment of the Indonesian authorities. A few weeks later, Gough Whitlam, the former Australian Prime Minister, made a hastily-arranged visit to Dili and went out of his way, after returning home, to discredit the Bishop in a series of vicious, unwarranted attacks. He accused the Church leader of perpetrating a 'wicked act' in sending this 'cruel letter', while Peter Hastings, the journalist who accompanied him, described the Bishop's letter as 'inaccurate and mischievous'.[65]

Not long after this visit, the military made yet another attempt to undermine the credibility of the Bishop and the clergy. Traditional leaders were summoned from all parts of the country and given a document, written in all the local dialects, branding the clergy as 'incompetent', 'too old', 'not mobile enough', and 'ignorant of the real situation'. The leaders were told to go back home and advise people to stop listening to the homilies of the priests. A Timorese Catholic layman was later quoted as saying that everyone knows the priests are critical of the Indonesians because they are faithful to the people.

It is not surprising then that the traditional leaders... are reported to have said: 'Who is going to tell the people that the priests are deceiving them? I don't think there will be anyone who wants to do that.' To which the layman quoted above added: 'The Timorese still believe in their priests, and anyone who says they are deceivers will himself be called a deceiver.'⁶⁶

In 1981 the Indonesian administration tried to force the Church to accept linguistic 'integrasi' by stipulating that Portuguese should no longer be used during Mass and should be replaced by Indonesian. The clergy rejected this request and asked the Vatican for permission for Portuguese to be replaced by Tetum. The Vatican gave its approval in October 1981. This change in language has helped integrate the Church even more closely with the community.

Thwarted time and again in their efforts to win over or discredit the Church leadership in East Timor, the military increasingly devoted their energies to trying to end the ecclesiastical independence of the Church in East Timor and bring about 'integrasi'. They tried to do this through the Indonesian Bishops Conference (MAWI) which was asked by President Suharto himself to make an approach to the Vatican in favour of integrating East Timor's church. In recognition of the supremacy of the Vatican's position in such matters, MAWI had hitherto remained neutral on the question of integration but on this occasion, under pressure from the temporal power, MAWI did make efforts in this direction. Not long afterwards, the Indonesian Government publicly claimed that the Vatican was of the opinion that the welfare of the people of East Timor would best be served by 'integrasi'. Whether or not this was true, it is reported that when the Pope visited Portugal in May, 1982, he agreed to a request by President Eanes not to transfer the Dili diocese to Jakarta's jurisdiction, nor would the Vatican recognize the integration of East Timor into Indonesia.⁶⁷ Since then, Jakarta has avoided any public interpretation of the Vatican's attitude on East Timor.

Even so, there is no reason to doubt that it was the Papal ambassador in Jakarta, Mgr Pablo Puente who played a critical role in bringing about the resignation of the Bishop of Dili in May 1983. The Pro Nuncio maintains a close relationship with General Benny Murdani, himself a Catholic. Within a month of Murdani's appointment as Commander-in-Chief of the Indonesian Armed Forces in late March 1983, pressure on the Bishop had become so great that he had no alternative but to resign. Some of the clergy of East Timor made a last-minute bid to prevent the Bishop's removal. In a statement issued on 13 May 1983, they affirmed their solidarity with Mgr da Costa Lopes, and declared:

> This group feels disappointed and profoundly hurt, knowing that members of the Indonesian Catholic church have joined in the chorus of campaigns carried on inside and outside Indonesia and the defamation of its Prelate, accusing him presumptively of falsehoods, exaggeration and irresponsibility in his affirmation and attitudes; when his is the only voice raised in defence of the people on whom silence and fear are imposed and for whom the exercise of freedom of expression will only result in imprisonment or disappearance.

The appointment of Mgr Carlos Philipe Ximenes Belo as the new Apostolic Administrator took place without any consultations with the local clergy. Logically, the choice should have fallen to Mgr A. Ricardo, the Vicar-General under Costa Lopes and a man who would have been very acceptable to the priests in the territory. Mgr Belo by contrast was virtually an outsider having lived and studied abroad for many years prior to his appointment. As a much younger man than his predecessor and an Indonesian citizen at that, it may have been hoped that his position would be less prestigious and more open to influence from Jakarta. The fact is that despite the ecclesiastical independence of the Church in East Timor, its relations with the Vatican and the crucial question of appointments are regulated through the Pro Nuncio in Jakarta, establishing a *de facto* dependence on an official whose ties with the leadership of the military high command are very close.

Commenting on Mgr Belo's appointment, the former Bishop of Dili said:

> He took up his new position with no experience of how the Indonesians have treated our people. He was not there during the invasion; he returned to Timor quite recently so he knows very little. But I strongly believe that he will, little by little, realise what is going on, and begin to do what he can. He said recently—I saw a report in a Macau newspaper—that when he went back to Timor, he thought that the process of integration with Indonesia was complete, but after working there for a while, he now realises that this is not true.[68]

Less than six months after the new Church leader had taken office, Costa Lopes' prediction proved true. In October 1983, two months after the Indonesian offensive was lauched, Mgr Belo delivered a sermon at Dili Cathedral in which he protested against Indonesian brutalities and condemned the many arrests being made by the Indonesian Army. He was strongly reprimanded by the Indonesian religious affairs office in Dili but in November, he used the occasion of a meeting of the Indonesian Bishops' Conference (MAWI) to draw the attention of the Indonesian Catholic Church to the alarming situation in East Timor.[69] MAWI responded by addressing a letter, signed by its president Mgr F.X. Hadisumarta and Secretary, Mgr Leo Soekoto, expressing 'solidarity and friendship with the Faithful and the people of East Timor who are being deluged by most bitter trials both physically and spiritually'.

> ...we cannot refuse to confront the events that are happening among the people, especially those affairs which determine the welfare or the misery of the masses who are involved in or who are the victims of cruel oppression.[70]

This is the first time the Indonesian Catholic Church made public its response to the conditions in East Timor, although the previous

Apostolic Administrator frequently attended MAWI meetings as an observer and is known to have appealed to it on several occasions to help stop the brutalities being committed by Indonesian troops in East Timor. Whatever the circumstances which convinced the MAWI that it was now time to speak out, the MAWI November 1983 letter, addressed to the Catholic community in East Timor, represents an important reaffirmation of its position of neutrality on the central issue of 'integrasi' and its concern for the victims of oppression. No direct reference is made to Indonesia's role as the cause of this oppression, although MAWI goes out of its way to dissociate itself from the motives of the Indonesian government:

> ...the role and competence of the Church being what it is, she must in no way be confused with the political community nor bound up to any political system.[71]

It acknowledges that sympathy and solidarity from the Catholic church in Indonesia and in other countries has been 'a drop of water when compared with the ocean of pain' suffered by the East Timor people 'in the past eight years'. MAWI undertakes among other things to provide material assistance to help the many orphans in East Timor.[72] The MAWI statement also promised help in education 'by revitalizing the (Catholic) schools'.

The Pro Nuncio in Jakarta made another move in 1983 to promote ecclesiastical 'integrasi' by suggesting to the newly-appointed Apostolic Administrator, Mgr Belo, that the church in the Oecussi enclave should be incorporated into the Diocese of Atambua which is part of the Indonesian church. Mgr Belo responded by paying a visit to Oecussi to test the views of the inhabitants. He was warmly welcomed and told that such a proposal was unacceptable; despite years of separation the people regarded themselves as part of East Timor. This gave Mgr Belo grounds to reject the Pro Nuncio's suggestion.[73]

When General Murdani visited Dili on Christmas Day 1983, four months after the 1983 offensive was launched, he wanted to have a meeting with priests and nuns. According to information from Jakarta, the religious boycotted the meeting and refused to budge despite efforts by local intelligence agents to persuade them to change their mind. They had heard that another offensive would be launched on 2 January.

> It would have been difficult for them if the people heard that they were meeting Murdani when everyone knew that a week later there was going to be a great slaughter.[74]

One of the most drastic moves against the Church is directed against the Catholic system of education. During the colonial era, virtually the entire education system was run by the Church. Since the invasion, the Indonesian administration had devoted a great deal of effort to imposing a thoroughly doctrinaire curriculum on the schools. Catholic schools represent the only alternative to this system but their scope is continually declining. Although in absolute terms there are more Catholics in the country now than before 1975, the number of children attending Catholic schools has fallen sharply. At the same time, there is a shortage of teachers which is being met by recruiting staff from West Timor. Dissatisfaction has been expressed over the quality of these teachers, particularly because they bring with them a strong sense of loyalty to Indonesian attitudes and practices.

The Catholic schools also face discrimination because their teaching staff are not accorded civil servant status, which denies them facilities enjoyed by other teachers—particularly *in natura* allowances. The Church has been warned that equal status for its teachers will not be granted until it accepts 'integrasi'.

The Protestant churches in Indonesia, through the Indonesian Council of Churches (DGI), has on numerous occasions tried to become involved in East Timor affairs through a variety of relief and missionary activities. Unlike MAWI, the DGI has never adopted an attitude of neutrality on the question of East Timor; on the contrary, it has solidly backed the Indonesian government on 'integrasi' since the start. The DGI's position has had a very negative influence internationally, preventing the World Council of Churches from making any public pronouncements against the Indonesian takeover of East Timor, and standing in the way of positive action in support of East Timor by Protestant churches abroad.

Stage-managed visits

Ever since the invasion, Indonesia has maintained rigid control over access to East Timor. No one, including Indonesians, can visit the territory without special permission and all visitors must comply with conditions set by the authorities regarding their itinerary, mode of transport, accommodation and choice of interpreter. This enables the military authorities to stage-manage visits, to prevent free and unfettered contact with Timorese people and to use the visits for their own propaganda purposes. Security officers are constantly present whether or not the visitors are aware of it. *New York Times* journalist, Henry Kamm, described how he was escorted everywhere by Major Benny Mandalika, a military intelligence officer from Jakarta who

> took notes during interviews not only with ordinary people but also with Indonesian officials of Timorese origin, and often peered openly at the notes the reporter was taking. Explaining his actions when challenged, he said: 'I must stay with you so you get the right information. My boss told me to go with you wherever you go. If you interview the man in the street you may get the wrong information'.
>
> In the presence of Major Mandalika and other officials and speaking through interpreters in the various languages of the island, the people of the mountain tribes interviewed at resettlement sites

appeared intimidated and blamed Fretilin for all the ravages they had visibly suffered. Conversations in Dili with educated Timorese and non-Timorese residents, as well as conversations out of Major Mandalika's earshot in the interior, provided other accounts.[75]

A Portuguese television crew that visited East Timor in February 1983 used their camera to expose a crudely concealed tape-recorder being held by a security officer, who recorded every word of the team's interviews with Timorese prisoners on Atauro island.[76]

Stage-management of visits is a high-level responsibility entrusted to Major-General Dading Kalbuadi who has been intimately connected with East Timor since 1975. In March 1983, he became Assistant for Logistics of the Armed Forces Commander-in-Chief, thus retaining a direct link with the affairs of East Timor. Like other army officers who have carved their military careers out of the violent annexation of East Timor, he has enjoyed rapid promotion. His particular 'contribution' has been making sure that foreign visitors see what the authorities want them to see and hear what they want them to hear.

East Timorese refugees feel particularly angry about the way visits are manipulated. They have described how Timorese people are forced at gunpoint to give displays of enthusiastic welcome, to shout 'hurrahs' and repeat slogans in favour of 'integrasi' for the benefit of foreign visitors. On such occasions, they testify, Indonesian soldiers, dressed to look like local people, take up positions among the crowds to make sure of a good performance. Great care is taken by the organizers to conceal tanks, armoured cars and other war material, and if necessary, they even go to the lengths of removing tombstones from the cemeteries of Indonesia's war dead to conceal the extent of their own casualties. Troops are kept well out of sight when visits are in progress, though such efforts do occasionally go wrong. The Portuguese television team succeeded in taking a shot of soldiers disappearing from the road ahead as the vehicle in which they were travelling approached.[77]

A Timorese refugee told the Australian Senate Inquiry that when he was operating a photocopier in a government office in Dili, he managed to remove copies of internal instructions.

> One document I got specified which battalion was to take responsibility for each area when the ambassadors and journalists came to Timor in 1978. It also said that thirty army members would dress up in plain clothes. This was to keep the Timorese under watch and make up numbers to welcome the delegation and yell out 'Viva Indonesia.'[78]

Local administration officials are given detailed instructions on how to handle visitors, how to answer their questions and even what to wear. For instance, they are told not to wear the traditional Timorese loincloth wrap which Indonesian officials regard as being 'improper'. Occasionally, foreign visitors are treated to a special performance of Timorese traditional song and dance without realising that when visitors are not present, Timorese folklore is actively discouraged; the Timorese are expected to develop an enthusiasm for the culture of other islands as part of their process of 'integrasi'.

The forms of stage-management used by the Indonesian military in East Timor are often crude enough to be detectable to any discerning visitor. Yet many journalists have come away to report favourably on conditions and to claim that things are nowhere near as bad as the critics of Indonesian annexation say. In an effort to confound the critics, they insist that their first-hand impressions must be worth more than 'second-hand' material smuggled out or information from sources who, for obvious reasons, refuse to be identified.

The military authorities do everything possible to check the credentials of journalists and their papers before granting entry; most who get in believe firmly that 'integrasi' is 'irreversible' and their reports reinforce this viewpoint. There have been a few major breaches of Indonesia's control of journalists, notably the damaging report written by Rod Nordland in *The Philadelphia Inquirer*, and the film made by Rui Araujo in March 1983 for Portuguese Television. One journalist, Denis Reichle, from *Paris Match* smuggled himself across the border from West Timor in late 1977 to report on the Indonesian offensive then under way, but all his documents and films were confiscated. He was arrested by Indonesian troops on 21 September then jailed and 'pushed around a bit' during stiff questioning by Indonesian army officers in Atambua (West Timor). He was deported four days later.[79] Two years before, in October 1975, five television journalists from Australia were murdered by Indonesian troops in Balibo, a border town.

Indonesia's overall success in manipulating media reporting from East Timor is enhanced by the territorial blockade which means that secret visits are virtually impossible. Analysis of conditions in East Timor cannot rely on the first-hand reports of journalists but must be based on information from a variety of sources. Enough is available to penetrate the curtain which shuts the country off from the world, to see through the facade created by Indonesian bureaucracy and to discover the reality of life in East Timor today.

6. Atrocities and Violations

The Lakluta Massacres

> During the months of June to September and especially in recent weeks, the atrocities of the Indonesian army have caused the deaths of thousands of people, including those who had surrendered. Even women have been killed very slowly by stabbings with sharp knives. Apart from those who have died of hunger, starvation, or illness, or been burnt to death and shot during encounters with the Indonesian army, none of them compare with the evil atrocities that occurred recently in Lakluta...
>
> Twenty trucks were needed to take the bodies away, so many were there...
>
> Indonesian soldiers took hold of the legs of small children and threw them around in the air a number of times and smashed their heads against a rock. A woman asked that one of the children be given to her after the mother had been killed. At that time, the soldier permitted the woman to take this small child but a few minutes later, he grabbed the child and killed him. The soldier said: 'When you clean your field, don't you kill all the snakes, the small and large alike?'[1]

Lakulta lies on the southern slopes of the Dilor mountain range, in central East Timor, surrounded by the Santo Antonio hills. It was here that the Indonesian 1981 Operation Security was concentrated. Hundreds of people were brought from surrounding districts and slaughtered along with local inhabitants. It was a place where no one dared drink the river water because it tasted of blood. The events of September 1981 turned Lakluta into a symbol of the worst atrocities perpetrated by Indonesian troops in East Timor.

On 2 September, writes one eye witness, 25 people—twenty men and five women—were brought there. The women were separated from the men, who were lined up and shot dead by soldiers. Their bodies were covered with dry leaves and grass and set alight. Then, the women were taken away by helicopter. Other Timorese who had been forced to join the Indonesian army patrols were forced to watch. They stood motionless, 'fearing even to shake their heads which was considered most dangerous lest they lose their own lives'.

Many massacres followed, culminating in the day that twenty trucks were needed to remove the bodies, so many people were slaughtered. This was the day when

> troops surrounded Lakluta, firing through the houses with automatic rifles; (they) did not know who was there. The Battalion was 744/5. There were also Timorese in it. Only in the morning did they discover that there were only women and children and no Fretilin army. The shame was so great, they confessed to the Bishop. Some took photos which have been seen. Battalion 744/5 was withdrawn to Klaten, Central Java. When the Bishop mentioned it in his sermon, *bupatis* (were) all forced to sign a letter declaring it did not happen. (General) Benny Murdani confessed there were at least 80 people. Deaths were possibly somewhere between 200 and 400 in this incident alone.[2]

The Bishop of Dili later denounced these massacres in a letter to Australian Catholic Relief. Five hundred Timorese had been killed, he said, in Lakluta during a four-day seige 'including innocent children, pregnant women and defenceless people without any crime except the desire to be independent of all oppression'.

Since those events, all the surviving inhabitants of Lakluta have been forced to resettle in a new concentration camp in Dilor, about ten miles south-east of Lakluta.

A Pattern of Terror and Brutality

Under Indonesian military occupation, the people of East Timor have become the victims of a regime of unparalleled terror and barbarism. Much has been written about the indiscriminate killings that occurred in the capital, Dili, on the first day of the invasion. Details of what happened were first documented by Jim Dunn, a former Australian consul in Dili, who interviewed East Timorese refugees in Lisbon in February 1977.[3] Dunn described the attack on the East Timorese capital in 1975 as 'one of the most brutal operations of its kind in modern warfare'.

> According to a Catholic priest who was in Dili after the invasion, as many as 2,000 citizens of the capital, some 700 of them Chinese, were killed in the first few days of the Indonesian invasion... Hundreds of Timorese and Chinese were gunned down at random... In one such incident, a large number of Apodeti supporters who had just been released from internment by Fretilin, went out to greet their liberators (the Indonesian troops, CB-LSL), to be machine-gunned for their trouble. A number of public executions were carried out by Indonesian troops, with some of the condemned being selected at random, and others with the help of Apodeti collaborators. One of the most bizarre and gruesome of these atrocities occurred within

24 hours of the invasion and involved the killing of about 150 people. This shocking spectacle began with the execution of more than 20 women who, from various accounts, were selected at random... The women were led out to the edge of the jetty and shot one at a time, with the crowd of shocked onlookers being forced at gun-point to count loud as each execution took place![4]

The horrifying events in Dili set the pattern of brutality that has characterized the Indonesian occupation ever since. The troops, egged on by their commanders, regard the Timorese with deep suspicion and mistrust, seeing everyone, even their closest collaborators, as actual or potential 'dissident remnants'. The Timorese respond to every new act of brutality with an even deeper hatred for the occupation forces. In such a situation, any act of violence perpetrated by an Indonesian soldier is considered to be justifiable. This attitude has been summed up by the former Bishop of Dili:

> There is not a spark of humanitarianism among the Indonesians. Perhaps the reason is that there are so many people in Indonesia—about 150 million isn't it?—so they simply don't value human life at all. The soldiers kill anyone without any sense of guilt at all. If they are asked why they killed so-and-so, they say the person was related to a Fretilin member. Their officers then say that's okay. Killing people just doesn't seem to matter. The Indonesians treat the Timorese like a colonised people. They treat them not like people but like slaves.[5]

The most notorious killers among the Indonesian troops in East Timor are the *nanggalas*, a name widely known to East Timorese people and used also in the secret army documents.[6] The *nanggalas* are troops of the para-commando regiment, Kopassandha, who have received special training in killing and violence. Kay Rala Xanana the President of the Revolutionary Council of National Resistance (CRRN), refers to the *nanggalas* as 'knife-killers', the red-beret (Kopassandha) assassins who

> extract fingernails, squeeze testicles with pliers. Under the table at which a red-beret assassin is sitting, the victims have their toes pressed by weights. All this is for interrogation in order to find out about the popular organisation in the concentration camps. And then comes execution by firing squad, and bludgeoning to death in front of the graves they have dug themselves, being drowned in drums of water head first, whereafter the dead person's family is told by the murderous authorities that they have 'gone to Jakarta to study'.[7]

The Kopassandha death-squads that unleashed a reign of terror in the cities and towns of Indonesia in 1983 under the pretext of 'combatting crime' were composed of 'veterans of the bitter war in East Timor'.[8]

In 1981, strong condemnation of the inhuman practices of the occupation troops came unexpectedly from the East Timor Regional Assembly

(DPRD). This body which was set up by the Indonesian military authorities to provide for figure-head Timorese participation in the administration of East Timor, produced a lengthy report in June, for submission to the President. While reaffirming their collective support for 'integrasi', the DPRD itemised numerous malpractices, and complained that it is

> continually, with deep sorrow, receiving verbal as well as written reports or complaints from the people about torture, maltreatment, murders and other unimaginable cases... irresponsible people or groups commit murders without due process of the laws concerning investigation.[9]

The Report specifically mentioned murders committed by troops of Battalion 745 in Los Palos, the murder of 'tens of inhabitants in the district of Viqueque after being tortured by having their sex organs slashed because they did not obey orders serving the interest of certain individuals or groups', the 'murders of tens of people by Kodim after having been tortured with electricity', and more murders by troops of Battalion 745 in Cova Lima.

The ability to commit atrocities and devise new techniques of torture has become a special accomplishment rewarded by quick promotion in the Army. Xanana, Chairman of the CRRN, drew attention to this practice in a special communication sent abroad in July 1983 giving details about massacres and atrocities. Non-commissioned officers at the Koramils, he says, have earned promotion from the rank of sergeant-major to that of commissioned officer, a promotion not normally possible except at a time of retirement. Major Williem da Costa, the Army's chief of intelligence in East Timor, rose from the rank of sub-lieutenant in 1979 to major in 1982, a jump of three ranks in as many years, 'because of the crimes he committed during the period of surrenders in 1978 and 1979 in the region of Same'. Another officer whose name frequently appears in reports of atrocities is Lieutenant-Colonel Iswanto, who rose from sub-lieutenant to lieutenant-colonel, a jump of no fewer than five ranks, in less than four years, from 1979 to 1983.[10]

The CRRN document on massacres and atrocities also makes the important point that the amnesties announced annually by the Indonesian military authorities since 1977, in an attempt to convince resistance fighters to surrender, are worthless. People who surrender, particularly if they are members of the armed resistance, are treated in just the same way as those who are captured. Many of the several hundred persons identified in the document as having been murdered or having disappeared without trace had surrendered under one or other of these 'amnesties'. Among those killed were many dozens of Fretilin members or supporters who were persuaded to defect during the Indonesian intelligence operation code-named 'Skylight' which was launched in 1978. The only person who appears to have survived the 'Skylight' defections is Alarico Fernandes, former Fretilin Minister of Information, now a prisoner on the island of Sumba. A statement by a Timorese who worked for some time with Indonesian Army intelligence, quoted by Amnesty International in a submission to the UN Decolonization Committee in August 1983, also emphasises that surrendering makes little difference to a prisoner's ultimate fate:

> The normal procedure was to interrogate the captives or those who surrendered. People who surrendered and were not soldiers who had engaged in battle with Fretilin would be permitted to go free after the interrogation but only after approval from intelligence headquarters in Dili.
>
> During the interrogations they were normally tortured, especially if the interrogators thought they were Fretilin soldiers or leaders. They would be tortured by hitting them with a blunt instrument, by jabbing lit cigarettes into their faces around the mouth or by giving them electric shocks, sometimes on the genitals.
>
> The senior authorities would then decide who was to be killed after interrogation. Most of the leaders or more educated ones, those who were talented, were killed. Their wives would also be interrogated, tortured and killed.[11]

Imprisonment, Torture, Rape, Murder and Disappearances

The July 1983 CRRN document groups Indonesia's human rights violations in East Timor into four broad categories:
1. Systematic persecution and intimidation: these include threats, surveillance, provocations, restrictions on freedom of movement, regular reporting orders, night patrols of private homes by armed troops, spreading false rumours, using fabricated statements, and so on. These are all daily occurrences everywhere.
2. Torture of people suspected of involvement in clandestine organizations. Even the act of talking to an Indonesian soldier with folded arms (deemed disrespectful and a sign of defiance) or refusal to hand anything over on demand to an Indonesian soldier (taken as a sign that the person harbours pro-Fretilin ideas) is sufficient to make a person suspect. The forms of torture include shooting at people, slapping them in the face, whipping them, bludgeoning them with rifle-butts, karate, cutting off an ear, punching, burning people with lighted cigarettes, stabbing or lacerating the flesh with sharp-pointed needles, daggers or knives, using electric shock and a variety of other forms of physical mutilation.
3. Imprisonment without trial: formerly, the prisons were concentrated in the district towns and were always over-flowing with detainees. More recently, most prisoners have been transferred to Atauro island prison camp and other places of detention, including nearby Indonesian islands, though some are still being concealed in sub-district administrative posts after having been interrogated and savagely tortured by Kodim officers. Sometimes prisoners are 'freed' on condition that they go to the bush and bring back the head of a resistance fighter. The 'released' prisoner is given from 7 to 14 days to carry out the order, failing which he is

sent to Atauro or simply disappears. Other prisoners are 'released' on condition that they return to their former resistance unit to spy for Indonesian intelligence.

4. Killings: these are committed in numerous ways; shot down in cold blood, beaten to death with rifles, shot by firing squad, burnt alive, buried alive, starved to death, or dumped in the sea from a helicopter. Many women are murdered after having been savagely raped by a number of soldiers. People are killed by poisonous injections or injected with water. As the result of persistent condemnations by international organizations, there has recently been a tendency to replace massacres and killings with disappearances, to intimidate the population. Countless people have disappeared from camps located throughout the country.

Detailed information about large numbers of murders, disappearances, and cases of torture and rape is now available. Already in the late 1970s, Amnesty International began to build a dossier of information about individuals who had disappeared, much of it supplied through the network of refugees living abroad who occasionally receive smuggled letters from home. In February 1983, a prisoner on Atauro prison island handed a list of 116 names to the Portuguese television team which visited East Timor to make a film. They were the names of people who had disappeared in the region of Los Palos and had not been heard of since 1980. Six months later, when an Australian parliamentary delegation visited East Timor, another list of names was secretly handed to Senator MacIntosh by prisoners on Atauro. It contained 71 names of people who had disappeared from Comarca, the main prison in Dili.

The document compiled in July 1983 by the CRRN provides the most comprehensive information about murders and atrocities yet available. In addition to providing a list of 73 names of people murdered by Indonesian troops, with details of the units responsible and the method of extermination used, the CRRN document describes the circumstances in which several hundred resistance fighters were murdered or disappeared. This document deals with atrocities in only three regions, the district of Same, the north coastal district and the Eastern Sector. As Xanana explains in his introductory remarks, the conditions of war and the intimidatory presence of Indonesian security forces in the concentration camps make it impossible to document more than a tiny fraction of the atrocities committed since 1975:

> (T)hick volumes would need to be written and endless lists drawn up to show the extent to which the Indonesian forces of occupation totally ignore internationally-accepted principles of human rights. The information included in the document... is confined to cases where it has been possible to carry out an investigation and where the victims can be identified. The vast majority of cases involving masses of ordinary people cannot be recorded, only a small minority of cases involving Fretilin leaders whose fate it has been easier to record.[12]

The cases described, a small selection of which are given below, reveal a pattern of extreme brutality. The public nature of many of the atrocities recorded prove that one of the main objectives is intimidation. There are even acts of cannibalism performed by Army officers quite deliberately in public, apparently with the intention of instilling the idea that people who oppose integration must be treated like animals.

In 1979, *Alberto* who was deputy-secretary of the Fretilin zone of Maubisse gave himself up in Hatubuiliku. He was brutally beaten up by military personnel, then sent to the town of Maubisse. On the way, the soldiers who were escorting him continually burnt his body with lit cigarettes. At the Maubisse Koramil, the officer in charge did nothing to protect him from such violence. On the contrary, the maltreatment continued after which he was driven to the town cemetery and shot with an MU-2. Not yet dead, Alberto shouted: 'You may kill me but other comrades will continue to struggle.' This infuriated the Koramil officer who then ordered *hansip* troops to cut him up. Even while there were still signs of life, Alberto was burnt.

On 24 August, 1982, a guerrilla also named *Alberto* was captured by Indonesian troops in Dare region, Bohaha-Hatubuiliku. He was taken to the Dare concentration camp where the Koramil officer ordered his troops to kill him. When he was dead, the officer ordered his body to be cut up, like the carcases of animals are cut up by butchers. The Koramil officer ate the flesh from Alberto's body for a week, telling people as he did so: 'This is what we do to Fretilin people.' The inhabitants at the Dare concentration camp are witnesses to this barbaric crime.

Francisco Barros, deputy-secretary of the Fretilin Zone, and *Antonio Adakay*, a health officer, were captured in Barike, Cassohan on 3 September, 1978. They were taken to Lakluta and tied to trees with their legs apart and their arms outstretched. They were burnt with lit cigarettes, then with red-hot irons. Then their penises were cut off and they were left to die in the sun.

On a Friday night in September 1979, two companies of Indonesian troops from Queliquai arrived in Laleia, and camped for the night on the Vemasse bank of the river Laleia. The soldiers asked their Timorese carriers to go and find two women. Two women were brought to them: *Melinda da Costa* and *Ana Vicenta da Costa*. They were brutally violated by all the soldiers throughout the night. By morning, the women who were both in very bad shape tried to escape, but they were caught. The raping was resumed till 12 noon that day. All this occurred by the roadside; people going along the road to market in Laleia could see what was going on.

Felicidado dois Santos Gandera, from Liquica (Ossu), had

studied at the Medical Faculty in Lisbon. She was a member of the Commissariat of the support base in the Ponta Leste Sector (Los Palos region) until its destruction by Indonesian troops in November 1978. She was arrested together with her husband *Victor* after the destruction of the base. Her husband was killed and dumped in the river Lura, at Txino. She was then dragged away by about half a dozen soldiers to the village of Lausepo, and violently raped. She was then shot dead with an UZI machine-gun.

Mariano de Sousa, Clementino Jose Branco Ximenes, Joao de Brito Ximenes, all of them platoon commanders; *Gregorio Soares, Antonio Rufino de Costa*, both section commanders; *Felisberto Viegas*, deputy-secretary of the Zone; *Joao Viegas*, in charge of the Fretilin youth organisation (OPJT) in the Zone; *Sebastiao Gusmao*, secretary of the *suco*; *Mario Ximenes*, in charge of a village; the fighters *Domingos Barto Ximenes, Sergio da Costa Gusmao, Felipe da Costa, Filomeno Gusmao, Jose Bento, Jose Von* and others, all surrendered and were taken prisoner in January 1979. After being tortured, they were released. Two weeks later, they were summoned to report and ordered to join *hansip*. After a week's training, they were summoned for 'night training' on 11 February 1979. The whole group was shot dead by soldiers of Battalion 745. Domingos Mau Ximenes whose name was also on the list of people to be shot heard about the planned shooting, so he escaped. He and other inhabitants are witnesses to this crime. (The location of this incident is not mentioned, but it comes under the section headed Laleia.)

Miguel Montiero, a native of Mehara/Tutuala, Los Palos, was commander of the Tutuala Zone. He was captured in 1977 and held, then released. In 1979, he was captured again by Battalion 745 because he had taken part in clandestine activities of the armed resistance. After several days in captivity, he was taken to a Battalion post at the former Catholic mission in Fuiloro where he was tortured, then killed. An Indonesian commander of the Battalion ordered soldiers to cut open his chest and take his heart out. They were told to grill the heart and serve it up for him to eat. The commander then ate the heart with relish, making sure that the people from the surrounding district were gathered there to watch this spectacle. After finishing this barbaric meal, he told the crowd who were standing around that whenever a Fretilin member was captured, the same thing should be done because, he said, human flesh is very tasty, especially when its the flesh of a member of Fretilin.

On 20 July 1983, Amnesty International publicly drew attention to an Indonesian army manual which instructs military personnel on the circumstances in which torture should be used during interrogation. This manual was in the file of captured secret documents which also show that it is common practice for interrogators to use death threats against their victims to extract information. The Amnesty exposure caused great embarrassment to the Indonesian government which responded with denials and even accusations of 'forgery'.

The manual is one of the few documents ever to have surfaced in any country providing conclusive evidence that violence and torture are officially sanctioned as a means for obtaining information. But it does not describe torture techniques to be employed by interrogators, and gives only the merest hint of the kind of instructions under which interrogators and torturers really operate. These written instructions are primarily concerned with warning interrogators not to allow other Timorese to witness acts of torture.[13]

White Sands Becomes A Sea of Blood

Ten kilometres or so along the coast to the east of Dili, the coastline bends inland making a group of shallow water inlets, called White Sands. It was here that Indonesian troops disposed of so many butchered corpses of their victims that White Sands was renamed the Sea of Blood.

'The prisoners are horribly beaten up and tortured. Some of them are even skinned and decapitated. The bodies are then left in the shallow sea, tied to heavy rocks to prevent them from floating away. Of course, there is a great deal of blood which discolours the water.' (*Neobere, in Tapol Bulletin, No 58, July 1983*)

Lake Tacitolo, on the western outskirts of Dili has also been used for executions. Many victims of the early 1979 round-ups were taken and killed here. This campaign of killing came to be known in Dili as Ramelau 41, the number of the truck used to take people from their homes to the paracommandos interrogation centre, then transport them to their place of execution. The people executed at White Sands and at Lake Tacitolo were all alleged Fretilin members, people who had been captured in 1977 or 1978, detained for some time, then released. Whenever the army considered the security situation to be under threat, 'suspects' were rounded up again and killed.

In one such period, so many victims were taken to Queliquai that 'going to Queliquai' came to mean going to your death.

Thousands Exiled to Atauro Island

During the 1981 Operation Security, parts of East Timor were to witness a mass exodus of people living in localities where the Army suspected villagers of giving support and sanctuary to the resistance. Whole families were driven from their homes which were then burnt down; many were forced to make their way to towns such as Ossu and Viqueque, and transported by truck to Laga on the north coast. From there, they were taken by ship to Dili, then in small boats to Atauro island. One Timorese source gave figures showing that 1,300 people were exiled from Los Palos, 1,100 from Baucau and 200 from Manatuto.[14] Later, when the International Red Cross gained access to Atauro, the figures they gave after registering all the prisoners tallied closely with this early information. Atauro has also become the place of detention for many prisoners who were previously detained in district and sub-district towns.

The Indonesians make no secret of the fact that most of the prisoners on Atauro were sent there to isolate the resistance. They are also regarded as hostages, being held in an attempt to force resistance fighters to surrender. When Portuguese television journalist, Rui Araujo interviewed Mario Carrascalao, the puppet Governor of East Timor, about the Atauro prisoners, the journalist was told:

> **Carrascalao:** People may leave Atauro as we gradually learn that their relatives who are in the bush have either died or joined us. Then there will no longer be any reason for us to segregate those people.
>
> **Araujo:** And if the relatives of those people who are held in Atauro today do not surrender, then what will happen?
>
> **Carrascalao:** Then they will continue to stay at Atauro. Or at least they will remain in the new settlement we are going to build...[15]

The prisoners themselves are well aware of their status as hostages. A written message secretly handed to the Portuguese television team by an Atauro prisoner said:

> In the first place, I wish to send my regards and respects... We have come here but our brothers and our families have remained in the bush, and it is only when they die that they will let us out of here.[16]

A small, arid and infertile island, Atauro lies about 15 kilometres north of Dili, and is clearly visible from the capital. It was first mentioned as a detention centre in September 1977, when Radio Maubere reported:

> The situation of the captured population in Dili (is) reported to be deteriorating. Shortage of medical supplies and food. Some people were recently transported to the island of Atauro.[17]

But for the first few years, the people captured by Indonesian troops who were not killed were mostly held at detention centres in the district or sub-district towns or in the numerous holding centres in Dili, including Comarca Prison. It was not until 1980 that Atauro began to be used on a large scale for the detention of political prisoners after mass arrests took place in Dili, following the armed raids in the capital in June. Many of the people arrested were killed, but those who survived were transported to Atauro.

The treatment of the people arrested in Dili in June 1980 was exposed by the Bishop of Dili in a letter to the Indonesian Bishops Conference (MAWI). Mgr da Costa Lopes named four men who were executed despite efforts by himself and other priests to intercede on their behalf. The Bishop told the Indonesian Bishops:

> After 10 June, many people in Dili were mistreated, then stabbed. The bodies of these people have been taken away in two trucks and thrown into one of the ravines not far from the city of Dili, by the side of the Dili-Baucau road. In Dili Prison, cruel torture is often performed. People are beaten repeatedly, and are forced to acknowledge or state something which they have not done.[18]

Amnesty International has described conditions on Atauro in 1980-81 as 'deplorable'.

> At that time detainees were being provided with no more than one can of maize a week... and were supposed to supplement this by growing their own food. In practice the infertility of the island and the composition of the population held there made this extremely difficult and most were forced to forage for leaves, roots and other edible matter. Official statistics put the number of deaths between June 1981 and May 1982 at 176. However, reports received by Amnesty International indicate that at least twice that number of persons were reported to have died of malnutrition, gastroenteritis and malaria in the second half of 1981.[19]

Information from the Bishop, about Atauro as well as about the Lakluta massacres and the precarious food situation caused by the 1981 Operation Security, was widely reported in the Australian press, following which preparations were made for the International Red Cross to commence an emergency relief programme on Atauro.

Since then, Atauro has been used as a show piece by the military authorities, included on the itinerary of every visiting foreign journalist, diplomat or politician. They are even expected to be photographed beside a board which reads, 'Welcome to Atauro' along with prison administrators, although not with prisoners! The International Red Cross has been allowed to supply and administer its own food and medical relief on Atauro in contrast with its operations on mainland East Timor where its delegates are only allowed to make occasional assessments of need and supply relief which is distributed by Indonesian personnel. The prisoners on Atauro are now solely dependent on ICRC food. In September 1983, the ICRC reported that the entire prison population on Atauro 'has been receiving a basic diet consisting mainly of maize, runner beans, butter oil and salt. But nevertheless there were, among the prisoners, 'young children, pregnant women, nursing mothers and persons (who were) suffering from malnutrition'.[20]

As for the Atauro prisoners, they have taken every opportunity to breach security and pass messages, at great risk, to foreign visitors. When the Portuguese journalist, Rui Araujo, visited the island, prisoners took advantage of the chance to speak to someone in a common language, without the intermediary of an interpreter. Araujo describes how a prisoner whispered, 'They are trying to get rid of us.'

> 'They are trying to get rid of us.' repeats another voice, behind me. The atmosphere is dreadful, stifling. I think to myself: all this misery is caused by hunger and despair. People look bewildered. The children never smile.[21]

After the 1983 offensive was launched, some Atauro prisoners were reported to have been transported elsewhere, to places of detention in Bali or other Indonesian islands. But in March 1984, Carrascalao admitted that there were still over 2,000 prisoners on Atauro and that nothing would be done 'to release' them until 'the situation is calm'.[22] Carrascalao also claimed that prisoners being held in Dili were now being put on trial. Twelve had been tried recently, he said, and another 40 were awaiting trial. 'All those held in gaol will be put on trial, nobody will be held without trial'.[23] So, in Carrascalao's view, the prisoners on Atauro are not 'being held without trial', they are just people who will be 'released' when circumstances permit. As several foreign visitors to Atauro have observed, the island is a 'prison without bars', where a much higher degree of security and segregation can be maintained at much less cost than in mainland East Timor. It is not likely to be dispense with soon.

Nothing is yet known about the trials Carrascalao mentioned in his interview of March 1984, but they are the first ever to have been held in more than eight years of 'integrasi'. One thing is certain. Charges will, like all political trials in Indonesia, be based on the draconian provisions of the regime's Anti-Subversion Law. They will be show trials, offering the defendants no chance to defend themselves properly.[24] They are an attempt to give Indonesia's repressive apparatus in East Timor a cloak of legitimacy at a time when the regime needs to swing world opinion decisively to its side in order to remove East Timor from the agenda of the UN General Assembly.

7. The Struggle For Self-Determination Continues

Operation Clean-Sweep, August 1983

In his letter to Xanana on 2 June 1983, Armed Forces Commander-in-Chief, General Benny Murdani warned of Indonesia's determination 'to destroy you if you are not willing to be co-operative'.[1] On 16 August, Murdani repeated the warning, this time in public; he declared that the Armed Forces would show 'no mercy' to the resistance movement and would use all the forces at its disposal. In fact, well before Murdani's public statement, the informal ceasefire that had been introduced as a result of the talks in March between Xanana and Colonel Purwanto, Commander of the Indonesian troops in East Timor, was virtually a dead letter.

Indonesia's 1983 offensive was code named *Operasi Persatuan* or Operation Unity but in military circles it was known more bluntly as *Operasi Sapu Bersih*, Operation Clean-Sweep. Although the Army maintained total secrecy about the operation, it did all it could to create the impression that the renewed fighting was sparked off by an incident near Viqueque when some Indonesian soldiers were killed. Western governments accepted this explanation despite all the evidence to the contrary. The British government used it in its standard replies to MPs who expressed concern about the offensive. The US State Department claimed in its *Country Reports on Human Rights Practices for 1983*[2], issued in February 1984, that 'the security situation in East Timor deteriorated after pro-independence Fretilin elements broke the ceasefire'. In fact, the decision to launch an offensive had already been taken by Murdani in June, and the preparations were well underway by the end of July. By this time the facilities for International Red Cross relief activities had also been withdrawn. For its part, Fretilin had not, as the Indonesians hoped, been lulled into passivity and acquiescence by the ceasefire but on the contrary was well prepared.

Although the ceasefire had been marked by incidents, the military had hoped that the more relaxed atmosphere would beguile Fretilin guerrillas into surrendering. Resistance fighters were allowed to move freely in Indonesian-controlled areas but a number of incidents occurred because Indonesian troops in some places resented the presence of the guerrillas. In some instances, paramilitary Timorese troops were ordered to harass or capture Fretilin people. The most serious incident occurred in late July when Indonesian troops arrested a group of Fretilin fighters in the central sector; despite Fretilin demands for their release, they disappeared and are believed to have been shot. Tensions rose. In early August, Indonesian soldiers gatecrashed a village party near Viqueque. They seized some women, ran off with them and raped them. In response, a group of ex-guerrillas in a nearby concentration camp seized a number of weapons and attacked their Indonesian guards. Fifteen soldiers were killed and another twenty were injured. In retaliation, Indonesian forces attacked a village. In the ensuing massacre, according to church circles, about two hundred villagers were killed. Gilles Bertin, the AFP correspondent in Jakarta, also reported this incident and the revolt that preceded it on 8 August. He described the 86 people in the revolt as deserters from an Indonesian paramilitary unit.[3]

Meanwhile troop reinforcements were being brought into East Timor in readiness for Operation Clean-Sweep. Timorese who left Dili for Lisbon in early September reported that military activity was greatly stepped up on 1 September. A curfew from 6 pm to dawn was imposed in the capital and there was an

> influx of waves of troops into the territory, accompanied by tanks, helicopters and planes... Trucks belonging to Chinese merchants in Dili had all been requisitioned to carry ammunition to the interior and... columns of thirty trucks at a time escorted by tanks were moving regularly out of Dili to all areas of the territory. They carried bullets, grenades and mortar shells.[4]

These movements had been going on since mid-August, one refugee said, and fighting had obviously already occurred on a large scale as 'helicopters had been bringing wounded—Timorese and Indonesians—into Dili Hospital "almost daily".'[5] Another refugee who left Dili at about the same time and identified himself only as Antoninho to protect relatives still in East Timor, reported that 'every day, new troops were being brought in, most of them wearing red berets'.[6]

The use of the red-beret paracommando troops, the elite Kopassandha corps, as the basic fighting force is a new departure in Indonesian military operations. In previous offensives, Kopassandha troops were only used as shock-troops in advance of regular troops; now they were taking the brunt of the fighting. This is indicative of General Murdani's desperation. He has concluded that only rigorously trained and ruthless men have the will and stamina to cope with the guerrillas. However this strategy could prove costly and self-defeating because even paracommandos need to be relieved after a few months of combat. Two Kopassandha battalions were deployed in West Papua in late 1983 with more flown in in February 1984 to cope with a resurgence of guerrilla activity by the Free Papua Movement (OPM). This limits the number of shock troops Murdani has at his disposal, and means that losses in the field could become difficult to replace.

Murdani conceived and planned the 1983 offensive, personally controlled the preparations, and visited the troops in December 1983, to boost morale and review tactics. As he has risen to the position of four-star general without a single conquest on the field of battle, he needs a victory in East Timor to establish his credentials as a commander. He is much younger than many generals subordinate to him. He owes his present position to his intense and undying loyalty to Suharto. As the editors of *Indonesia* point out in the latest of their 'Current Data on the Indonesian Military Elite',

> Suffice it to say that the appointment as Commander-in-Chief of the Armed Forces of an intelligence specialist who has never personally commanded any unit larger than a battalion is extraordinary and defies all the norms of professional modern militaries.[7]

Murdani's strategy at the outset of the 1983 campaign was to isolate the guerrilla units from each other, hoping thereby to destroy them one by one. Falintil is very familar with this strategy which was successfully used in 1977 and 1978, and tried again in 1981. The initial assault took place with some 12,000 troops concentrated in the central sector, along the road network from Baucau in the north to Viqueque in the south. The troops struck east supported by air and sea bombardment, hoping to destroy the Falintil forces in the eastern sector, which the Indonesian intelligence regarded as Fretilin's chief support base and operational area.

Unable to pinpoint guerrilla units because of their mobility,

> enemy forces made massive use of land and sea artillery to shell civilian and economic targets indiscriminately in the regions of Laga, Viqueque, Uatolari, Luro, Venilale and Fuiloro where thousands of people were taking refuge and living under precarious food and health conditions.[8]

A letter from Dili, written several months earlier reported that:

> Indonesian red-beret commandos were leading the operation in the countryside, following a strategy of encircling villages thought to be harbouring Fretilin sympathisers and burning all within the area encircled... this was being done on a zone-to-zone basis and Timorese between the ages of 15 and 50 were conscripted to join the operation. Some who refused had been executed.[9]

A report from Jakarta described the devastating effect this onslaught had on the people living in the concentration camps scattered throughout the eastern sector:

> Church sources said that the military move had completely disrupted already precarious food supplies... Crops have been destroyed and

farmers have been unable to get to their fields or to forage food in the forest, they said. In the central region of Viqueque and the eastern region of Los Palos, food shortages have been aggravated by a flood of refugees, with about 3,000 living around the city of Viqueque.[10]

Fretilin's responded by launching a number of attacks on Indonesian troop emplacements, columns and convoys in other parts of the country, 'forcing the Indonesian army to reconsider its initial strategy and accept the tactical superiority of Falintil in the theatre of operations'.[11] Making use of their mobility, the guerrillas took the offensive where they chose. In mid-November, the Australian press reported that OV10 Broncos operating from Baucau and A4 Skyhawks operating from Madiun in East Java were attacking targets as far apart as Bobonaro, Ainaro, Venilale, Uatolari and Los Palos.[12] The Armed Forces were now being forced to wage operations in many parts of the country. Four days later, the newspaper reported that twenty helicopters and a number of C130 Hercules transport planes were shuttling regularly between Dili and Java to provide logistical support for embattled troops in East Timor.[13] Timorese refugees in Lisbon reported in March 1984 that contacts back home had spotted two F.5E Tiger jets based in East Timor.[14] AMX tanks supplied by the Dutch Goverment were also in use.[15]

The Fretilin communique in January 1984 reported a number of guerrilla attacks in November and December: an assault on an Army unit five kilometres from Barique in the south central sector where three combat vehicles were destroyed and a large quantity of heavy and light war material captured; the ambush of an Indonesian convoy on the road from Alas to Fatuberliu; a series of attacks on military posts in Taitudak, Mane Hat, Aimale Fu and Loi Hunu; more strikes in the southern border regions of Aitalik, Dare (Hatu Builico) and Rotutu; and an attack on an enemy column travelling from Zumalai to Mape when two assault vehicles were destroyed. Several of these attacks inflicted high casualties on the Indonesian army: five dead near Barique, 17 dead in the attacks near the border, and 'a high number of deaths' in the assault between Zumalai and Mape. After several of these engagements, Fretilin forces were compelled to retreat by air bombardment.

The ability to spread the fighting to the central, southern and border regions was undoubtedly the reason for General Murdani's visit to East Timor on Christmas Day. On this occasion, he was accompanied by top Defence Department and Armed Forces generals including Lieutenant-General Himawan Sutanto, Assistant for Operations, Lieutenant-General Gunawan Wibisono, Inspector-General of the Defence Department and Lieutenant-General Bambang Triantoro, Deputy Chief-of Staff of the Army. The team visited several 'isolated areas' such as Ossu (near Viqueque), Natarbora (district of Manatuto), and Alas, near Same in the west.[16] But even as Murdani was visiting the areas where Falintil troops had been exerting pressure in the previous weeks, the guerrillas had already switched their area of operation to the north-west. Starting on the very day of Murdani's visit, they launched a series of attacks in Talo, Fatubessi (coffee-producing regions in the north-west) and in Balibo, close to the border with West Timor, one of the first towns captured by the Indonesians in October 1975. At the same time, guerrillas units were on the offensive in the eastern sector where several Timorese collaborators were captured and killed, one of them a sub-district chief (*camat*). The January communique also reported that 269 members of Ratih, Indonesia's new-style militia force, had deserted and joined the resistance.

On his Christmas Day visit, General Murdani was forced to acknowledge the strength of the resistance movement when he made an appeal to 'everyone in the hills, the forests, the caves and the towns to halt their efforts and surrender to the authorities.'[17] His troops meanwhile were told to emulate the nobility and glory 'of Christ's lowly birth' in the midst of suffering and hardship.

By contrast with the blackout usually imposed on happenings in East Timor, Murdani's visit was widely reported in the Indonesian press. As an editorial in *Merdeka* commented, this had set people wondering what was going on there. Nothing had been heard of the security situation in East Timor since the president of Fretilin, Nicolau Lobato, was killed in December 1978, said the paper, and if armed resistance groups had held out for so long, they must have 'support from inside, that is to say, from the people'. The paper warned that 'if such support is to be handled, it cannot be done only by military means'.[18] This represents the only public expression of criticism of Murdani's offensive which is known to have been voiced privately, both within the Armed Forces and outside. The soldiers who have to fight in East Timor, said one private communication,

> do not agree with the operation not only because the risks of being killed are great but also because they think the chances of winning the war are remote. And they feel reluctant to kill people or wipe out whole villages consisting of unarmed civilians.[19]

When the offensive started, Murdani confidently predicted that it would be completed by Armed Forces Day (5 October); when that passed, by the start of the rainy season in November. On 17 October, AFP in Jakarta quoted the Govenor of East Timor, Mario Carrascalao as predicting that the campaign 'should succeed within a few months', but in another report filed on 19 February 1984, AFP reported official military circles as saying that the offensive 'would certainly' last until April. The foreign editor of a leading Dutch daily wrote in March that, according to reliable information from refugees and church circles in Jakarta,

> heavy fighting is still going on, particularly in the mountains... In the past few months, the fighting has greatly intensified. The Indonesian troops are ill-prepared to cope with the tactics of the guerrillas and are not hardened enough for the fight.[20]

A Canadian daily paper reported a western military analyst's comment after a recent visit to East Timor:

It's a running sore. They have tried the hearts and minds approach and it didn't wash. Now they have gone back to the bigstick policy and it doesn't seem to be working... This thing is going to go on and on until we all get old.[21]

In a report designed to give an account of the offensive after the first six months and to provide an estimate of losses on both sides, all the AFP correspondent could obtain from official military sources in Jakarta was that 'the fighting had been far more bitter' and 'the casualties far higher' than had been expected, and that thirty Indonesian soldiers had been killed, including an officer, during fighting at the end of December and the beginning of January.[22]

No figures of Falintil losses are available. In June 1983 the Fretilin representative abroad reported that there were 6,800 people under arms in the resistance movement. Some East Timor observers regard this figure as exaggerated, but what they fail to take into account is that the resistance forces not only consist of the ten regular Falintil companies, each around 120 people, but the far larger militia (*Miplin*) units. Taken together these comprise the fighting men and women who move freely in the bush, some of them with their families. This figure does not appear to include the *nureps* or popular resistance nuclei members, who are not armed and many of whom operate inside the Indonesian-controlled camps. Even with substantial losses, the number of guerrillas and militia may have increased since August 1983 as a result of the many desertions of Timorese troops from the Indonesian army. In any case, as the former Bishop of Dili has said, the vast majority of East Timorese support Fretilin. 'There are no opposition parties; Fretilin is the only movement that has stood up for the rights of the people. They regard it as their only friend.'[23]

Along with Indonesia's military campaign came new sweeps against the population in the towns, more arrests, executions and other violations. AFP reported that

> six hundred people were brought in for questioning recently in Dili, 125 in Baucau and 34 in Viqueque... Eight schoolchildren aged 14-15 were arrested in Viqueque and 'held for several days in a room so narrow they could not sleep'. Dozens of people including three children were hauled away by unknown abductors in civilian clothing...[24]

Letters smuggled out of East Timor gave a similar account. One said:

> Timor is now in a state of great insecurity, especially in the east. The Javanese have removed prisoners from the Comarca prison and are sending them to other parts.[25]

Another reported:

Everything is more complicated, more confused, more exhausting in the widest sense... The Red Cross are now only allowed to work in Atauro; the programme elsewhere is cancelled. Little can be done to help. The Catholic Church is passing through difficult moments. The military are making life hell for them. Many prisoners are sent to Bali to be interrogated. Some have returned to Timor but nothing is known of the others. Over 2,000 prisoners are still on Atauro. I point out that Bali is the tourist centre of Indonesia...[26]

On 20 February, Amnesty International announced the names of 23 people who had 'disappeared', among them Father Domingos Soares, a priest from Ossu, near Viqueque, who was arrested at the end of January 1984. Others on the list were arrested after the offensive commenced and most were public servants or working with the Indonesian army. A new prison has been constructed at Becora on the outskirts of Dili, according to Amnesty.

The Timor War and the Indonesian Army

Because of the highly secretive nature of the Timor War as far as the Indonesian public is concerned, no documents have appeared from the Indonesian side analysing or relating the development of the war. In a detailed account of the structure, intake and curriculum of the Army's Staff and Command School, Seskoad, an American writer points out that eight years after the war commenced, 'there are virtually no professional articles on the (Army's) activities in East Timor' and that the 'military aspects of the integration of East Timor into Indonesia remain undocumented.[27]

The Army's reluctance to produce such documents is hardly surprising since the war itself has never been officially acknowledged. In June 1983, when Amnesty published extracts from Indonesian military documents indicating the use of torture in East Timor,[28] a Defence Department spokesperson denied that such a manual existed claiming that 'there are no manuals especially written for East Timor, only those for Indonesia as a whole',[29] implying that there are no special military activities in the territory.

A period of service in East Timor helps officers to obtain a much-coveted place in Seskoad; roughly half the officers on the 1982-83 course were East Timor veterans, according to McFetridge. He described the pivotal role of Seskoad:

> Indonesia is dominated by military; the armed forces are dominated by the army; the army is dominated by graduates of Seskoad.[30]

These Seskoad graduates, shaped by battle experience in East Timor, are bound to rise quickly in the military hierarchy. Already many of the generals who occupy key strategic posts have served in East Timor. Murdani, who was there from the start, is now Commander-in-Chief of the Armed Forces, head of the Strategic Intelligence Agency (*Badan*

Inteligen Strategis) which incorporates all wings of military intelligence, and Commander of Kopkamtib, the Operational Command for the Restoration of Security and Order. The most vital and strategic posts in the Army are now held by Timor hands.[31]

> *Major-General Soeweno*, now Commander of Kostrad, the Army Strategic Reserve, the position from which General Suharto seized power in 1965, was Commander of Kodam XVI, the regional command which includes East Timor, from 1976-78 and in 1979 headed the Joint Task Force for *Operasi Seroja* in East Timor.
>
> *Major-General Dading Kalbuadi*, now occupying the strategic post of Assistant for Logistics of the Armed Forces, was in charge of the attacks mounted across the border from West Timor and the capture of Maliana and Balibo in the months preceding the invasion of Dili. He then became Commander of Korem 164, the sub-regional command of East Timor and from there rose to command Kodam XVI, the regional command of Nusa Tenggara which includes East Timor.
>
> *Major-General Try Soetrisno*, now in command of Kodam V, the military command of Jakarta, was Chief-of-Staff of Kodam XVI/Nusa Tenggara from 1978 to 1979. The top command post in the capital is of utmost strategic importance to the preservation of the regime.
>
> *Major-General Eddy Sudradjat*, who now commands the equally strategic Kodam VI/West Java, was Chief-of-Staff of the East Timor Joint Task Force for *Operasi Seroja* in 1978 and 1979. The West Java Siliwangi Division which controls Kodam VI has a long history of operations in support of Army supremacy.
>
> *Brigadier-General Sahala Rajagukguk*, is now Deputy Governor of Seskoad. For two years he was Commander of Kodam XIII, the regional command for North and North-east Sulawesi, important for its control of the northern approaches to Mindanao in the Philippines and a much-prized 'wet' post for the profits to be made from smuggling copra. Up to 1982, Rajagukguk was Commander of Korem 164/East Timor. His name appears as the signatory of several of the documents reproduced in this book.
>
> *Brigadier-General Meliala Sembiring*, is now Commander of Kodam XVII, the military command of the troublesome and rebellious territory of Irian Jaya (West Papua) which is also embroiled in a military campaign against a liberation movement, the Free Papua Movement. He was in charge of Combat Team 18 of the Joint Task Force of *Operasi Seroja* up to 1979.

The Army is using the East Timor war to give troops combat experience and to groom officers for positions of seniority in the Armed

Forces. But the inability of the Armed Forces to defeat the resistance despite the many campaigns, offensives and changes of strategy since 1981 is turning the war into the Achilles' heel of the Suharto regime. Moreover, resentment over Murdani's appointment as Commander-in-Chief could be reinforced by the growing criticism of his 'big-stick' strategy as the chances of crushing Fretilin become more and more remote.

East Timor Self-Determination at the United Nations

Since December 1975, the issue of East Timor self-determination has been repeatedly raised at the United Nations, twice on the Security Council—in December 1975 and April 1976—and at every General Assembly session from 1975 to 1982. Despite vigorous lobbying by Indonesia actively assisted in particular by Australian diplomats, the UN has continued to uphold the right of the people of East Timor to determine their own future. For the past few years, the annual resolutions have incorporated more references to human rights abuse and the need for humanitarian relief in order to retain the support of as many countries as possible, but self-determination has continue to be the central issue upon which the voting has been cast. The fact that resolutions continued to win majority support even during the grim years when the resistance movement was having to overcome the setbacks of 1977 and 1978 and when it was virtually impossible for people outside to obtain information about the strength of the resistance inside, is testimony to the degree of international support for the people of East Timor.

Government attitudes towards East Timor fall into several categories: The first is the self-determination lobby whose leading advocates are the five former Portuguese colonies in Africa. A number of newly independent countries have reinforced this lobby, notably Nicaragua, Zimbabwe and Vanuatu, while several socialist countries have continued to support East Timor. Portugal as a state officially committed in its Constitution to 'promote and safeguard' the self-determination and independence of its former colony has also voted in favour but it was not until 1982 when the UN resolution for the first time included a call for consultations with the 'parties concerned' that Portugal became a sponsor. Most other supporters of self-determination are African countries and a few Latin American states.

The second category—the anti-self-determination lobby—consists of countries which fully accept Indonesia's claim that a valid act of self-determination took place in 1976. They even find no difficulty supporting the view that Indonesian troops invaded the country at the invitation of the East Timorese people. This group includes all the members of ASEAN and Third World countries like India and Saudi Arabia which added their weight in giving 'integrasi' an air of legitimacy by attending the 'People's Assembly' meeting in Dili in May 1976 when the petition requesting 'integrasi' was adopted. Countries expressing Islamic solidarity such as Pakistan, Bangladesh and the Gulf States, as well as other repressive regimes like Chile, Guatemala, Paraguay and Turkey are also part of this lobby which loyally supports Indonesia's efforts to vote down the East Timor resolution each year. Japan, Indonesia's chief trading partner, has always been in this lobby.

A third category includes states which acknowledge that no act of self-determination has taken place but for reasons of global strategy, political expediency and economic interest have no qualms about accepting 'integrasi'. They try to justify their betrayal of principle by arguing that 'integrasi' has become 'an irreversible fact' and therefore it would not be in the interest of the East Timorese people to try to change things. Foremost among these countries which accord no absolute value to the principle of self-determination are the USA which has voted with Indonesia every year since 1976, and Australia which has voted with Indonesia since 1978.

The abstentionist lobby which has always consisted of a large number of UN member states include some who appear to have no interest whatsoever in the matter, often not even bothering to vote at all. Some countries drift in and out of the abstentionist group for no apparent reason. Most West European countries also abstain as a way of registering the fact that they do not formally accept 'integrasi' but neither do they want to antagonize Indonesia by supporting East Timor. Their apparent concern over the issue of self-determination does not prevent them however from supporting Indonesian aggression with military supplies to the Indonesian Armed Forces.

The 1982 resolution, adopted by 50 votes to 46 with 50 abstentions, called on the UN Secretary-General 'to initiate consultations with all parties directly concerned with a view to exploring avenues for achieving a comprehensive settlement of the problem'.[32] It was based on recognition of the 'inalienable right of all peoples to self-determination and independence', and stipulated that 'The Question of East Timor' should again be discussed at the 1983 General Assembly.

In the first half of 1983, the forthcoming UN debate became a topic of intense public debate in Australia after a Labour government took power in March committed to withdrawing recognition of 'integrasi' which had been granted by the Government of Malcolm Fraser in January 1978 and to halting military assistance to Indonesia until its troops were withdrawn from East Timor. Nevertheless, the new Prime Minister, Bob Hawke, and his Foreign Minister, Bill Hayden immediately set about dismantling pro-self-determination policy by proclaiming that 'East Timor must now be put behind us' in order to safeguard bilateral ties with Indonesia. Strong opposition to this sellout was building up inside the Australian Labour Party and the Government was also subjected to considerable criticism in some sections of the press. The controversy was expected to reach a climax at the end of the year when the 1983 General Assembly was due to vote on an East Timor resolution for the eighth year running. The Hawke Government was saved the embarrassment of revealing its stand by a decision in New York to defer discussion on East Timor till 1984.

All this was happening at a time when developments inside East Timor were helping to reinforce the international campaign in favour of self-determination. The negotiations with Fretilin initiated by the Indonesian military command provided the best possible proof not only that resistance continued to exist, but to use Fretilin's own phrase, that it had 'conquered the right to dialogue'. The veritable flood of information from inside East Timor made it abundantly clear that resistance was and is nationwide. The former Bishop of Dili, Mgr Martinhu da Costa Lopes, left East Timor in May 1983, after being forced to resign, and almost immediately set out on a world tour to publicize conditions inside, to speak about the scale of resistance, and to lobby for support at the UN. A man with no tradition of political radicalism, he spoke unreservedly in support of the resistance movement under Fretilin's leadership.

> Fretilin is fighting for an ideal. For freedom, justice and independence. They are the symbol of national resistance and have the support of the people until we get our independence like other small Pacific islands. Xanana says Fretilin is the people and the people is Fretilin. It's true.[33]

With developments moving in favour of another majority for East Timor at the UN, Indonesia engaged in a major diplomatic offensive to ensure that voting at the 38th session of the General Assembly would this time finally remove East Timor from the UN agenda. The Indonesian Foreign Minister, Mochtar Kusumaatmaja, visited the Solomons, Fiji, Western Samoa, New Zealand and Papua New Guinea as well as Norway and Denmark 'to explain Indonesia's position on East Timor'.[34] In some cases, these were countries that already supported Indonesia but effective lobbying during the Nuclear Free and Independent Pacific Conference in Vanuatu in July had helped increase awareness in government circles in several Pacific countries of the reality of the East Timor situation; hence the Mochtar mission. Other missions were sent from Jakarta to eight African countries—Burundi, Kenya, Uganda, Rwandi, Guinea, Ivory Coast, Liberia and Togo, of which five supported the resolution in 1982 and one abstained. Lobbying missions also went to several Latin American countries and to Haiti and Jamaica in the Caribbean.

On 19 August, the UN Secretary-General unexpectedly announced that he would not be submitting a report to the 38th General Assembly on consultations carried out under the terms of the 1982 resolution 'because of the recent developments'. What these developments were remained a mystery. On 23 September, the steering committee of the General Assembly decided without discussion to defer the debate on the question of East Timor until the 39th session in 1984. Norway's Ambassador, Tom Eric Vraalsen who proposed this deferral is reported to have observed:

A confrontation in the Assembly at this time would not have been helpful and might possibly have had a negative effect on the contacts that are going on'.[35]

No one explained what contacts had been going on. Certainly, the party most directly concerned in the conflict, the East Timorese people, had not been involved. In fact, by this time, they were once again plunged into a bitter new conflict with their Indonesian aggressors, a matter which should have had the attention of the UN Security Council, let alone the General Assembly.

For its part, Fretilin had already shown its willingness to accept the terms of the 1982 UN resolution. On 11 April 1983, Xanana sent a message to the UN Secretary-General declaring that:

> Fretilin supports the last resolution and is mobilizing all forces in search for a just solution in which the following basic questions are defined:
> - the right of the Maubere people to self-determination,
> - the total withdrawal of occupation forces.[36]

Fretilin was moreover ready with a comprehensive peace plan which was first set forth in a document made public in May that year, in preparation for the ninth anniversary of the foundation of Fretilin on 20 May:

> We resist with arms but we don't refuse dialogue... dialogue cannot be restricted to only Portugal and Indonesia. Fretilin is the party with the highest interest, the wronged party in the conflict... We are very aware that the problem of East Timor affects the geopolitical zone in which we live, particularly Australia and Indonesia. We agree that Portugal must have an influential role... However, we remember that Australia can have an even more influential role because of its interest 'post-solution'.[37]

Fretilin's Peace Plan was launched internationally in Lisbon on 25 March, 1984:

1. The holding of direct negotiations between Portugal, Indonesia and Fretilin under the auspices of the UN and with the intermediary of the UN Secretary-General, in accordance with the principles enunciated in Resolutions 1541 (XV) and 1514 (XV) of the UN General Assembly, to discuss the following:
    a. The constitution of a truly impartial UN Peace Force or Multinational Force as the indispensable condition to safeguard and ensure:
    - the functioning of a transitional administration,
    - the proper implementation of decisions reached during dialogue about the stationing of the two belligerent forces,

Falintil and the Indonesian Armed Forces.
  b. The holding of a free and democratic consultation of the Maubere people.
  c. Fixing the date for the transfer of sovereignty.
2. Reserving the right for Australia to participate in the negotiations as an observer.
3. Other observers may be chosen on the proposal of the parties mentioned in point (1), in equal numbers, each of which shall be subject to the approval of the other two parties.

Fretilin also re-affirmed its policy of non-alignment, stressing in its statement of 20 May 1983 that East Timor should not become a focus for spreading conflict in South East Asia:

> A policy of peaceful co-existence regulates its relations with all countries... The Maubere people know that they must respect the interests of their neighbours.

However, there is a very real danger that the 1982 UN resolution will be used to exclude Fretilin from the international dialogue on ending the war. Western powers, rejecting Fretilin as the representative of the people of East Timor, seem to believe that a solution can be left to East Timor's former and present colonial rulers. The Australian Foreign Minister, Bill Hayden expressed the hope in his address to the 1983 General Assembly on 4 October that:

> Indonesia and Portugal will be able to use the time between now and the next General Assembly to reach a lasting settlement on this question, a settlement which will take account of the best interests of the people of East Timor.[38]

It is foolish and provocative for the international community to ignore the rights of the East Timor people, and to imagine that these rights can be safeguarded by Portugal. Portugal's policy towards East Timor in 1974 and 1975 consisted of little more than a series of prevarications and betrayals; since then, successive Portugese governments have done nothing to redress this nor indeed to implement the terms of their own Constitution. The UN still recognizes Portugal as the administering colonial power with responsibility to complete the decolonization process it so abruptly abandoned in August 1975. Fretilin also recognizes Portugal's role, as its Peace Plan indicates.

Portugal must direct its efforts to bringing about the necessary conditions for this decolonization process to be completed, the first and foremost of which is the withdrawal of Indonesian troops. Nor can Portugal deal with this issue without acknowledging the strength of resistance inside East Timor and insisting that the resistance movement participates as an equal partner in international negotiations. Secret negotiations leading to a deal between Indonesia and Portugal can only mean betraying yet again the people of East Timor. When in September 1983, the Indonesian Government publicly claimed that Portugal had agreed to enter into direct negotiations, the Portuguese Foreign Minister, Jaime Gama, quickly denied it:

> There is no justification for the solution of the East Timor question to be a matter for talks between Portugal and Indonesia. The solution rests with the UN and the mandate of its Secretary-General. This does not mean that Portugal will not keep its channels open through the intermediary of third parties such as the ICRC, Holland or other channels, to the other party in this conflict. But the Portuguese position has always been one of not regarding Timor as being a conflict between Portugal and Indonesia.[39]

Yet at the end of March 1984, the Portuguese government announced that it was seeking direct negotiations with Indonesia with a view to 'safeguarding the identity of the Timorese people and protecting Portuguese cultural and diplomatic interests in the region'. Nor would Portugal make self-determination or any other issue a condition for negotiating with Indonesia', said Foreign Minister Jaime Gama.[40] Jill Jolliffe reported that the Portuguese government's policy proceeds from the belief that the best way to 'alleviate the suffering of the Timorese (is) by recognising Indonesian sovereignty and by opening a consulate in Dili, one of the main aims of which would be to promote Portuguese culture'. She quoted Foreign Minister Gama as saying:

> Timor is an affair between Portugal, Indonesia and the international community represented by the UN member states although Portugal is concerned to safeguard the rights of the Timorese.[41]

He also claimed there was 'no mechanism to consult the Timorese people'.

Fretilin's response was unequivocal. Abilio Araujo described this position as 'completely immoral... A betrayal of everything the politicians have been saying in past years. The Timorese people will not accept any solution in which they do not take part.'[42]

Indonesia's inability to crush the resistance movement during the 1983 offensive has made it far more difficult to remove the question from the UN agenda. In such circumstances, it is very much in Indonesia's interests to obtain Portugal's acquiescence to 'integrasi' by whatever face-saving formula that can be concocted. Western powers would only be too glad to accept a deal of this nature. Indonesia also hopes to use its new assertive attitude towards international affairs as a lever to win support over East Timor from the countries of Western Europe who have so far abstained. The issue over which Indonesia has been particularly assertive is Indochina where it is trying to establish a special relationship with Vietnam. This is an issue over which diplomatic horse-trading could also affect the votes of eastern bloc countries such as Vietnam, most of whom voted against Indonesia. In late 1983, Indonesia was again busy lobbying Pacific countries to shore up its position in the UN. The governments of Western Samoa, Kiribati, Niué and the Solomons have been offered attractive economic benefits in exchange for a vote against East Timor.

Fretilin and the international solidarity movement have always attached great importance to keeping East Timor's self-determination before the UN. The annual debates at the General Assembly's Fourth Committee on decolonization afford an opportunity for many non-government organizations and individuals to expose Indonesia's wanton disregard for the wishes of the East Timorese people and to condemn the persistent violation of human rights. This also keeps open the possibility for international initiatives in favour of a genuine act of self-determination. At the same time it would be foolish to ignore that power politics generally prevail at the UN. The history of UN intervention on decolonization provides many instances where the very principles enshrined in the UN Charter have been breached.[43]

If despite everything the vote at the UN goes against self-determination, the international solidarity movement will have to take the issue to other forums. A defeat for East Timor at the UN would be a severe blow to that body itself. For East Timor, it would be yet another act of betrayal in a long history of betrayals committed ever since the Portuguese governor fled in August 1975 and the western powers consciously decided in mid-1975 not to oppose Indonesian aggression. It would not be a fatal blow to the resistance movement in East Timor which owes its inspiration and encouragement not to 'incitement from outside the country' as some people claim,[44] but to the refusal of the people of East Timor to acquiesce to subjugation by Indonesia. Resistance in East Timor has always been waged against tremendous odds, against a very powerful military regime that enjoys the support of the West, a regime that the eastern bloc would also prefer not to upset.

The Fight for Self-Determination

The resistance is well aware that it has little chance of driving out the invaders by military means alone nor can the aggressors ever hope to assert their will over the people of East Timor. The Indonesian Armed Forces have met more than their match in the combined armed and unarmed resistance of the Maubere people. It is a conflict which contributes towards weakening the stranglehold of the military throughout the archipelago and bringing its downfall closer.

For the third time in their history, the people of East Timor are fighting for independence from a foreign aggressor. They fought against the Portuguese colonialists, they offered powerful resistance against the Japanese at tremendous human cost during the Second World War. Their rejection of the latest attempt to subjugate them and the bitter war they have been compelled to wage is in the tradition of these past anti-colonial struggles. East Timor's right to self-determination and independence is non-negotiable.

Indonesia's invasion and occupation contravenes the UN Charter and international law. Self-determination is recognised as a fundamental international norm in the Charter (Articles 1, 55 and 56) and international law has recognised that the principle of self-determination applies to all non-self-governing territories, which describes East Timor's status under both the Portuguese and the Indonesians.[45] The UN Declaration on the Granting of Independence to Colonial Countries and Peoples (General Assembly Resolution 1514 (XV) 14 December 1980) states:

> The subjection of peoples to alien subjugation, domination, exploitation constitutes a denial of fundamental human rights, is contrary to the Charter of the United Nations and is an impediment to the promotion of world peace and co-operation. All peoples have the right to self-determination; by virtue of that right, they freely determine their political status and freely pursue their ecomomic, social and cultural development.

In·addition, upholding East Timor's right to self-determination means safeguarding the sovereignty and integrity of other states which share common borders with the Republic of Indonesia. Indonesia seeks to justify 'integrasi' by claiming that East Timor is an integral part of the Indonesian archipelago; that there are historical, ethnic and cultural ties between Indonesia and East Timor; and that in any case, East Timor is too small to be economically viable or survive as an independent state. These claims could, with equal cynicism, be used by Indonesia to justify the annexation of other neighbouring states, Papua New Guinea, Brunei or the State of Eastern Malaysia. Many people, particularly in Papua New Guinea are well aware of this threat. The PNG government has succombed to intimidation from Jakarta on numerous occasions over issues concerning the liberation movement in West Papua and Indonesian infringements of the border. It has even supported Indonesia on East Timor at the UN although prior to 1978 it abstained.

International support for East Timor has been especially strong in Australia, Portugal, the Netherlands, the USA and the UK. In Australia, a network of solidarity campaigns and support groups, some of which are closely linked to the Catholic church and to relief and development agencies, have kept up a flow of information about East Timor to the rest of the world which was instrumental in keeping the East Timor issue alive even during the most difficult period. One of the greatest achievements of this movement was the adoption in July 1982 of a pro-self-determination resolution by the Australian Labour Party and the decision of the Australian Senate later that year to hold an inquiry on East Timor. Despite the betrayals that followed the Labour election victory in March 1983, intensive campaigning has persisted and East Timor is now a major foreign policy issue in Australia.

Solidarity groups in Portugal have worked hard to exert pressure on a series of reluctant Portuguese governments in a situation where all political parties tend to treat East Timor not as a matter of principle but as a means for fighting their own domestic political battles. Nevertheless, Parliament found it necessary to set up a special commission on East Timor. Solidarity groups in Portugal have convened several important international meetings on East Timor and hosted the important People's Tribunal on East Timor in June 1981 which heard testimony from a wide range of witnesses and experts.

In the Netherlands, East Timor has been a constant focus for solidarity groups which have worked since the late 1960s to expose the true nature of the Indonesian military regime. One of the climaxes was the campaign to oppose the export to Indonesia of three naval corvettes. There has been consistent pressure in Parliament on successive Dutch governments over their support for Indonesia, and a large number of Dutch Parliamentarians from almost all political parties signed a joint appeal by parliamentarians from eight European Community countries calling on the governments of the Community:

> to work collectively for the self-determination of the people of East Timor, in accordance with the United Nations Covenant on Civil and Political Rights and the Resolution of the UN General Assembly adopted in November 1982.

This appeal, published on 29 July 1983 was signed by 170 parliamentarians from Holland, the UK, Belgium, Denmark, France, Germany, Ireland and Italy.

In the USA, there have been no fewer than six congressional hearings since 1977 on various aspects of the East Timor question. On several occasions, notably in October 1982 when President Suharto was on a visit to Washington and in December 1983, a large number of members of Congress signed letters to the Administration stressing the need for action on East Timor's behalf against Indonesia. The December 1983 letter had the support of 105 members. It called on the Reagan Administration to 'add the suffering of the people of East Timor to America's foreign policy agenda', and expressed concern over the offensive launched in August and the exclusion of the International Red Cross since before the offensive was launched.

The Parliamentary Human Rights Group in London took the initiative in launching the appeal to governments of the European Community to which reference has already been made. There is a sizable lobby of parliamentarians both in the House of Commons and the House of Lords ready to take up issues related to East Timor. In December 1983, no fewer than 128 Members of Parliament from all parties signed an Early Day Motion which reads as follows:

> That this House, concerned at the new military offensive launched in August by Indonesia in East Timor which has been under illegal

Indonesian occupation since 1975, and distressed that the International Red Cross had to suspend its much-needed food relief operations in East Timor a month before the offensive began because the Indonesian authorities had withdrawn the necessary facilities, calls upon Her Majesty's Government to halt the sale of arms and military equipment to Indonesia and to take other urgent steps to press Indonesia to halt military operations.

The central issue of international campaigning over East Timor has at all times been self-determination. The people of East Timor exercised their right to self-determination by their unilateral declaration of independence on 28 November 1975 when Fretilin proclaimed the establishment of the Democratic Republic of East Timor. That historic event has not been diminished by anything that has subsequently happened. When Fretilin made its call in the Peace Plan launched in March 1984 for a referendum on the future of East Timor, it was in no way reversing the events in Dili eight years before. However great the support for independence was in those early days, it has become immeasurably greater and more deep-rooted after years of brutality and suffering at the hands of the Indonesian occupation forces. The struggle for East Timor's self-determination will not stop, inside and outside the country, until Indonesia has been forced to withdraw its troops and the people are able to give free expression to their desire for independence.

The Fretilin leader, Xanana addressing a gathering of guerrillas in the Central sector, May 1983.

A militia unit on the move.

Fighting and studying. An illiteracy class in one of the many mobile bases of the resistance movement.

Health care. A Red Cross unit of the Fretilin forces.

Agriculture. Tending a garden in a jungle clearance. Guerrillas grow their own food wherever they are.

Communication. Several Falintil commanders listening to reports from other regions.
On the left: Mau Hunu, Deputy Chief-of-Staff of of Falintil

Solidarity actions abroad
(Top) A picket-line in front of the UN Headquarters in New York.
(Bottom) Demonstrating outside the Dutch Parliament against weapons export to Indonesia.

Notes

Chapter 1

1. J. Dunn, *Timor, a People Betrayed*, p.24.
2. *Ibid.*, p.28.
3. *Ibid.*, pp.29-30.
4. M. Leifer, *Indonesia's Foreign Policy*, p.155.
5. J. Dunn, *op. cit.*, p.166.
6. *Ibid.*, p.113.
7. G.J. Munster and J.R. Walsh, *Documents on Australian Defence and Foreign Policy, 1968-75*, Hongkong, 1980.
8. *Ibid.*, p.199.
9. *Ibid.*, pp.199-200.
10. *Los Angeles Times*, 7 December 1975.
11. *The Australian*, 22 January 1976.
12. *The Guardian*, 10 February 1984.
13. Munster and Walsh, *op. cit.*, pp.192-3.
14. For a more detailed account of these events, see chapter 5.
15. R. Clark, 'The "Decolonization" of East Timor and the United Nations Norms of Self-Determination and Aggression', in *The Yale Journal of World Public Order*, volume 7:2, 1980.
16. From 'The Timor Papers', see p.16
17. *The Age*, 10 February 1977.

Chapter 2

1. 'The Timor Papers', in the *National Times*, 30May/5 June 1982.
2. *The Age*, 8 December 1975.
3. H. McDonald, *Suharto's Indonesia*, p.207.
4. 'The Timor Papers', in the *National Times*, 30 May/5 June 1982.
5. *Ibid.*
6. *TAPOL Bulletin*, No.60, November 1983.
7. J. Dunn, *op. cit.*, p.220.
8. *Melbourne Herald*, 5 September 1975.
9. 'The Timor Papers', in the *National Times*, 30 May/5 June 1982.
10. 'The Timor Papers', in the *National Times*, 6-12 June 1982.
11. J. Jolliffe, *East Timor: Nationalism and Colonialism*, p.207.
12. 'The Timor Papers', in the *National Times*, 6-12 June 1982,
13. *Boston Globe*, 8 December 1975.
14. J. Dunn, 'East Timor, Notes on the Humanitarian Situation', Parliamentary Legislative Research Service, Canberra, 26 September 1979, pp.2-3.
15. *Timor Information Service*, No.9/10, 6 May 1976.
16. *Far Eastern Economic Review*, 21 April 1983.
17. 'The Timor Papers', in the *National Times*, 6-12 June 1982.
18. H. McDonald, *op. cit.*, p.212.

19. *The Australian*, 4 May, 1976.
20. *Timor Information Service*, No.9/10, 1976.
21. Xanana's message to the UN General Assembly, 14 October 1982, reproduced in *East Timor News*, No.78-80, Spring 1983.
22. J. Jolliffe, *op. cit.*, p.300-301.
23. US Congressional Hearings, 10 June 1980.
24. J. Dunn, *op. cit.*, p.325.
25. *The Age*, 8 October 1977.
26. Xanana's message to the UN General Assembly, 14 October 1982.
27. *East Timor News*, No.29, 23 March 1978.
28. *East Timor Information Bulletin*, British Campaign for an Independent East Timor, May 1978.
29. *The Age*, 29 April 1977.
30. *Kompas*, Jakarta, 17 July 1978.
31. *Far Eastern Economic Review*, 29 September 1978.
32. *Ibid.*
33. Quoted by John Waddingham in *Official Hansard Report* of the Australian Senate Inquiry on East Timor, May-October 1982, pp.726-27. The *Report* is hereinafter referred to as *Senate Inquiry Verbatim Records*.
34. *Hadomi*, Victoria, August 1982. This special issue of *Hadomi* reproduced anonymously extracts from the evidence of Timorese who testified to the Australian Senate Inquiry. These testimonies were not included in the Senate Inquiry Verbatim Records because they had been submitted *in camera*.
35. Xanana's message to the UN General Assembly, 14 October 1982.
36. *Kompas*, 23 April 1979.
37. Xanana's message to the UN General Assembly, 14 October 1982.
38. Quoted in Dunn, *op. cit.*, p.318.
39. Xanana's message to the UN General Assembly, 14 October 1982.
40. *Dossier on East Timor*, Australian Council for Overseas Aid (ACFOA), 1982.
41. Xanana's message to the UN General Assembly, 14 October 1982.
42. *Dossier on East Timor*, ACFOA, 1982.
43. *Ibid.*
44. *UCAN News Agency*, Hongkong, quoted in *East Timor News*, No.71-73, Summer 1981-82.
45. *Dossier on East Timor*, ACFOA, 1982.
46. Xanana's message to the UN General Assembly, 14 October 1982.
47. *Sinar Harapan*, Jakarta, 25 January 1983.
48. Xanana's message to the UN General Assembly, 14 October 1982.
49. *Tempo*, Jakarta, 22 January 1983.
50. See pp.193-204
51. *Fretilin Conquers the Right to Dialogue*, published by Fretilin in Lisbon, June 1983.
52. *Radio Netherlands*, 2 July 1983.
53. *Tempo*, 22 January 1983.
54. Interview in Lisbon, 2 December 1983.
55. *ICRC Situation Report No.10*, September 1983.
56. *The Age*, 17 August 1983.

Chapter 3

1. J. Jolliffe, *op. cit.*, p.75.
2. Helen Hill, *Fretilin: The Origins, Ideologies and Strategies of a Nationalist Movement in East Timor*, Melbourne, 1978, p.98 (Mimeographed).
3. *New Perspectives*, 7 (4), 1977, p.27.
4. *Southeast Asia Chronicle*, No.74, August 1980.
5. Grant Evans, quoted in Hill, *op. cit.*, p.99.
6. *Tribune*, Sydney, 26 November 1974.
7. Hill, *op. cit.*, pp.186-7.
8. *Ibid.*, p.192.

9. *Ibid.*, p.193.
10. 'Report of Visit to East Timor', ACFOA, quoted in *ibid.*, p.193.
11. *East Timor News*, No.47, December 1978.
12. *TAPOL Bulletin*, No.60, November 1983.
13. Interview with *Vox do Povo*, reproduced in *East Timor News*, No.60, November 1979.
14. Hill, *op. cit.*, p.86.
15. Elizabeth Traube, 'Cultural Notes on Timor', quoted in *ibid.*, p.87.
16. Quoted in *Southeast Asia Chronicle*, No.74, August 1980.
17. *Far Eastern Economic Review*, 3 November 1983.
18. Quoted in Hill, *op. cit.*, p.157.
19. Interview with one of the authors, 29 November 1983.
20. Xanana's message to the UN General Assembly, 14 October 1982.

Chapter 4

1. *US Congressional Hearings*, 6 June 1977, p.17.
2. *Ibid.*, pp.21-22.
3. Joachim K. Metzner, *Man and Environment in East Timor*, Australian National University, 1977, p.17.
4. *Ibid.*, p.130.
5. Neobere, in *TAPOL Bulletin*, No.58, July 1983.
6. Arnold Kohen and John Taylor, *An Act of Genocide: Indonesia's Invasion of East Timor*, TAPOL, 1979, p.85.
7. *Far Eastern Economic Review*, 29 September 1978.
8. *Melbourne Herald*, 12 September 1978.
9. 'East Timor: Some Experiences and Reflections', 25 April 1979. (Mimeographed).
10. *Sydney Morning Herald*, 1 November 1978.
11. 'Aid and East Timor', Australian Council for Overseas Aid, July 1979.
12. See *US Congressional Hearings*, 4 December 1979, p.28.
13. *Ibid.*, p.24.
14. US Department of State, *Situation Report No.1*.
15. Henry Kamm, *New York Times*, 28 January 1980.
16. Testimony of Benedict R. O'G. Anderson to the US Congressional Hearing on 6 February 1980, pp.20-21. (Mimeographed)
17. *TAPOL Bulletin*, No.59, September 1983.
18. Donald Weatherbee, 'The Situation in East Timor', Institute of International Studies, University of South Carolina, 1980, p.21.
19. *The Philadelphia Inquirer*, 28 May 1982.
20. *Ibid.*
21. *Ibid.*
22. *Far Eastern Economic Review*, 6 August 1982.
23. *Ibid.*
24. See p.201.
25. See p.216.
26. See Document 4, p.211.
27. *Australian Parliamentary Delegation Report*, p.163.
28. *Ibid.*, p.77.
29. See p.177.
30. *Tempo*, 22 January 1983.
31. *Australian Parliamentary Delegation Report*, p.45.
32. *Ibid.*, p.45.
33. *West Australian*, 4 May 1983.
34. *The Philadelphia Inquirer*, 28 May 1982.
35. *Australian Parliamentary Delegation Report*, p.47.
36. *East Timor After Integration*, Jakarta, 1983, p.116. This is an official publication of the Indonesian Government and is referred to as their 'White Book'.
37. D.J. Richardson, 'Report on Visit to East Timor', point 22. (Mimeographed).
38. *Situation Report No.9*, May 1983.

Chapter 5

1. *UN Document 3/12011*, 29 February 1976.
2. *UN Document S/12106*, 22 June 1977.
3. Dunn, *op. cit.*, p.298.
4. *Tempo*, 12 June 1976.
5. *Indonesian Times*, 26 June 1976.
6. *Australian Parliamentary Delegation Report*, 1983, p.66.
7. Dunn, *op. cit.*, p.71.
8. *Tempo*, 22 January 1983.
9. *Timor? Timor?* Grande Reportagem, Portuguese Television (RTP), 1983.
10. *Tempo*, 22 January 1983.
11. *Ibid.*
12. *Senate Inquiry Verbatim Records*, p.1709.
13. *Far Eastern Economic Review*, 6 August 1982.
14. Donald Weatherbee, 'The Indonesianization of East Timor', Paper to the 20th Annual Meeting of the Southeast Conference of Asian Studies, 21 January 1981.
15. *Far Eastern Economic Review*, 6 August 1982.
16. Barry Wain in *Asian Wall Street Journal*, 16 June 1982.
17. Michael Richardson in *The Age*, 15 March 1977.
18. *Ibid.*
19. Mario Carrascalao in an interview with Leigh Mackay, *West Australian*, 20 March 1984.
20. *East Timor After Integration*, p.117.
21. Barry Wain, *op. cit.*
22. *Ibid.*
23. *Ibid.*
24. *Dossier on East Timor*, ACFOA, March 1982.
25. *West Australian*, 20 March 1984.
26. *Tempo*, 23 August 1980.
27. *Asian Wall Street Journal*, 16 June 1982.
28. *East Timor After Integration*, p.117.
29. *Sinar Harapan*, 29 March 1984.
30. *Tempo*, 8 October 1983.
31. *Sinar Harapan*, 26 January 1983.
32. Metzner, *op. cit.*, p.136.
33. Mario Carrascalao in *Sinar Harapan*, 17 October 1983.
34. *TAPOL Bulletin*, No.59, September 1983.
35. *East Timor After Integration*, p.116.
36. *Senate Inquiry Verbatim Records*, p.1168.
37. Donald Weatherbee, in *West Australian*, 2 February 1982.
38. *Senate Inquiry Verbatim Records*, p.1431-2.
39. *East Timor After Integration*, p.133.
40. *Senate Inquiry Verbatim Records*, p.1707.
41. *Ibid.*, p.1714.
42. *Ibid.*, p.1702.
43. *Ibid.*, p.1717.
44. *Ibid.*, p.1715.
45. *Ibid.*, p.1715.
46. *Ibid.*, pp.1702-3.
47. *Ibid.*, p.1706.
48. *Australian Parliamentary Delegation Report*, p.46.
49. *TAPOL Bulletin*, No.58, July 1983.
50. *East Timor After Integration*, p.92.
51. *Asian Wall Street Journal*, 14 June 1982.
52. *TAPOL Bulletin*, No.58, July 1983.
53. Report of Mr Richardson's Visit to East Timor (mimeographed), point 31.
54. *Australian Parliamentary Delegation Report*, p.190.
55. *Asian Wall Street Journal*, 14 June 1982.
56. *TAPOL Bulletin*, No.58, July 1983.

57. *Ibid.*, No.59, September 1983.
58. *Carta Pastoral*, 25 January 1975.
59. Jill Jolliffe, AAP Dispatch, Dili, 6 November 1975.
60. *TAPOL Bulletin*, No.59, September 1983.
61. Pat Walsh, *National Outlook*, January 1982.
62. Pat Walsh, 'Notes on the East Timor issue, based on an International Visit', 1980. Action for World Development.
63. *East Timor Report*. ACFOA, No.5, November 1983.
64. See p.194.
65. *The Age*, 6 March 1982.
66. Pat Walsh, *op. cit.*, November 1982.
67. *Ibid.*, pp.11-12.
68. *TAPOL Bulletin*, No.59, September 1983.
69. *The Age*, 27 December 1983.
70. Letter from the Bishops' Conference of Indonesia (MAWI) to the Diocese of Dili, 17 November 1983.
71. *Ibid.*
72. Catholic parishes in East Timor now care for some 13,000 orphans.
73. From an interview by the authors with a Timorese priest, Lisbon, 25 March 1984.
74. Communication from Jakarta, early March 1984.
75. *New York Times*, 28 January 1980.
76. *Timor? Timor?* Grande Reportagem, Portuguese Television (RTP), 1983.
77. *Ibid.*
78. *Senate Inquiry Verbatim Records*, p.1717.
79. *The Australian*, 8 October 1977.

Chapter 6

1. Eye-witness reports from East Timor, 1981, in *Dossier on East Timor*, ACFOA, 1982.
2. *Ibid.*
3. See Dunn, 'Report on talks with Timorese Refugees in Portugal', 11 February 1977, (Mimeographed).
4. Dunn, *Timor, A People Betrayed*, p.283.
5. *TAPOL Bulletin*, No.59, September 1983.
6. See p.239.
7. Xanana's message to the UN General Assembly, 14 October 1983.
8. *Far Eastern Economic Review*, 29 September 1983.
9. Report of the East Timor Regional Assembly, 3 June 1981. The document is translated in full in *TAPOL Bulletin*, No.47, September 1981.
10. Report of the Revolutionary Council for National Resistance, sent out from East Timor in July 1983.
11. Amnesty International Submission to the UN Decolonization Committee. *UN Document* ASA 21/09/83, August 1983.
12. Report from the *Revolutionary Council for National Resistance*, July 1983.
13. See Document 8, especially p.236-7.
14. *Dossier on East Timor*, ACFOA, 1982.
15. *Timor? Timor?* Grande Reportagem, RTP, 1983
16. *Ibid.*
17. *Timor Information Service*, No.22, December 1977.
18. Letter, 12 July 1980, to Bishop Leo Sukoto, Secretary of MAWI. Reproduced in *Dossier on East Timor*, ACFOA, 1982.
19. Amnesty International Submission to the UN Decolonization Commission, August 1983.
20. *ICRC Situation Report No. 10*, September 1983.
21. *ABC Monthly*, Lisbon, April/May 1983.
22. Interview in *West Australian*, 20 March 1984.
23. *Ibid.*
24. See J. Southwood and P. Flanagan, *Indonesia: Law, Propaganda and Terror*, by Southwood and Flanagan, 1983, especially chapter 5.

Chapter 7

1. *The Age*, 17 August 1983.
2. *Country Reports On Human Rights Practices*, p.775.
3. *The Age*, 27 December 1983.
4. *Timor Newsletter*, volume II, No.3, October 1983.
5. *Ibid.*
6. Interview with one of the authors, Lisbon, November 1983.
7. *Indonesia*, No.36, October 1983, p.111.
8. *Fretilin Communique*, 18 January 1984.
9. *Timor Newsletter*, October 1983.
10. *The Age*, 27 December 1983.
11. *Fretilin Communique*, 18 January 1984.
12. *Canberra Times*, 15 November 1983.
13. *Canberra Times*, 19 November 1983.
14. Authors' conversations with Timorese refugees, Lisbon, March 1984.
15. *The Australian*, 6 January 1984.
16. *Sinar Harapan*, 27 December 1983.
17. *Ibid.*
18. *Merdeka*, 29 December 1983.
19. Communication from Jakarta, early March 1984.
20. *NRC Handelsblad*, 3 March 1984.
21. *Toronto Globe and Mail*, 10 February 1984.
22. AFP, 19 February 1984.
23. *Trouw*, 23 February 1984.
24. *The Age*, 27 December 1983.
25. Letter, 12 October 1983, quoted by Jill Jolliffe in *The Age*, 28 January 1984.
26. Letter, 13 January 1984, quoted by Jill Jolliffe in *The Age*, 28 January 1984.
27. Charles McFetridge, in *Indonesia*, No.36, October 1983, p.97.
28. These were taken from the documents reproduced in Part II.
29. *Far Eastern Economic Review*, 4 August 1983.
30. *Indonesia*, No.36, October 1983, p.87.
31. The following draws heavily on information in 'Current Data on the Indonesian Military Elite' in *Indonesia*, No.36, October 1983, pp.99-134.
32. UN Document A/C.4/37/L.8, 4 November 1982.
33. *East Timor Report*, ACFOA, No.5, November 1983.
34. *Jakarta Post*, 22 September 1983.
35. *Far Eastern Economic Review*, 6 October 1983.
36. *Timor Newsletter*, volume II, No.3, October 1983.
37. *Ibid*
38. *East Timor Report*, ACFOA, No.5, November 1983.
39. From the verbatim report of an interview of Jaime Gama in London, 18 September 1983, by Gilberto Ferraz.
40. *The Washington Post*, 31 March 1984.
41. *Canberra Times*, 1 April 1984.
42. *Ibid.*
43. See *West Papua: The Obliteration of a People*, published by TAPOL, 1983. Also Brian May, 'The United Nations Fiasco' in *The Indonesian Tragedy*.
44. For example, the Australian parlimentarian, Bill Morrison, said: 'I feel very sorry for the Fretilin supporters. Thanks to so-called support from other countries, they still cling to the belief that the "resurrection" is in sight. People overseas, especially in Lisbon, give them false hopes and that in principle is very unjust.' Interview in *Volkskrant*, 10 October 1983.
45. For a comprehensive account of the international legal aspects of the East Timor case, see Roger Clark, 'The "Decolonization" of East Timor and the United Nations Norms on Self-Determination and Aggression', in *The Yale Journal of World Public Order*, volume 7:2, 1980.

PART II
THE INDONESIAN ARMY'S SECRET INSTRUCTIONS FOR COUNTER-INSURGENCY OPERATIONS IN EAST TIMOR

Introduction

Indonesia's Counter-Insurgency Operations in East Timor

On 31 December 1982, Fretilin forces captured a set of nine documents giving instructions to Indonesian troops on how to deal with the resistance in East Timor. Some of the documents were issued by Colonel Rajagukguk, the commander of Indonesian troops in East Timor, and some by Major Williem da Costa, the officer in charge of intelligence operations. The folder was the property of the Baucau/1628-06 District Military Command (Kodim 1628/06 Bakau). All these instructions were issued in the second half of 1982.

The documents provide an invaluable source of information on the strategy and tactics of the Indonesian Armed Forces at the time and prove conclusively that in stark contrast to their claims that Fretilin was a 'spent force', the forces of occupation were very conscious that they confronted a powerful and well-organized resistance. Apart from a few sections that have been excluded because of their very technical nature or because of difficulties in deciphering the contents, the documents are reproduced in full. Some of the diagrams have been omitted for reasons of space. The following introductory remarks are provided to help the reader understand the military structures of the two sides in the war and to follow some of the highlights in Indonesia's counter-insurgency strategy at the time the documents were issued. Documents 1 to 8 are marked 'Secret' at the top and bottom of each page. Document 9 is marked 'Restricted' at the top and bottom of each page.

The Indonesian Military Structure

The Indonesian Army is divided into seventeen Regional Military Commands, (*Komando Daerah Militer*) known as Kodams. Many Kodams bear the names of figures in Indonesian history or names evoking some mythical virtue. Some Kodams are equivalent to a province, some cover more than one province. Kodam XVI/Udayana incorporates the eastern islands of Indonesia known as Nusa Tenggara as well as the 'province' of East Timor. Its headquarters is in Den Pasar, Bali. The Army's structure in East Timor is as follows:

Kodam XVI/Udayana
↓
KOREM (Komando Resort Militer), 164/Wira Dharma
the Sub-Regional Military Command
which covers the whole of East Timor.
↓
Thirteen Kodims (Komando Distrik Militer),
the District Military Commands each of which cover
an area equivalent to the 'kabupaten' or district
in the local government administration.
↓
Koramils (Komando Rayon Militer),
the Sub-District Military Commands equivalent to the
'kecamatan' or sub-district in local government administration.
↓
Babinsas (Bintara Pembina Desa),
the Village Guidance NCOs or **Team Pembina Desa (TPD)**,
the Village Guidance Teams, who represent Army control
of the resettlement areas or villages. The criteria
for determining why some villages need only one officer
whilst others need a team are related to security conditions.

Fretilin's Military Structure

In the national liberation struggle, Fretilin's military wing, Falintil, *(Forcas Armadas de Libertacão de Timor Leste)* has developed a structure at two levels, one concerned with the armed guerrilla struggle and one concerned with the clandestine struggle inside enemy-occupied territory. The two are closely interlinked. The Fretilin military structure described in the Indonesian documents is concerned primarily with the clandestine network and its connections with the military structure as a whole. The outline reproduced below is based on information contained in Indonesia's counter-insurgency documents without implying that it is in all respects accurate.

East Timor is divided into *three military regions,* each of which is under a political commissar and a military commander. The three regions are:

- Funu Sei Nafatin, the eastern sector.
- Nakroman, the central sector.
- Hacsolok, the western sector.

Military Sub-Regions
The documents only provide a description of the Funu Sei Nafatin Military Sub-Region, which is said to be divided into two sub-regions each of which has its own armed Red Brigade or Company, Company I and Company II. A third company, Red Brigade Company III is also said to operate in one of these sub-regions.

The Militia (Milicia Popular Liberacão National), referred to as Miplin
The Militia are armed members of the population, not full-time resistance guerrillas. According to the documents, each Miplin consists of one detachment with four or five companies. Each of the companies has three platoons composed in turn of three teams. According to figures given in the documents, the numerical strength of each Miplin would appear to be about 270 armed men and women.

The Cernaks (or Celula) are the Centro de Resistencia Nasional
The Cernaks are each responsible for districts existing below the three main sub-regions. Each Cernak is run by a co-ordinating group, the Orgão Co-ordinator, and an Orgão Directivo.

The NUREPs (Nucleos de Resistencia Popular)
These Nuclei of Popular Resistance are groups of unarmed resistance members whose task it is to establish and maintain contact with people living in Indonesian-occupied villages and concentration camps. The Nureps are responsible to the Orgão Directivo of the Cernaks. These are the resistance fighters who confront the troops in charge of the population centres and who therefore figure most prominently in the counter-insurgency documents.

The New Form of National Resistance

As has been explained in Chapters 2 and 3, after the setback suffered by the resistance movement in 1977 and 1978, the vast majority of East Timor's surviving population entered Indonesian-occupied territory and became virtual captives in the concentration camps set up by the Indonesians as the central feature of their population control. But as Xanana, Commander-in-Chief of Falintil has said, the Maubere people had to accept 'to enter into the control of the aggressor' which 'only made the people transfer their support bases from the mountains to the villages'. The new form of resistance 'revolved round the centre of the Maubere people who consolidated their forces in clandestine organizations that were primary and vital necessities for the struggle'.*

The captured Indonesian Army documents provide convincing evidence that this new form of resistance is recognized by the enemy as having been resoundingly successful. The strategy presented in the documents is directed at dealing with this new form of struggle. The following are some of the main points that emerge.

Recognizing the Strength of the Resistance
Of all the documents in the collection, Document 3 presents the most comprehensive survey of Fretilin's strategy and tactics. The resistance is shown as basing itself firmly on the support of the people. Even though the people are physically under Indonesian Army control, the resistance

---
* *Xanana's message to the United Nations*, 14 October 1982

can rely on the people's support because it is inspired by 'regional ideals' (in other words, national independence), because it is better able to win the people's confidence due to 'family ties' or 'custom and tradition', and because it can exploit the weaknesses of the Indonesian army as a colonial army.

Document 3 also presents a detailed description of Fretilin's guerrilla tactics emphasizing their skill in outmanoeuvring the enemy, their mobility and stress on keeping the initiative and the tremendous importance attached to going onto the attack and keeping on the attack at all times. The objectives of the resistance are described as being mobilization of the whole people, destruction of Army units, establishing a broad resistance front and dissipating enemy forces from within.

Document 3 is clearly the result of successful intelligence activity, based probably on a combination of studying captured documents and extracting information from captured fighters by means of torture. But this successful intelligence work has only provided the theoretical framework; experience in the field of battle is the real basis for the Army's intense concern that its troops should understand the strategy and fight accordingly. In other words, the Army knows that Fretilin's strategy is working very well.

Focusing all attention on the village
In several places, notably Document 3 and Document 4, the Indonesian Army acknowledges that resistance support networks exist in all resettlement areas, villages and towns. By focusing attention on the village (meaning essentially the resettlement areas) which is the subject of Document 4, the Indonesian military hope to put an end to resistance in their own backyard. Under the Indonesian Army's 1982 strategy, it became the central task of all military units, from top to bottom (i.e. no longer only the task of the Babinsas and Koramils), to prevent the resistance from 'wresting control of the village'. Whereas the resistance wages this struggle through the Nureps, the critical link between the armed guerrilla movement and the population in Indonesian control, 'The Indonesian Army must try to gain control of the village via the Babinsas. In other words, every village will become a contest between ourselves and the (resistance), and whoever wins that will win the guerrilla/anti-guerrilla war.'

The instructions issued to Babinsas and Koramil officers on how to 'gain control of the village' which appear in several of the documents leave no doubt that mistrust and repression are the keynotes to their attitude towards East Timorese.

Coping with armed and unarmed resistance
The Documents abound with instructions to military personnel on how to deal with opposition inside the resettlement areas. The Babinsas are told to keep a close watch on every inhabitant, particularly persons who have relatives still fighting in the bush. All formal and informal leaders must be constantly watched and scrutinized. Some attention is given to

the need to consult with the population on matters of security and development because it is recognized that 'what is good for us is not necessarily good for the local people'. Time and again, military personnel are warned not to trust anyone, even the 'most trustworthy' Timorese. They must 'always remain vigilant and suspect everyone in the community of the area for which they are responsible'.

Army personnel are told to determine the degree of 'troublesomeness' of each and every village according to nine criteria, and even in the absence of all these criteria, never to regard any village as 'safe'. Guidelines to Babinsas and Koramil officers require them to isolate everyone suspected of being in contact with the resistance, to control people's movements and patrol the villages regularly, to undertake interrogation, using force 'where necessary'. Combat units are instructed on ways to detect resistance concentrations, conduct spy missions, examine conditions in advance of battle and attempt to preempt guerrilla forces bent on keeping the initiative and staying on the attack. A special set of instructions for non-military administrative personnel includes such points as 'ferreting out two-faced officials in the administration' and exercising vigilance against government officials who make 'negative or dubious remarks'. Acknowledging the close links between guerrillas in the bush and populations under Indonesian control, the instruction on *razzias* or raids (Document 7) stress the need to raid villages simultaneously with operations launched against guerrilla units in the vicinity.

Central to the counter-insurgency strategy is the need to 'protect the people' against the propaganda of the resistance. Under an instruction entitled 'Intensifying Control of the Population' (Document 5, p.218), military personnel are told to set up systems to spy on the population, to check and control everyone's movements, to patrol the plots and gardens where people cultivate food and regulate the location of these areas of cultivation in accordance with security needs. (The need to ensure that people are able to produce enough food for their basic requirements is never once mentioned.)

The guidelines on information work to neutralise the propaganda of the resistance reveal the problems of an army of occupation surrounded by Timorese who they do not trust. Even information officers specially trained to give lectures in Portuguese or Tetum on the benefits of 'integrasi' must be spied on while at work, to make sure that they 'say the right things'.

Organizing Timorese Paramilitary Forces
(Timorization of the War)

Document 6 explains why the present form of paramilitary units, the *Wanra (Perlawanan Rakyat,* or 'people's resistance'), more commonly known as Hansip (Civil Guard) needs to be replaced by a new structure because 'Experience shows that Wanra participation in operations for the restoration of security is not yet supported by a profound consciousness of the need to defend the state'. Another reason for this is a financial one because Wanra forces are paid a regular wage whether on operations or not, whereas the new forces, known as *Ratih (Rakyat Terlatih* or Trained People) will only receive material support when out on operations. Ratih members are expected to display a 'reasonably high level of consciousness... so that they are prepared to fight for and defend integration without reserve.' But in the last resort, neither Wanra nor Ratih are to be trusted. There are special guidelines for controlling these units—constant indoctrination, careful control of weapons, continual scrutiny to weed out pro-resistance suspects. Particularly worrying is the question of weapons control without which 'their weapons could be mis-directed, and could for instance be used to strike fear among the people or could even become a boomerang against the people and the Indonesian Armed Forces'.

Ratih units were first used during *Operasi Keamanan* (Operation Security), sometimes referred to by the Army as *Operasi Kikis* (the 'Chipping-Away' Operation) when fence-of-legs operations were used in 1980 and 1981 in an attempt to drive the guerrillas into the open. (See chapter 2). These unwilling recruits who in the event often helped the guerrillas so much that the Operation was a fiasco, are seen as the forerunners of the new-style Ratih units.

Document 9 returns to the question of Ratih units and gives details of their numerical strength in the Baucau district. Logistical support for these units is far below needs; material support is enough for 250 Ratih members whereas the Baucau command claims no fewer than 2,392 Ratih forces. This had led to these forces feeling neglected and dissatisfied particularly when rice rations were replaced by moldy corn. Army personnel must beware of making empty promises, and are warned that there is a lack of indoctrination with the result that 'many people are still not conscious over the question of integration and state affairs'. The wives of Army personnel are also required to help in the propaganda war because 'through the women, information work among the people can be far more effective'.

The *Tenaga Bantuan Operasi* (Operational Support Forces) are the Timorese who are used to carry weapons and supplies when Indonesian troops are out on operations. These men are presented as being closer to the Indonesian cause, having mingled more with the troops, being able to speak Indonesian and so on. Though they are described as having a strong sense of loyalty, they too can be a 'source of trouble'. They have a 'precise knowledge about the weaknesses and strengths of the troops with whom they operate' and many 'have fled to the bush and joined forces with the (resistance) because of lack of proper guidance'.

Raiding the Settlements
Document 7 establishes procedures for conducting raids or 'razzias' on settlements to prevent them from being used as hideouts for guerrilla forces during or after operations. Raids can be conducted against a number of settlements either simultaneously or in succession, to isolate the guerrillas from support or to 'cut off their line of retreat'. Raiding

techniques are described in detail. At night, all inhabitants are ordered to remain at home while the raid is in progress; in the daytime, they must be ordered out of their homes to 'listen to a lecture' while their homes are being raided. Anyone acting contrary to orders will be 'regarded as the enemy' (and presumably shot).

Note on Spelling

The spelling for the names of people and places used in the Documents is often incorrect. No corrections have been made in translation.

Note on Reproduction of Diagrams

The diagrams that are reproduced in the text that follows are taken from photocopies of photocopies of the original documents; this is the reason for the regrettable poor quality of reproduction.

Document 1

Military Resort Command (Korem) 164
Wira Dharma
Intelligence Section

Instruction Manual
Subject: The Way for Babinsa or Team Pembina Desa to Expose/Break Up (Membongkar) GPK Support Networks

I. Introduction

In Instruction Manual no. JUKNIS, dated 30-8-82 on the activities of the Babinsa in territorial intelligence, it was stated that there are 'Degrees of Troublesome-ness (kerawanan)* of Villages' which are determined by several factors, including:

1. Villages that are birth-places of GPK leaders. For instance, Saelari is the native village of Mauk Muruk, Bualale/Laoserolai is the native village of David Alex.

2. Villages whose liurai have sons or daughters who are still in the bush.

3. Villages many of whose inhabitants are still in the bush.
For example, there are still 91 from Maluro, 84 from Saelari, 66 from Atelari, 18 from Samalari, 28 from Tekinomata, and so on.

4. Villages where most of the inhabitants have just come down from the bush.
For example, villages where many of the people came down in 1979 and 1980 are certain to be more troublesome than villages whose inhabitants came down in 1977.

5. Villages most of whose inhabitants consist of ex-GPK and who came down on the basis of plans to destroy ABRI/TNI from within.

6. Villages many of whose inhabitants are disgruntled because of past deeds on the part of ABRI-TNI.

---

*kerawanan: carries the idea of restlessness, instability, cause of trouble. The closest English word to the meaning here intended is the adjective 'troublesome'. To retain this meaning, the derived abstract noun 'troublesome-ness' is used in these translations.

7. *Villages that are not yet able to provide sufficient foodstuff for their own inhabitants.* For instance, villages in the kecamatan of Laga, Baguia and Queliqai.

8. *Villages the composition of whose population is (completely) heterogeneous, and there is no unity or harmony within the village.*

9. *Villages whose entire population consists of people from other villages that have not yet been rebuilt, so that the land which they are now cultivating is not their own.* For instance, villages whose inhabitants still live in the kecamatan [meaning here, town capital of sub-district.]

Such villages are 'troublesome' because there is a greater possibility for 'GPK support networks' to exist. Even so, this does not mean that other villages are clean of GPK support networks. Every possibility exists. Therefore, the Babinsa who work in villages in general as well as Team Pembina Desa (TPD) who work in 'troublesome' villages must be able to break-up support-networks in their villages. Until these GPK support networks have been exposed/broken up, the efforts to eradicate the GPK remnants will not succeed. What is the way to do this? This will be explained in this Instruction Manual.

II The structure of GPK support networks

1. *The division into regions by the GPK*

The GPK divides East Timor into three military regions which they call:

    a. the Funu Sei Hafatin Military Region (the region of Baucau-Viqueque and Los Palos).
    b. The Nakroman Military Region (the region of Manatuto).
    c. The Haksolok Military Region (the western sector).

2. *The Funu Sei Hafatin Military Region*

    a. Their region commander is Marcur (Rubileki) who comes from Ualili.
    b. Their Political Commissar is Tito Ililawa (Loro Timur Anan) who comes from Iliomar.
    c. This Military Region is sub-divided into two sub-regions:
        i. The Funuk sub-region (to the east of Matabean Mountain).
        ii. The Nafatin sub-region (to the west of Matabean Mountain).
    d. Company I Red Brigade, led by Falo Chai (Iliomar Komlek) is located in the Funuk sub-region. In addition to Company I, the Red Brigade commander, Mauk Muruk (who comes from Saelari village) together with his bodyguard, is also in this region (the Saelari complex).
    e. Company II Red Brigade, led by David Alex (who comes from the Bualale village/Laesorolai), is located in the Nafatin sub-region. In addition to Company II, the Company III Red Brigade which is led by Kalisa together with Ologari (deputy of Mauk Muruk), often operates in this sub-region (Uaibobo-Builo complex).

3. Cernak (Celula)

a. Each of these sub-regions is further divided into districts which they call Cernak, or Centro de Resistencia Nacional (Centres of National Resistance) which is a body that collects data from several Nureps.
b. The Cernak or Celula in some regions of the Funuk sub-region have been exposed/broken up; these are Celula 111, 112, 113, 114 and 115.
c. Those in the Nafatin sub-region still have to be exposed/dismantled by both the Babinsa and the TPD.

4. The Nureps

a. Each Cernak coordinates several Nureps (Nucleos Resistencia Popular) or Popular Resistance Nuclei, the bodies which organise and guide the villages and resettlement areas.
b. Some Nurep members live in the resettlement areas (people who help the GPK covertly) and some live in the bush (we normally refer to these as 'Rakyat GPK'—GPK People). It is the task of these Nureps to help the GPK by supplying information, food and clothing, and to try and influence the people so that they sympathise with the GPK's struggle and if possible subsequently become cadres.

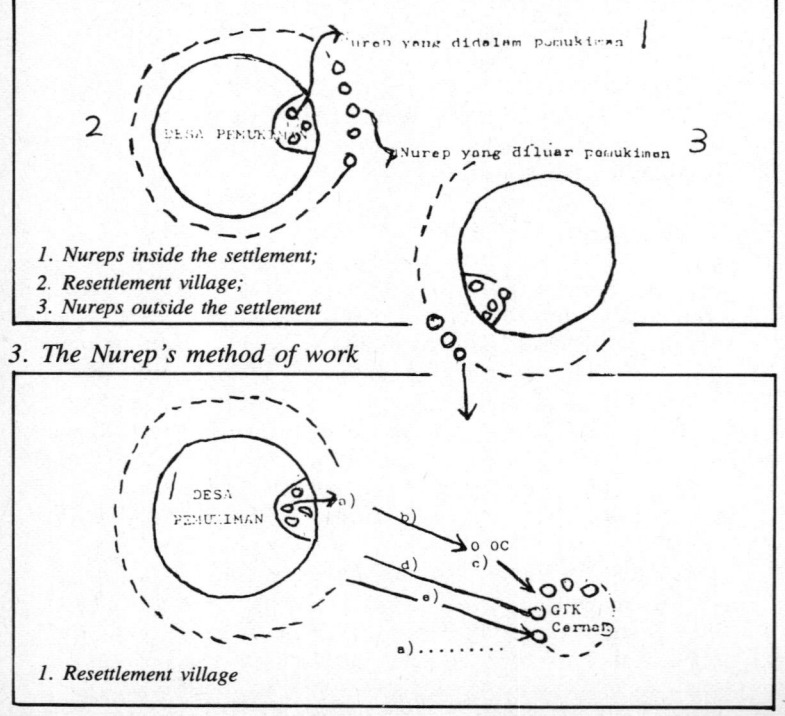

1. Nureps inside the settlement;
2. Resettlement village;
3. Nureps outside the settlement

3. The Nurep's method of work

1. Resettlement village

a. Nurep members in the settlements (they include ordinary people, Hansip/Ratih members and even community leaders; they are motivated by family ties, because they feel disgruntled towards ABRI/TNI, they fear being intimidated, and so on) look for and collect anything needed by the GPK (information, clothing, food and so on), and these things are given to Nurep members outside the village or settlement. These meetings can take place in gardens, in forests or places agreed by them.

b. The Nureps who are outside the settlement then report the information or hand over the clothing or food to the OC (Orgão Coordinator) who is a member of the Cernak and operates as a Political Assistant who is the 'ajunto'. The OC members and Cernak members are in the GPK and they are in the bush.

c. With the help of this information, clothing and food, the GPK is able to continue with its guerrilla activities.

d. If GPK members fall ill and are no longer able to carry weapons, they are appointed to become Nurep.

e. Conversely, if a Nurep is restored to health, or if there is a cadre (someone in the settlement who has been influenced), that person returns to a GPK unit of troops.

III How do the Babinsa or TPD expose/break up these GPK support networks?

1. By investigating each of the persons from the village who are still in the bush, together with their relatives.

[*There follows a table setting out the kind of information needed: age, sex, education, occupation, firearms, family and other remarks, such as whether any relative is now in Atauro*]

2. Try to capture a Nurep or GPK member by making investigations about the GPK family still in the village or by making patrols around the settlement, or by asking those GPK who have surrendered or been captured and who come from the village in question.

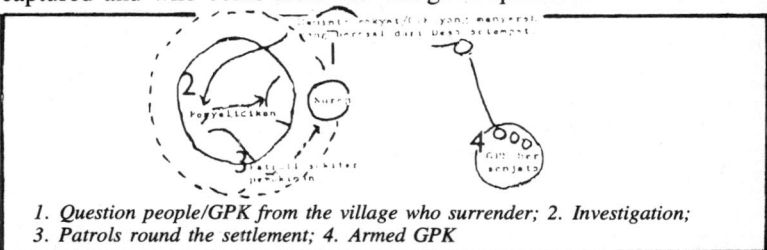

1. Question people/GPK from the village who surrender; 2. Investigation; 3. Patrols round the settlement; 4. Armed GPK

3. Interrogate/investigate the person in question to find out who is it who helps them in the settlement, who are the Nurep or GPK who are in the Cernak.

Instructions regarding interrogations

    a. Use a native-born interpreter who can be trusted.
    b. Show the person (under interrogation) that his friends are still alive because they made honest confessions and were prepared to help ABRI/TNI for the early restoration of security.
    c. Avoid using violence that would result in the person under interrogation sealing his/her lips or giving false information and creating anxiety in the community.
    d. Questions should be asked about the following
    — who are still helping them in the settlement;
    — who are the Nureps operating outside the settlement;
    — who are still members of GPK in the Cernak or with the troops;
    — the organisation and method of operation of the above three. For instance, who is the commander, chairman, person in charge, the one who issues orders. Where and how do these people meet their members.

4. Transfer to Atauro or to other places designated for this purpose those in the GPK support network who are still in the settlement and the relatives of GPK who have not yet been sent away. In this way, we can cut the ties between the support networks in the settlements and the Nureps.

5. Try to capture the Nureps and the GPK members who are outside the settlement:

    a. Nureps and GPK members who surrender or are captured should be asked to bring down their comrades who are still outside the settlement with the movement.
    b. Those Nureps or GPK who surrender or are captured should be told to call to their comrades through loud-speakers.
    c. Hold *tebe-tebe** festivities so as to make the Nureps still outside the settlement feel a longing for their village and then come down.
    d. Disseminate information to show that those who genuinely come down will be well received (won't be killed).
    e. Other methods can be cultivated by the Babinsa or TPD.

Those Nureps or GPK members who come down must be put in places that are separated from other people so as to prevent any contact. Even so, they must continue to be 'guided' as well as possible so as to give them a better picture of things, and ensure on the one hand that they don't try to take to the bush again, whilst on the other hand bringing over their comrades who are still in the bush.

---

*tebe is a Timorese dance. The word has been Indonesianized by giving it the Indonesian plural form.

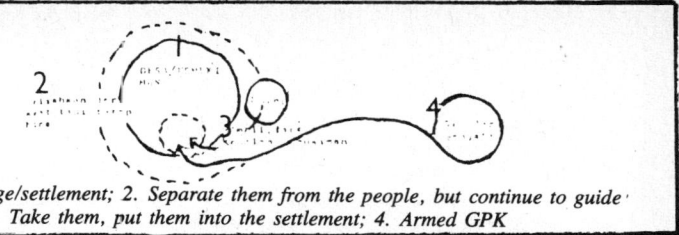

1. Village/settlement; 2. Separate them from the people, but continue to guide them; 3. Take them, put them into the settlement; 4. Armed GPK

6. In order to break the link between the Nureps and the armed GPK members as well as bringing the Nureps down, patrols should be organized round the settlements particularly round the people's gardens which are suspected of being meeting places.

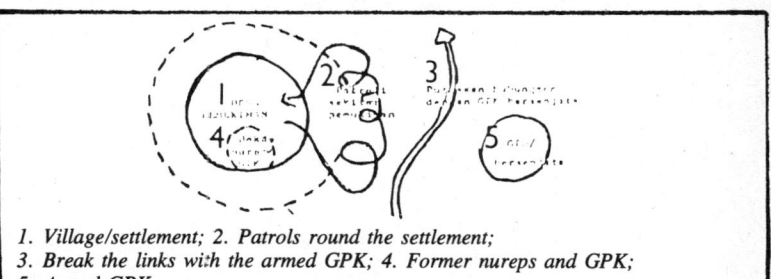

1. Village/settlement; 2. Patrols round the settlement;
3. Break the links with the armed GPK; 4. Former nureps and GPK;
5. Armed GPK

7. Whilst exposing the GPK support networks, simultaneously carry out efforts to win the sympathy of the village. Remember that people's sympathy is based first and foremost on the stomach, on their customs and on giving them a picture of a better life.

    a. Help people tend their gardens or fields.
    b. Help overcome food shortages (report to the Kodim commander if food supplies are indeed needed).
    c. Help set up cooperatives if possible.
    d. Show respect for local customs.
    e. Build the village by setting up sanitary facilities, schools, village halls or other facilities needed by the people to give them a picture of a better life.
    f. Other activities that can be developed by the Babinsa or TPD which are basically aimed at attracting people's sympathy.

8. In addition, undertake measures to safeguard and protect the people from GPK disturbances, whether thefts of cattle, thefts of crops, or murders.
    These measures should include:

    a. Creating an effective Trained People's Unit (*Ratih*) organisation.
    b. Bringing into being a Village Security System that can cope with various kinds of GPK disturbances.

c. Conducting patrols round the village so as to make sure that the village remains safe.

IV. Final Section

If Korem 164/WD and its components are likened to the human body, with Korem as the head (or brains), the Kodims as the trunk and the Koramils as the arms and legs, the Babinsas and Village Guidance Teams are the fingers. If the brains have made plans for the capture of the GPK and the body has caused the muscles in the arms and legs to move but the fingers do not function, then the GPK will escape. So, remember that your role and share as Babinsa or Village Guidance Team *is not insignificant*. Think this over! All the best in the fulfilment of your duties! May you succeed for God is with you all!

Head of Intelligence Section
Williem da Costa
Infantry Major no. 24293

Document 2

Instruction Manual No. Juknis/05/I/1982
System of Security in Towns and Resettlement Areas

I. Introduction

1. General
In their efforts to wage 'protracted war', the GPK has worked out a 'Guerrilla Strategy' as discussed in Instruction Manual Number: JUKNIS/04/XII/1981, of 28 December 1981 regarding the activities of the Babinsa (Village Guidance Officer) in Territorial Intelligence. This guerrilla strategy plans, among other things, to achieve the following guerrilla objectives.

    a. To stay alive by avoiding decisive combat and to wait for a good moment to re-emerge.
    b. To maintain and develop support networks in the Towns and Resettlement Areas.
    c. To show signs of their existence or presence (showing that they still exist) particularly in the months prior to the UN General Assembly).
    d. To create conditions in which the TNI-ABRI feels insecure wherever they are.
    e. To create mobile bases in many regions, particularly in formerly fertile villages that are now abandoned by their inhabitants.
    f. To inflict casualties on the TNI.
    g. To get the people's support.

These objectives, particularly point 1.c, 'to show signs of their existence', have already shown results in such incidents as the attack on Dili (the TVRI—Television Station) on 10 June 1980, the attack on Baguia on 21 August 1980, the attack on Baucau on 25 December 1980, and the planned attack on the village of Mulia on 20 June 1980. Such actions are likely to be taken by the GPK when we are off guard or our vigilance flags.

    In addition, the existence of networks of their supporters in the towns as well as the resettlement areas will make it possible for them to ircite the people and thus cause disorders both in the towns and resettlement areas.

Other disturbances that can occur in the towns and resettlement areas are natural disasters such as fires, whether as a result of sabotage or by accident. Bearing in mind moreover that in both the towns and resettlement areas there are various ABRI elements such as the Military District Command (Kodim), Resort Command/Police (Kores), other Departmental Service Units, the Civil Guard (Hansip/Wanra) as well as the Trained People's Unit (Ratih), conflicts are possible among ABRI elements or between ABRI elements and the people which could disturb public order or create unrest in the community. In order to cope with such possibilities, well-coordinated efforts by all units and authorities, preventive as well as repressive, are needed in the event of such incidents occurring. So as to safeguard such coordinated efforts in the field, a special Instruction Manual is needed.

2. Objective

This Instruction Manual is aimed at regulating the coordination between (combat) units, (government) authorities and the community to cope with threats and disturbances that occur in the towns and resettlement areas throughout the territory of District Command 1628/Baucau.

3. Scope

This Instruction Manual will describe the various threats and disturbances that are likely to occur, the measures that must be taken to cope with them, and technical implementation of these measures in the field. It is organised according to the following systematic:

    I. Introduction
    II. Threats and disturbances that are likely to occur and the measures to be taken.
    III. Measures to cope with threats and disturbances against the town of Baucau.
    IV. Measures to cope with threats and disturbances against the sub-district (*kecamatan*) towns.
    V. Measures to cope with threats and disturbances against resettlement areas.
    VI. Final section.

4. Basis

[A list of military documents given here is omitted]

II. Threats and disturbances that are likely to occur and measures to be taken to deal with them.

5. General

As has already been stated in the Introduction, threats and disturbances are likely to occur in the towns as well as in the resettlement areas, originating both from external forces (GPK) as well as from internal forces (disorders that can spread unrest in the community). Such threats and disturbances must be overcome by systematic measures so that 'uniformity of action' in the field is achieved by all existing forces.

6. Threats and disturbances

The various threats and disturbances which can be caused by the GPK in the towns and resettlement areas include:

    a. Attacks by the GPK on vital objects in the towns as well as attacks on the resettlement areas, such as those launched in Dili, Baguia, Mulia village and the planned attack against the town of Baucau that was foiled.
    b. Disorders in the towns and resettlement areas by masses of people who have been incited by GPK support networks.
    c. Natural disasters such as fires, earthquakes, floods and hurricanes, which must be speedily overcome so as not to spread unrest in the community.
    d. Disturbances of the public order such as scuffles between members of ABRI and the people or among the people themselves can, if not speedily handled, create unrest in the community.

7. Framework of Measures

In order to cope with such threats, the following is the framework of measures:

    a. Preventive measures, and repressive measures when the incident has occurred.
    b. The measures are based on *Sishankamrata* and *Siskam Swakarsa** according to which all potential forces are mobilised.
    c. Close coordination between army units, the government authorities and the local community.
    d. Defensive-active in the sense that the measures are not concentrated solely on defence.
    e. Speed of action in the sense that within a short time, forces are ready to cope with the threat or disturbance that has occurred.
    f. Flexibility in the sense of avoiding rigidity and always conforming with the situation being faced.
    g. Organised into security systems for the town of Baucau, the sub-district towns and other settlement areas.
    h. The town security system of Baucau will include one for the town of Baucau itself and one for Lanu Baucau, mutually assisting each other. In other words, if the town of Baucau is under threat, the security system of Lanu can come to its help, and vice versa.

---

* These are military acronyms implying 'total and self-generated' involvement of the population in security measures.

III. Measures to Cope with Threats and Disturbances Against the Town of Baucau.

8. *General*
In dealing with various threats and disturbances, the security system of the town of Baucau shall be organised as follows:

a. *Responsibility for town security.*
i. For the town (excluding Lanu), responsibility rests with Military District Commander 1628/Baucau, with the Police Resort Commander 11.32/Baucau as his deputy.
ii. For the region of Lanu, responsibility rests with the Commander of Lanu Baucau. The security system shall be controlled solely by the Commander of Lanu Baucau.

b. *Joint Action Command*
i. This is the day-to-day executor of town security, responsible to the officer responsible for Town Security.
ii. It shall consist of an officer, one NCO and one enlisted soldier taken in turn from District Command 1628/Baucau, Police Resort Command 11.32/Baucau, Infantry Battalion 745/Bs, Lanu Baucau, elements from Departments/Services and Combat Units in Baucau.
iii. On duty for 24 hours and located for the time being at the headquarters of District Military Command 1628/Baucau.
iv. Transfer of duties shall take place at 08.00 every day in the presence of the Officer Responsible for Town Security or an officer appointed by him.

c. *Security Posts*
i. Civil defence (Hansip/Wanra) posts shall encircle the town.
ii. Police posts shall guard installations and vital objects in the town such as the Television Station, the munitions arsenal, the electricity plant, the Hospital, the Flamboyant Hotel and so on.
iii. People's guard-posts shall encircle the villages (localities) and town.
The locations of these posts shall shift round to make them less open to detection by the enemy. Throughout the night, these posts shall strike a bell on the hour with the number of strikes denoting the hour.

d. *Forces at the ready*
i. ABRI units, the Civil Guard (Hansip/Wanra) and Trained People's Forces (Ratih), which shall be located for the time being at the headquarters of the District Military Command, the Resort Police Command, the Subdistrict Military Command and the Infantry Battalion 745/BS, and shall be ready at all times to go into action.
ii. Trained People's Forces (Ratih) in every locality in the town which can be deployed for out-of-town patrols and reconnaisance and as readiness forces for use at any time.

e. *People's Forces*

Male inhabitants armed with spears and *katana* (knives) who can, in times of danger, be summoned to one place in their village or locality in the town.

9. Measures to be taken if threats or disturbances occur

   a. In the case of GPK attacks
   Preventive
   i. The Joint Action Command shall at all times control the readiness of the Civil Guard posts encircling the town, the police posts guarding vital objects and the people's patrols round the villages or localities in the town.
   ii. The Joint Action Command shall organise out-of-town patrols and reconnaissance, using the Trained People's Units (Ratih) in the villages and towns.
   iii. The Joint Action Command shall at all times control the state of readiness of the forces deployed at the Headquarters of the District Military Command, the Resort Police Command, the Subdistrict Military Command and Infantry Battalion 745/Bs.

   Repressive
   i. Posts under attack will resist and sound the danger-gongs with continuous strikes, taken up from post to post, to report to the Joint Action Command stationed at District Military HQ 1628/Baucau.
   ii. Upon hearing this danger signal, the Joint Action Command will immediately engage the Readiness Forces closest to the location of the incident. Other Readiness Forces must be at the ready in their posts, and the Joint Action Command will immediately report the incident to the officer responsible for Town Security who will go straight to District Military Command HQ 1628/Baucau to issue further orders.
   iii. At the same time, all members of military units and government services will immediately muster at their headquarters, each bringing their weapons. Members of each Command will report to their respective HQs to await further orders. Specifically for government employees and teachers:

   If the incident occurs in the daytime:
   - District government employees will gather at the government office, with the exception of those who work at the electricity plant, the Hospital, the health centres (who will muster) at their respective offices.
   - Teachers will keep their pupils inside the school building.
   - Officials will keep people in the market who will not be permitted to leave the market complex.

   If the incident occurs at night:
   - Officials living in town will muster at the government office.
   - Officials living out of town will muster with the people of their village.

iv. The Babinsas, Regional Police Officers and Village Heads will also make ready the Trained People's Units (Ratih) and all male inhabitants armed with spears and *katanas* (knives) at places previously determined in their villages to receive further orders.
v. The officer responsible for Town Security will issue further orders in accordance with the current tactical situation. If the attack is severe, reinforcements may be brought in from Lanu-Baucau.
vi. When the danger has been overcome, the gong will be struck with interrupted strikes, on the orders of the officer responsible for Town Security.

b. *In the case of unrest*
Preventive
i. The Joint Action Command will conduct patrols (using Joint Military Police Units) at places where the community congregates, for instance at markets and other busy places.
ii. If any unrest occurs, it should be quickly halted before the mass of people become uncontrollable.

Repressive
i. The Joint Action Command will quickly prepare all Readiness Forces and will also immediately report the incident to the officer responsible for Town Security.
ii. The Joint Action Command will quickly contact the Town *Tripida* for them to issue orders to the Babinsas, Police commanders and village heads to confine people to their homes so as to prevent them from being influenced by the incident.
iii. The officer responsible for Town Security will come immediately to issue orders to calm things down or halt the unrest.

c. *In the case of natural disasters*
Preventive
i. The Joint Action Command, through Town *Tripida* channels and army unit commanders, must continually draw attention to the danger of fire.
ii. At every office and vital object, the fire-fighting equipment must always be at the ready, at the very least a number of buckets filled with sand.
iii. The Joint Action Command will have ready places to accomodate inhabitants who are struck by a disaster (fire, hurricane, etc).

Repressive
i. Posts located closest to the disaster will immediately sound the danger-gong with three groups of interrupted strikes.
ii. Upon hearing this signal, the Joint Action Command will immediately report to the officer responsible for Town Security and mobilise Readiness Forces and people's forces close to the place of the disaster in order to put out the fire.
iii. Inhabitants affected by the disaster will be evacuated to accommodation made ready for the purpose.

d. *In the case of security disorders*
Preventive
Through army unit commanders and *Tripida* channels, the Joint Action Command will warn of the need for:
i. Compact unity among all elements of ABRI.
ii. Togetherness between ABRI and the people.
iii. Vigilance against the possibility of trouble-making by the GPK. Besides this, to conduct patrols of the Town (deploying joint Military Police units) at all times so as to prevent any outbreak of disorders.
Repressive
i. Upon hearing of incidents, for instance scuffles between people, between members of ABRI, between people and members of ABRI, the Joint Action Command will quickly separate the contending parties, report immediately to the officer responsible for Town Security and also report to the commanders of the units whose members are involved in the disorder.
ii. Every unit commander will immediately take preventive measures to prevent the incident from growing.
iii. The Joint Action Command will intensify Town Patrols to prevent undesirable events from occurring.

10. The Responsibilities of each element in the Apparatus
[This section lists the personnel that must be summoned into action at all levels of the command structure. It is too technical to be of interest in the present context.]

IV. Measures to Cope with Threats and Disturbances Against the Subdistrict (*Kecamatan*) Towns

11. General
As with the Town of Baucau, there is the possibility of threats and disturbances against the subdistrict (*kecamatan*) towns. A security system needs to be prepared to cope with such eventualities.

12. Responsibility
The officer responsible for security of each subdistrict town is the Commander of the Subdistrict Command assisted by the Sector Commander as his deputy.

Principles of Implementation
These are basically the same as the system of measures for Baucau Town Security:

    a. Preventive and repressive
    b. Based on a 'total' and 'self-generated' security system in which all forces are mobilised.
    c. Close coordination between army units, government authorities and the local communities.

d. Defensive-active in the sense that the measures are not only concentrated on defense.
e. Speed of action in the sense that forces become available at short notice to cope with the threat or disturbance.
f. Flexibility in the sense of avoiding rigidity, at all times being able to adapt to the situation being faced.

Implementation
Each Subdistrict Commander, assisted by the local Section Commander, will speedily create a security system for his Subdistrict capital, including among others:

a. Civil Guard (Hansip/Wanra) posts, Trained People's Unit (Ratih) posts and people's posts round the town at non-permanent locations.
b. Readiness Forces which can be mustered at all times to go to the location of the incident.
c. People's forces that can be fully mobilised to defend the town in the event of danger.
d. A good system of Command control so that all potential forces can be well organised.

Once the system has been created, it should be reported to the Commander of District Command 1628/Baucau: the system should be constantly exercised to ensure it is in a state of readiness to face any threats or disturbances that may occur.

V. Measures to Cope with Threats and Disturbances in the Resettlement Areas

General
As shown by the examples mentioned in Section I, the Introduction, it is always possible for threats and disturbances to occur in the resettlement areas or villages. For this reason, every resettlement area and village needs to prepare a security system capable of coping with these eventualities.

Responsible Officer
The responsible officer is the local *Babinsa* assisted by the *Binpolda* (Local Police Officer) as his deputy.

Principles of Execution
In principle, the same as in the District and Subdistrict towns, namely:

a. Both preventive and repressive. That is to say, preventive action must be taken to avoid threats from occurring, for instance by conducting patrols round the village at all times, by planting informers so that every enemy attempt to attack the village can be discovered in advance. But if these preventive measures are not successful and an attack is launched against the village, repressive measures must be made ready to cope with this.

b. Based on the principle of 'totality' and 'self-generation'. This means that the village security system must mobilise all existing forces, military, police, Civil Guard (Hansip/Wanra), Trained People's Units (Ratih), the male inhabitants and so on. 'Self-generated' means that the efforts to safeguard the village must emerge from within the village itself.

c. Well coordinated which means that all the existing forces, including combat units that happen to be stationed in the village, must be regulated in such a way as to be mobilised altogether and properly co-ordinated into a force that is capable of coping with all threats and disturbances that may occur.

d. Defensive-active which means that the forces are not directed only to defensive purposes but must also play an active role in the sense of foiling efforts by the enemy forces which are about to attack, or by conducting patrols and so on.

e. Speed of action which means that there are at all times forces that are ready to act: as soon as anything happens, it can be speedily overcome.

f. Flexibility which means that the security system is not rigid but is capable of dealing with every event in accordance with the situation being confronted at the time.

Execution

Each Babinsa assisted by the local Binpolda must immediatly draw up a security system for his village, which includes among others:

a. Civil Guard (Hansip/Wanra) posts, Trained People's Unit (Ratih) posts and people's posts around the village at non-permanent locations.

b. Readiness Forces composed of armed Hansip/Wanra and Ratih members which are situated in such a way as to be ready to be mobilised at any time and taken to the location of the incident.

c. People's forces armed with spears and *katanas* (knives) which can be mustered the moment an incident occurs, and can be mobilised to wage opposition.

d. A good system of command control so that all forces in the village, including the patrol posts encircling the villages, the readiness forces as well as the entire population, can be mobilised quickly and effectively.

As soon as the security system has been drawn up, this must be reported to your Subdistrict Commander. In addition, to keep the system in a state of constant readiness, exercises should be held.

VI. Final Section

19. Other matters
Matters not included in this Instruction Manual will be regulated separately on a point-by-point basis.

20. This Instruction Manual comes into force at the moment of issue and is an Established Procedure.

Issued in Dili on 10 September, 1982

(signed by)
Williem da Costa
Infantry Major No.24293

Document 3

Military Regional Command XVI
Udayana
Military Sub-Regional Command 164/Wira Dharma

Established Procedure (PROTAP) on Intelligence
No. 01/IV/1982
Subject: Instructions for Territorial Intelligence Activities in East Timor

Section I: Introduction

1. General
The anti-guerrilla operations which are now in progress for the restoration of security in East Timor, based on instructions for territorial activities as already implemented, have not yet, it is felt, ensured an overall settlement and the achievement of the objectives of the Operation. It is a fact that the GPK's underground networks have not yet been finished off. Although it is known that these networks are closely related to customs and to the family system, it is clear that special treatment is required if they are to be broken up. In order to be able more speedily to crush the GPK remnants to their roots and to prevent their re-emergence, it is considered necessary to develop Territorial Intelligence in the Territory of East Timor.

2. Purpose
This Procedure on Intelligence is issued to provide technical instructions for APTER (Territorial Apparatus) and SATPUR (Combat Units) to undertake intelligence activities so that all information available in their region can be used at the right time and aimed at the right target.

3. Framework and System of Presentation
The framework of discussion in this PROTAP includes the conditions being faced, the concept of the GPK's covert network, the target being confronted and its connections with activities and Territorial Operations, and the techniques of Territorial Intelligence.

The system of presentation in this PROTAP is:

a. Introduction
b. Prevailing conditions
c. The GPK's guerrilla strategy
d. The target of Territorial Intelligence
e. Instructions for activities
f. Final section

Section II: Prevailing Conditions

4. General

The continued existence of GPK support networks in the resettlement areas is a concrete condition that must be faced. The factors which influence the resilience of these networks are the ties between the GPK and the people, whether based on customs or more specifically on the family system.

5. *Condition of the Community*

a. *Customs and tradition*
According to custom, a person feels guilty if he/she does not help a relative in difficulty. By custom and tradition, too, people feel a great reluctance to oppose former leaders or oppose their own children. This relates to the fact that some GPK leaders are liurais or the offspring of liurais.

By custom and tradition, people will take revenge on anyone who has behaved badly or not behaved well towards him/her or towards his/her family.

b. *Traditional leadership*
Some traditional leaders were replaced as leaders of tribes as a result of the upheavals and new leaders were appointed by Operation [ie. Indonesian] commanders. Some of these traditional leaders feel very resentful because they have lost their wealth and now find themselves in positions of disadvantage and moreover are being led by people who are not descendants of liurais.

c. *Church leadership*
Many people still tell the Church Leadership good and bad things about the State Apparatus and tell them about actions taken by ABRI. This Leadership can still be asked to establish contact with the GPK in the bush under conditions where lives are safeguarded.

The open character of the Church is of great value for information-gathering by APTER (Territorial Apparatus). Ideas that are conveyed through church channels, if these tally with their own policies, reach the community fast and are obeyed.

d. *Local government leadership*
Vestiges of party groupings that existed prior to the upheavals still remain. Some government employees are former GPK members whose political loyalty needs to be watched. ABRI members often treat local government officials in ways that upset the people or the

official himself. The local government apparatus sometimes regards the Territorial Apparatus as an obstacle to its pursuit of a feudalistic style of government. Attempts are made by certain groups to prevent local government from taking an active part in efforts to restore security.

e. *Condition of APTER (Territorial Apparatus)*
Some people in this Apparatus have not had special training in territorial activities or Territorial Intelligence. Many members still lack the spirit of Territorial Officers with the result that many actions offend the people. In addition, many members obtain information but pass it on too late or do not pass it on at all because they draw conclusions from their own analysis.

6. Condition of the GPK

Motivation   Despite the heavy pressure and the disadvantageous conditions under which they operate, the GPK has nevertheless been able to hold out in the bush. The motives that make this possible are:

a. Some of their leaders want a government of their own without Indonesia.
b. Feelings of fear because they have made many mistakes and if they were to come down from the bush, others would take revenge.
c. They are afraid because the GPK leadership have warned them that if they come down, they will be murdered by ABRI.
d. Family solidarity and ties with traditional leaders.

Such motives prove to be very shallow because once they are captured and given the chance to live, the very same day they will start opposing the GPK or their comrades still in the bush.

GPK activities   The GPK now operates (a system of) total pacification and resists when cornered. They are quick to notice when we are off guard and also quick to exploit our weaknesses. The efforts they make in order to prolong their guerrilla operations are:

a. Trying to win the people's sympathy by not doing anything to offend them.
b. Always developing covert networks in areas where Indonesian Army activities are reduced in profile. These networks provide support in information, logistics and personnel.
c. Cultivating an understanding of Marxism amongst a very thin layer of their leadership.
d. Occasionally revealing their presence by attacking places that are not being defended or are being inadequately defended by ABRI.
e. Robbing food from people's gardens.
f. Waging intimidation and terror against leaders and people who do not want to help the GPK or who help ABRI in such a way as to cause casualties for the GPK.

g. Waging propaganda by making use of ABRI's misdeeds committed by irresponsible elements in the regions.

h. Reminding former GPK members who have come down of the joint oaths they took when they were in the bush.

GPK areas of operation

a. The *Falo Txai group* operates from the Paichau Mountain to the estuary of the Lapa-Lapa river, the Chai village and Koaliu village complex.

b. The *Mauk Moruk group* operates from the Dau Dere complex to Atamami, the village of Saelari, Kuda Gula Lagarata up to Sirimana and the village of Nunira.

c. The *group of Alex, Ologari and Kalisa* sometimes unites in the Builo complex region. Sometimes, they separate, with the Kalisa group operating in the Macadiqui-Builo region down to the south coast, the Ologari group operating in the region of Uai Bobo-Nahareka and the Alex group operating in the area surrounding the district capital of Queliquai.

d. The *Kilik group* is still trying to find the leadership that was smashed in the Aitana region complex.

e. The *Mauhunu (Bukar) group* which operates in the Kabulaque area and in the Mamalau area complex.

f. There are still small, unorganised groups operating, among others:

    i In the Saburai area complex, district of Maliana.

    ii In the border district of Ermera, and in the districts of Dili, Liquica and Ailiu.

    iii In the Daramata area along the banks of the river Suhi in the district of Manufahi.

    iv In the regions of Home and Souro in the district of Lautem.

g. At certain times, they can meet together at pre-determined places. This is usually around Aitana because of its historical significance for the growth of the GPK. Meetings in the eastern region can be held in the regions of Koaliu, Matabean, Macadique or Builo. On such occasions there is a very sizeable concentration of forces in one place.

Section III: The GPK's Guerrilla Strategy

7. General

By making use of regional circumstances and exploiting ABRI's weaknesses, particularly those committed by irresponsible elements, the GPK is trying to wage protracted guerrilla warfare. They are convinced that they can do this because they are waging guerrilla warfare in regions where they were born and where some of the people still want to help them. Besides, although they have no contact with the outside world, they are convinced that some of their friends abroad are still trying to make sure that the United Nations does not acknowledge and legitimise the integration of the Territory of East Timor into the Unitary State of the Republic of Indonesia. The GPK realises that without the help of people, they would be nothing more than groups in difficulty roaming wild in the forests. This is why the GPK is convinced that this guerrilla war is also a war to win the sympathy of the people. The GPK's guerrilla war is aimed at diminishing and smashing the capability of ABRI/TNI so as eventually to be able to bring about its total destruction. In their guerrilla war, the GPK uses the guerrilla tactics of the Vietnam war and some aspects of the guerrilla struggle in Cuba and Angola as well as a combination that they have worked out themselves in the past three years.

8. Objectives of the Guerrillas

The following are the objectives that must be achieved by the GPK in this protracted war:

> a. To keep alive by avoiding decisive combat so as to have the time to restore their forces, whilst at the same time cultivating a high spirit of motivation and strong discipline.
> b. To preserve and develop support networks in the resettlement areas and in the towns.
> c. To show their presence or existence, particularly in the months before the UN General Assembly.
> d. To create conditions in which ABRI feel unsafe wherever they may be.
> e. To establish mobile bases in many regions, particularly in formerly fertile villages now abandoned by their inhabitants.

9. GPK Guerrilla guidelines

The tactical principles of guerrilla warfare used include skill, initiative, going on to the attack, tenacity and secrecy, speed and total destruction, and perfection of implementation.

Implementation in the field is itemised as follow:

Skilful in battle

> a. This is done by attacking then disappearing, by feigning an attack on one position whilst in fact another position is to be attacked, or by consolidating a position in another place so as to distract the enemy's attention from themselves.
> b. Avoid the enemy's strong positions and attack his weak positions.
> c. Advance or retreat as necessary.
> d. Fast action so as to give the enemy no time to react or ask for help.
> e. Never to engage in an action that cannot produce results.
> f. Never use the same tactic (twice).

Retain initiative of action

This principle is aimed at forcing ABRI to follow the wishes of the GPK, this is done by:

> a. Looking for places where ABRI/TNI are present in large numbers

or are weak.
b. Studying ABRI's practices so as to be able to predict their reactions to actions taken by the GPK and (know) ABRI's weaknesses.
c. Considering the safety of the population when engaging in battle and also keeping the battle away from the GPK bases.
d. Reducing their own weaknesses because of the balance of forces by doing intensive training whenever the opportunity arises.
e. Doing things that are impossible for ABRI.
f. Pushing ABRI to the point where they become exhausted and off-guard so as then to hit at them.

Going on to the attack
Great emphasis is placed on encouraging every GPK member to go onto the attack even when the balance of forces is not in their favour. This is done because they understand that:

a. This principle is the pre-condition for retaining the initiative.
b. Emphasising this principle means all GPK members will feel that destroying the enemy is one of the finest achievements for every member.
c. Going onto the attack must be preceded by information about the strength of the enemy. The guidelines for this are:
　　i. Set out to attack; keep on the attack so as to weaken ABRI/TNI, then go on to the attack again.
　　ii. If the TNI advances, the GPK retreats; if the TNI stops, the GPK hits it without respite and if the TNI retreats, the GPK pursues it.

Tenacity
This can be achieved by each member training himself/herself so as to be able to:

a. take action without hesistation and in good time.
b. always make a situation analysis and take action fast.

Secrecy
Secrecy is the key to surprise and also the key to the concentration of forces. In relation to its control and guidance of the population, the principle of 'secrecy at all costs' is crucial to the overall success of guerrilla warfare. Implementation is as follows:

a. The population must help protect the GPK from ABRI scrutiny.
b. Every GPK member must guard secrets strictly, before, during and after an operation is launched.
c. Whenever a GPK member enters a resettlement area or goes behind enemy lines, he/she must immediately adapt to local conditions and discard all signs of GPK identity.
d. The GPK tries to destroy all ABRI/TNI agents who are dangerous to them.

Speed

Speed is a decisive factor in achieving the element of surprise. By speed is meant that the GPK always uses time to the best possible effect and uses any opportunities arising from the TNI/ABRI being off guard or weak in order to launch a successful attack on ABRI, among other things by:

> a. Keeping all weapons and equipment in a constant state of readiness.
> b. Every time an attack or onslaught is launched, all GPK members must engage themselves in it in a high spirit of militancy.
> c. After an action is finished every GPK member always cleans the weapons and equipment he/she has used. The GPK always studies very carefully the regions to be used as the location for an action.

Total Destruction

This principle means that every time an action is undertaken, the maximum number of casualties inflicted on ABRI is determined without incurring casualties of their own, so as to be able to improve the balance of forces in the GPK's favour. In applying this principle, it is always stressed upon each and every member of the GPK that they must:

> a. Be convinced that every operation undertaken will succeed.
> b. Always remember that a powerful strike will result in destruction for the ABRI-TNI.
> c. Realise that, if necessary, some members will have to be sacrificed to achieve an important victory.
> d. Press on with an attack if the circumstances are favourable even though the target previously fixed has been accomplished.
> e. Always seek out and exploit TNI-ABRI's weak points.

Attack as hard as possible so as to achieve results quickly. This is done by the GPK striking continual blows wherever possible, from all directions and in all areas. In this way, the GPK hopes to keep the TNI in a position of passivity and expectation. To do this, the GPK must always obtain information about the deployment and activity of ABRI units. To achieve this they always instil:

> a. Militant fighting spirits.
> b. Self-confidence.
> c. Readiness to make sacrifices.
> d. The need for speed of movement.
> e. Preservation of good relations with the command.

10. Support of the population

> a. From the very start, the GPK realised that guerrilla struggle can only survive if it is supported by the people. If there is no people's

support, they say that they are nothing but wanderers in distress. Therefore, the people must by all possible means remain in the hands of the GPK. In the early days, the people were taken off with the guerrilla troops into the bush. But then, after this had gone on for a long time, they came to the conclusion that waging a guerrilla struggle with the people in the bush was not suited to conditions in East Timor. They therefore adopted the policy of sending the people down from the bush with the understanding that they would be given food and protection by TNI-ABRI. Even though this meant that the people were physically with ABRI units, the GPK was convinced that people would support them because:

    i The GPK are natives of the region, inspired by regional ideals.
    ii The GPK works for the regional cause so that they are better able to win the confidence of the people than ABRI units.
    iii The GPK will always be able to exploit the weaknesses of ABRI elements, make use of these weaknesses and spread propaganda to the effect that the TNI-ABRI is a colonial army.

b.. The GPK uses the following channels through which to obtain the support of the people:

    i GPK leaders' and members' relatives who are in the settlement areas.
    ii Former GPK members, by reaffirming the oaths they have already taken.
    iii Groups that have grievances because of treatment by ABRI elements.

Besides these channels which emerge spontaneously (*sukarela*) among the people, other methods are used, namely intimidation and terror. In this way, they hope that the people will help them as a result of compulsion or will at least be neutral and passive in critical situations.

c. In order to preserve and cultivate people's support for the GPK, they organise themselves clandestinely so that:

    i ABRI units will have difficulty discovering them.
    ii If they happen to be discovered, only a section will be captured.

Organisation of people's support also takes account of cultural factors so that:

    i It is difficult for ABRI units to take action because of their stupidity or naivety.
    ii If ABRI units do decide to take firm action, this will only arouse people's antipathy because people help them according to traditions based on values acceptable to the community.

d. It is in the eastern sector that people's support is the most militant and most difficult to expose. This is because of the very strong, close family ties and also because it has been possible for the GPK to consolidate its political leadership in this region for several years. This is also because a large part of the population in this region fled to the mountains and only came down to the new villages at the beginning of 1979. In such circumstances, the GPK has consciously chosen the eastern region as its hinterland and reserve base.

e. In waging guerrilla activity, this people's support is used:
  i. As a source of information, logistics and personnel replacement.
  ii For sanctuary during times of pressure.
  iii As guides during times of attack and retreat.

11. *The GPK's Underground Organisation*

a. In developing and ensuring people's support for the GPK, they organise the people and themselves in ways that make it difficult for ABRI units to bring about their total destruction; the importance of information to the conduct of the war is always stressed among all their members. Points particularly emphasised in this connection are:
  i Knowledge of the field of operations and information that makes it possible to have detailed mastery of the situation before launching an operation or setting up guerrilla bases.
  ii Comprehensive, accurate, meticulous and up-to-date information can only be obtained if they can set up networks for military information. These networks must rely on inhabitants who become the eyes and ears of the guerrillas, everywhere and at all times. Great emphasis is placed upon keeping secrets, especially regarding organisation, personnel, contacts, and codes.
  iii Methods of detection used are by moving and living in the midst of the people or by carrying out direct reconnaisance. They can also disguise themselves as, or infiltrate into the ranks of operational support troops (TBO) attached to ABRI units.
  iv The system of communications is linked to the settlements system, so that facilities from the Government and ABRI units can be harnessed both to supply information and to give logistical support as well as to draw people into action. Moreover, to unify their territory in East Timor, they shift round their activists and contacts in the process of guiding the population; many leaders from the east are transferred to the west.

b. In conceptual terms, the GPK undertakes the following covert activities with the support of the people in the following ways:

  i *Integrated mobilisation of the people for the purposes of resistance.*

Here, the GPK realises that the people are the only ones who can turn the guerrilla war they are waging into a revolutionary war. They also realise that without the participation of the people, their military actions will be of minimal significance for ABRI units, nothing more than a few pinches for ABRI.

  ii *Smashing the life forces that are with ABRI*

The targets are members of ABRI, members of the civil guard (Hansip/Wanra) or leaders who are with ABRI. These actions must be carried out by militant GPK members within our midst or amongst our population. If this is successful, the networks will exist right inside ABRI.

  iii *Expanding organisation of the front.*

The door is opened to anyone who does not agree with the Government or ABRI to join the GPK or to take part in its activities. Differences of political opinion or differences in social status or religion are no obstacle to unity. In this connection, the targets are the liurai, the sub-district chiefs (camat), members of the civil guard, the district chiefs (bupatis), members of the provincial assembly, the Army, and others.

  iv *Destroying the enemy*

Organising GPK people's resistance in various regions will result in the dissipation of TNI/ABRI forces. Infiltrating the GPK's covert organisation into the rear will seriously unnerve Operational Command (KOREM 164/WD). Acts of disloyalty among people living around Dili and other large towns will give an image that benefits the GPK's struggle internally and externally.

c. (Having) illegal/covert GPK organisations in the villages is the way to be able to wage protracted guerrilla war.

  i By the use of good organisational techniques, an underground organisation framework has been set up with a complex system of codes. (See Diagram 1, appended) [*This diagram was not included in the captured file.*]

  ii Around every Nurep, a control group is formed which is known as the OD or Orgao Directivo with the following composition:

- Each OD consists of three to six persons.
- The OD members must be chosen from patriots who understand politics, understand the need for secrecy, and are active and ready to sacrifice for the good of the organisation.

iii Furthermore, every Nurep must be in contact with Miplin (*Milicia Popular Libertacão Nacional*—People's Militia for National Liberation) which is the place for fighters with Falintil who have a patriotic spirit, who understand the political line, who are disciplined and have the courage to sacrifice for the sake of the organisation. Each Miplin is set up and organised as follows:
- 1 team composed of five people plus a commander.
- 1 platoon composed of 3 teams plus a commander.
- 1 company composed of 3 platoons plus a commander.
- 1 detachment composed of four or five companies plus a commander.

iv The activities and responsibilities of each section are as follows:
- Each Responsible Chief (*Responsavel Principal*) is responsible to his/her leadership for the activities of the community.
- The AGI and PRO are at all times responsible to the Region Committee for information about the enemy, for the propaganda undertaken, for spreading false information, counter-propaganda information and other underground activities.
- Information connected with military activity (operational movements, arms, routes and so on) is sent direct to the Region Committee as soon as such information is obtained.
- Regarding logistics, all the needs of the RED ZONE are supported by the WHITE ZONE,* in the form of clothes, food, medicines, writing equipment and so on. Implementation is carefully concealed, carried out in relays, and with sealed lips. In addition to catering for direct needs, such activities are directed towards stocking up special stores if conditions permit.

v At the same time, the Miplin also carries out such activities as:
- Secret patrols.
- Infiltration as members of operational support forces (TBO) in Koramil, Kosek, Kodim, as domestic servants in the households of district chiefs and so on.
- Penetration of the civil guard, the police force and the army.

vi The people in charge of the OD/Orgao Directivo and the control bodies try to work at the offices of bupatis, camats, police and Kodim, so as to become well acquainted with the enemy.

---

* Red Zone means Fretilin-held territory. White Zone means Indonesian-occupied territory.

vii Some officials of the Democratic Revolutionary Council are given the task of organising security as well as taking care of espionage, lookout posts, meetings and correspondence.

viii There are Court officials whose duty it is to resolve contradictions that occur within the community so as to prevent negative factors that could jeopardise the interests of the political line.

ix Finally, it is the task and duty of those responsible for the OPMT (Popular Organisation of Timorese Women) to give guidance to women in the kampungs in the struggle, as well as to stamp out prostitution.

x To obtain a clearer picture, Diagram 4 is attached showing the structure of a clandestine organisation which was broken up and the persons holding positions in it, in the District of Baucau. [*This diagram was not included in the captured file.*]

Section IV: The Target of Territorial Intelligence

12. General

The intelligence function includes investigation, consolidation and security. Intelligence activities are concerned with the field of operations, the weather, the GPK and the community which is the object of the contest between the GPK and ABRI units. Specifically in these anti-guerrilla operations, activities are centred on the inhabitants in the communities of the resettlement areas and of the towns which are under ABRI units as well as those which are under the government control.*

Control over all aspects of the life of the community is the key to efforts to separate the GPK from the people. Achieving these objectives is the starting point for operational plans of destruction and at the same time for creating more favourable conditions for operations to restore security in East Timor.

13. Targets

a. The break-up of all support networks in the towns and resettlement areas.

b. Conditions in which all attempts to make contact from the bush can be discovered.

c. Conditions in which all attempts to create new forces or consolidate existing ones in the resettlement areas to support the GPK can be discovered.

d. Conditions in which all attempts by the GPK to hide in the resettlement areas can be discovered.

e. Conditions in which leaders who are neutral and who help the GPK change to siding with TNI-ABRI.

---

* This distinction means that only some towns are run by the provincial government structure. Other towns and population centres are thus under ABRI control, ie. military government.

f. Conditions in which every attempt by inhabitants or the GPK to set up gardens to provide logistical support for the GPK can be discovered.

g. Conditions in which every support network of the guerrillas in the towns and the settlement areas and between several settlement areas can be destroyed.

h. When every attempt by the GPK to recruit members of the civil guard and members of ABRI can be discovered.

Section V: Instructions for Action

15*. General
Various efforts and activities are needed if we are to be able to accomplish certain objectives. They not only include intelligence work, they are an integral part of territorial activities and operations. Moreover, bearing in mind the actual capacity of the existing organisation, it is necessary in the course of implementation to develop the intelligence apparatus and make effective use of the organisation already existing for intelligence operations. Territorial intelligence activities to back up anti-guerrilla operations in East Timor require that special emphasis be placed on extraordinary support procedures so as to ensure that all efforts and activities undertaken are well and truly coordinated. This instruction is intended for every section of the apparatus which is directly connected with the life of the community.

16. Instructions for KODIM activities
a. Establish the level of troublesome-ness of the village according to the following factors:
  i Whether the village is the place of origin of a GPK leader.
  ii Whether the *liurai* or his children are still in the bush.
  iii Whether many of the villagers are still in the bush.
  iv Whether most of the villagers only recently came down from the bush.
  v Whether there are many ex-GPK people in the village who came down expressly in order to smash the TNI from within.
  vi Whether there are many villagers who harbour grievances against members of ABRI because of past misdeeds.
  vii Whether the village is not yet able to produce enough food for its own needs.
  viii Whether the village population is heterogeneous and lacks internal harmony and unity.

---

* The numbering in the original skips 14.

ix Whether all the inhabitants originate from another village that has not yet been rebuilt, so that the land they are now cultivating is not their own land.

b. *Determine the strength of resistance in the following ways:*
   i Interrogate captured GPK members.
   ii Study the results of patrols and contacts from the GPK.
   iii Study confessions made by people who have been in contact with the GPK.
   iv Make an inventory of GPK people still in the bush and people supporting them in the settlement by means of interrogation and isolation and by hunting down people based on interrogation results and espionage patrols.

c. *Physically isolate the GPK supporters by:*
   i Smashing the GPK underground organisation in the settlement area.
   ii Conducting regular and continuous patrols in the vicinity of the settlement area.
   iii Transferring to other places any people who have family ties with GPK members who are in the bush, particularly if they are classified as leaders.

d. *Guarantee security for the people against disturbances from the GPK, including their personal safety and the protection of their property* by:
   i Conducting security patrols.
   ii Setting up alarm-bell systems.
   iii Using danger signals and codes as a means of communication, for instance, by striking bamboo gongs.

17. *Instructions for KORAMIL and PEMBINA DESA activities*
    a. To expose and break up all support networks of the GPK in their regions:
       i Check on how many inhabitants are still in the bush, and find out how many are armed and how many are not armed (Nurep members are not armed).
       ii Look for information about particular Nurep members, for instance GPK people who have recently surrendered or been arrested.
       iii Collect the names of Nurep members who are already in the village or are still in the bush.
       iv Collect information about GPK locations in the bush, and the people who are the Nureps for such places.
       v Discuss and collect information about the approaches leading to GPK locations.
       vi Discuss and draw up methods for capturing Nurep members who are still in the bush.
       vii Isolate all these Nurep members from the rest of the people and keep them in a secure place. Carry out this custodial

system to prevent them from contacting other people and to prevent any leaks about future mopping-up operations.
viii Whenever information about other Nureps is obtained, pass this on immediately to the TPD or Babinsa in question.

b To safeguard village security
   i. Set up posts at places normally used for traffic between villages and on roads leading in and out of the village to the forests and gardens.
   ii Draw up lists of inhabitants, particularly former GPK members and their families.
   iii Send out patrols twice a week to make sure that there are no hidden GPK groups in the vicinity of the village. These patrols should take up positions up to one kilometer from the outskirts of the village. Inform the neighbouring unit whenever a patrol is sent out.
   iv Select and appoint some people to work as agents of the TPD/Babinsa, and make sure that none of them has family ties with the GPK.

c. Some methods or instructions about interrogation techniques.
   i Use interpreters from local people who can be trusted.
   ii Secure confessions in accordance with operational needs in the field, concerning leading members of the organisations or support networks in the town or village, including their known military strength.
   iii Guarantee continued survival to people who are being interrogated if they make honest confessions and are willing to assist further operations.
   iv Begin by telling them that there are colleagues of theirs who are still alive because they made honest confessions and provided positive assistance.
   v Avoid using violence that could result in the person under interrogation sealing his/her lips or giving false information to suit the wishes of the interrogator, and which could spread anxiety in the comn.unity.
   vi Give the person the opportunity to show dedication by participating in a limited operation to give information on pathways or on GPK leaders.
   vii Examples of questions to be asked of a prisoner:
   • What is your work or duty.
   • Who are your friends in the bush or in the village. (If the suspects are village inhabitants, then they are part of the GPK organisational network of the village, but if the person is from another village, it is very likely that this prisoner is a Nurep or a Political Assistant.)
   • The next question is about who gives him/her orders.
   • Where does the prisoner have to meet the person who gives him/her orders.

- What is the position of the person who gives orders.
- Are there any community leaders or civil guard members who are involved in the network.
- How long has he/she worked for the Nurep/Cernak.
- Additional questions can be developed to help uncover the underground network organisation.

d. Instructions for Special Unit (Sat-sat Gas) activities
   i Step up the number of patrols in order to detect GPK concentrations and ensure security in the area of operations, and to prevent the GPK from making contact with the inhabitants.
   ii Maintain contact when a GPK location is detected.
   iii Create security in your respective areas by conducting patrols, setting up spy posts and so on.

e. Instructions for activities of the Battalions
   i Conduct spy patrols continuously in order to discover GPK tracks.
   ii Follow these tracks until you make contact with the GPK.
   iii Preserve these contacts in order to discover the combat units of the enemy/GPK.
   iv Make a thorough survey of your battlefield, the critical battlefield, as well as the approaches, the shooting area, the observation area, and examine all obstructions so as to ensure that there is not an inch of territory with which you are not thoroughly familiar.
   v Study carefully the climatic conditions, including the temperatures, winds and level of humidity in the area of operation.
   vi Make use of prisoners to obtain information about climatic conditions and about the GPK in your area of operation.
   vii The companies, platoons and teams in each battalion must carry out the instructions implemented by the Battalion in greater detail, in conformity with their own field of operation and operational area, as well as the conditions and situation of each respective area of responsibility.

f. Instructions for Police Force activities
   i Keep a check on all law infringements and crimes committed in your region.
   ii Investigate them so as to decide whether they are purely criminal or not.
   iii If they are purely criminal, deal with them quickly according to the law, whilst not overlooking the possibility that they may need to be developed for operational purposes, and if not, hand them over quickly to the nearest territorial unit or combat unit for more thorough investigation. All measures taken should support the objective of coordinating

       activities to deal with the GPK.
     iv Explain to the community the need for law and order.
     v All these activities should be carried out comprehensively and aimed at achieving security in East Timor.
  g. Instructions for the regional administrations (Pemda)
      i Use political/social channels to ferret out two-faced people/officials in the administration, among others, by screening and by exercising supervision over all people under suspicion.
     ii Be vigilant of government officials who sometimes or often make negative or dubious remarks.
     iii From the sub-district (*kecamatan*) down to the village (*kelurahan*) level, conduct activities to detect people who may be under suspicion.
     iv Discover people who are still in contact with the GPK by closely watching everyday activities of their people and if anything suspicious is found, report it to the local territorial unit.
     v Draw up a complete list of all inhabitants, giving their respective occupations.
     vi Continually remind people of the criminality and danger posed by the GPK for community life so as to arouse the community to feelings and acts against the GPK.
     vii Educate the community to be conscious of the need to report anything they know about the GPK or about GPK underground support networks.

Section VI: Final Section

18. The criteria of success

Success in creating the required conditions, both by setting up a system of detection or organising the inhabitants, can be evaluated on the basis of the following criteria:
  a. *Conditions are favourable to us if:*
      i The inhabitants feel that any attempt by the GPK to approach or enter their settlement area is thoroughly disruptive of their life.
     ii Every time contact is discovered between the inhabitants and the GPK, people in the place feel disconcerted and unity in the village is undermined.
     iii Every attempt by the GPK to make contact with the settlement area is considered as being a source of suffering and unrest for the GPK.
     iv Every inhabitant who discovers anything about links between other inhabitants and the GPK quickly reports this to the local military authority.
     v All community leaders are willing and courageous enough

to resist the GPK with or without ABRI units encouraging them to do so.
vi All former GPK people can be used as people's units to resist the GPK.

b. *The apparatus is working well if:*
i Every change occurring in the community is known. To achieve this, every official must be sensitive to his environment.
ii Every time an inhabitant goes out of the area, the direction, destination, time and reason are known.
iii Any time goods that could be used as logistics for the guerrillas are shifted to or from the area to places suspected as GPK areas, information of this is speedily available and preventive action is taken.
iv No inhabitant's home is being used as a hideout for the GPK, with periodic checks being made.
v In all fields of life, it is possible to discover efforts to set up GPK support networks and detect the existence of such networks, and to keep informed of the relationship between these two aspects of life.

19. All people, from those in positions of top leadership down to the lowest ranking members, bear a responsibility to implement and control the terms of this Established Procedure (Protap) and to do so with flexibility, so as to ensure that implementation in the field can attain good results according to conditions.

20. Everyone in charge must understand the contents of this Protap, and implementation in the field must represent a combination of all the instructions and incorporate every intelligence matter referred to in this Protap.

21. There must be close coordination between all parts of the apparatus in each region, and every step must be taken after consultations so as to ensure that implementation is efficient and comprehensive, in accordance with the conditions prevailing in the region.

22. Matters encountered in your region which are not dealt with in this Protap should be channelled to your superiors so that they can be used to improve this Protap.

23. This Territorial Intelligence Protap is valid throughout the area of Korem 164/Wira Dharma.

24. The end.

Issued in Dili on (date not given)

Commander:
(signed)
A. Sahala Rajagukguk
Infantry Colonel No. 18805

Document 4

Instruction Manual No: JUKNIS/01-A/IV/1982
Subject: The Village as the Focal Point of Attention
and How to Guide It Comprehensively.

I. Introduction

Until now, we have tended in our territorial activities to be guided by the following way of thinking:

- The District Command (Kodim) commander and his staff pay attention in general to the whole district for which they are responsible and pay attention in somewhat more detail to each of the Sub-district commands (Koramil)/kecamatan;
- The Sub-district Command (Koramil) commander and his staff pay attention to the sub-district (kecamatan) for which they are responsible and pay attention in somewhat more detail to each village/Babinsa.

Meanwhile, the 'whys and hows' of the inner workings (*isi perut*) of the village fall completely under the competence of the Babinsas.

This hierarchical or 'ladder-like' way of thinking is suitable if all parts of the territorial apparatus are able to function effectively and can handle a society where conditions are stable and where problems do not arise.

But in dealing with the guerrillas in East Timor, this way of thinking needs to be improved upon, by making the village the focal point of attention for all sections of the territorial apparatus. In other words, the District Commands, the Sub-district Commands and the Babinsas must all have a clear understanding of the inner workings of each and every village, the problems they face, and the way to guide them so that the communities have a better picture of things.

II. Why the village as the focal point of attention?

The previous instruction manual explained how the remaining GPK are trying to 'wrest control of the village' by establishing support networks via the Nurep. Conversely, we too are trying to guide the village via the Babinsa, so as to immunise it against such GPK influence. In other words, every village will become the object of a contest between ourselves and the GPK. And whoever wins that will also win the guerrilla/anti-guerrilla war.

1. The Babinsa guides; 2. The nurep creates a network

That is why every level of the territorial apparatus, the Kodims, the Koramils and the Babinsas, must focus attention upon the village. And this is why Team Pembina Desa (TPD) have lately been sent into those villages specially thought to be troublesome.

III. How to guide the village comprehensively

By 'comprehensively' is meant knowing the village inside-out, in its entirety—its conditions, the problems faced by its inhabitants—and also guiding it in the sense of painting a better picture of life.

Activities to be carried out for this purpose:

1. Looking at the 'inner workings' of every village:
Instruction Manual No. JUKNIS/01/XI/1981, of 15-11-1981 concerning the keeping of a book for the Babinsa's data and events, explains that in order to know a village well, it is essential to have data and notes on events within the village. These include:

  a. Sketch map of the old village (pre-upheaval).
  b. Sketch map of the present village.
  c. Village security system.
  d. Genealogy of the chieftain.
  e. List of village government officials.
  f. List of catechists.
  g. List of other community figures.
  h. Etc., (refer to the above-mentioned manual).

It is not only the Babinsa who needs to have such data, but also the Koramil and Kodim. Thus every level of the territorial apparatus will know for certain the inner workings of the villages.

Example of looking at the inner workings of Bualale village:
  a. Bualale consists of two kampungs, Lia Lura and Ossomeca. In the time of the Portuguese, the inhabitants were spread between the two kampungs. With the upheavals, they fled into the bush. Once they had returned, they were resettled in the present location—the kecamatan town of Quelicai—in May 1979. But this led to their being unable to grow food on their own land, so that food shortages have occurred. Thus efforts are currently being made to get the people back to their original lands—about 4km. to the south of

Quelicai—as part of a programme for the settlement of 30 villages.

b. Bualale is the native village of the GPK figure David Alex (Commander of Red Brigade Company II), and thus has always been an area in which he operates. Moreover the area is extremely fertile—another reason for the move back to the original lands. While the people will be able to grow things, thus preventing food shortages, the move will also cut down the GPK's area of operations, especially that of the David Alex group.

c. Village inhabitants number 413: 206 male, 207 female.

d. The number of villagers still in the bush is 15, including David Alex.

e. Regarding the relatives of these villagers who are still in the bush:
    i 13 have been sent to Atauro
    ii 2 have not yet been sent to Atauro
    iii None has yet returned from Atauro

f. Ex-GPKs currently living in the village number 17 persons.

g. The former village head, Francisco Freitas, is at present in Buibao, while the new one, Batholomeus, carries a fair amount of authority with the inhabitants and is assisting the operation for the restoration of security.

h. Apart from the village head, there are two community figures with quite a lot of influence, i.e. a religious teacher (catechist) and an elder. If they are properly guided, they should both be very useful.

i. The people's participation in security and development is fairly good; even so, it is believed that there is still a network of GPK supporters, either because they are afraid, are being forced, or for other reasons.

j. Hansip/Wanra strength stands at 10 persons with 7 weapons.

k. A Ratih unit of one platoon with 10 weapons has been set up.

l. There are four Hansip/Wanra/Ratih widows requiring special attention.

m. The number of people outside Hansip/Wanra/Ratih who could be mobilised at any time is 50.

n. Additional data which could be compiled and which would depict the condition of the village.

2. *Identifying problems faced by the villagers:*

Bring together the local community figures, the village head, the kampung heads, teachers and any other influential figures, and invite them to discussions identifying the problems the community faces in security and development. The results of such discussions will help to complete the picture of the village's inner workings obtained from the earlier data.

This kind of discussion should be carried out not only by the Babinsa/TPD, but also by Koramil and Kodim when they go to the village. Thus each level will really get to know the conditions and problems faced by the village concerned.

These discussions are most necessary, so that guidance plans which we formulate really accord with the needs of the local people. We often have plans which are in our own opinion good, but what is good for us is not necessarily good for the local people. That is why the opinions of the local community figures have to be listened to. If a plan is drawn up jointly, the easier its subsequent implementation will be, because the people will feel they have been involved.

Example of conducting a discussion:
Throw out some questions, e.g. How do the community figures think security could quickly be restored? What should be done so that there are no longer people who support the GPK? What do they think is the best way to get remaining GPK back in from the bush? What type of development do they think the village needs?

A variety of questions like these will produce opinions we had not previously thought of. If these are in line with our planned operations, so much the better, and we can go ahead as planned. If not, e.g. if they request the return of relatives from Atauro, then we will have to explain once again the reasons for their relatives' having been removed to Atauro.

3. Drawing up guidance plans:
Based on the outcome of the aforementioned discussions, draw up a good guidance plan dealing with security and development. Because such a plan is the result of consultation, it will obviously gain the people's support in its implementation. In this way the people will not just feel that they are being dictated to. A plan of this type must basically paint a better picture of life for the people.

4. Carry out evaluation (reassessment):
Once a plan has been implemented, carry out reassessment. Have things gone as planned? What were the shortcomings, what was the outcome? And so on. This is important as source material for further planning.

IV. Control command of the village must also be comprehensive

There may be a variety of officers in the village, eg. Babinsa and Binpolda; members of Battalion 745 charged with guiding the Ratih; a Territorial NCO (*Bater*) from another unit; an intelligence NCO (*Ba Intel*) from the Satgas Intel or other units, and the Team Pembina Desa. All these officials must be able to coordinate so as to form a 'comprehensive team'.

The oldest person will take over leadership of the Team. If it so happens that there is a TPD member of officer rank in the village, this officer will be leader of the Team. Nevertheless, the Team Leader will use the available personnel in accordance with their respective duties— the Babinsa, Binpol and Territorial Officers from other units will be used to undertake territorial activities as well as *kamtibmas* (public security and order) activities. Members of Battalion 745 will be used to give guidance to Ratih forces. Intelligence Officers from other units as well as from *Sat Gas Intel* (Special Intelligence Unit) will be used for intelligence activities. In those villages where there is a *Team Pembina Desa* (TPD), command control will be directly in the hands of the District Command commander(*Kodim*). Even so, the TDP must coordinate with the local Sub-District Command (*Koramil*) commander as well as with villages nearby.

If there is no member of the TPD of officer rank, the oldest non-commissioned officer will be the one to lead the Team. If it so happens that an NCO from Battalion 745 is the oldest, then he is the one who will lead the Team. If the territorial NCO or the intelligence NCO happens to be the oldest, then he is the one who will lead the Team. In villages where there are no TPDs, command control will remain in the hands of the Sub-District Command commander (*Koramil*). Even so, he must coordinate with neighbouring villages and the nearest TPD.

In this way, command control in each and every village will be comprehensive.

Final Section

By making the village the focal point of attention at every level of the territorial apparatus—for the Kodims, the Koramils, the TPDs or Babinsas—and by giving comprehensive guidance because there is comprehensive command and control (*Kodal*), it is to be hoped that it will be possible to speed up operations to restore security. May we be successful because God is with us all.

Issued in Dili, 10th September 1982

Chief of Intelligence,

(signed)

Williem da Costa,
Infantry Major, NRP No. 24293.

Document 5

Instruction Manual No: JUKNIS/04-B/IV/1982
Subject: How to Protect the Community from the Influence of GPK Propaganda

I. Introduction

In Instruction Manual Number JUKNIS/04/III/1982 issued on 19 March 1982, it was stated that GPK 'support networks' exist in all settlements, the villages as well as the towns. The present Instruction Manual will describe the experience of how one such GPK support network was set up in a settlement, with propaganda through which they succeeded in influencing the people. By knowing how the GPK support networks are set up, it will be possible for us to take measures to prevent this from happening.

II. The Process of Setting Up a Support Network in a Settlement

> a. In every settlement, there are people, people's gardens as well as *Nureps* (GPK members responsible for guiding the settlements).
> b. Guidance or propaganda can be undertaken by the Nurep by means of writing letters or by making direct contact, that is to say, by coming to meet people when they are tending their gardens.
>
> At the first meeting, the Nurep/GPK explains:
> > i That GPK forces elsewhere are getting stronger.
> > ii That these forces include not only people but weapons and equipment as well.
> > iii More help will soon come from the towns as well as from other countries such as Russia, China, Vietnam, Africa and elsewhere.
> > iv That the GPK will soon be victorious.
> > v For this, the people and former GPK members who have come down from the bush do not need to go into the bush; they should stay in the villages to create forces so as to be ready to take action at any time. To develop these forces, future battles will be waged in other places.

c. When the people return home from their gardens, they don't report this to the Babinsa/village chief for fear of being interrogated, asked questions and so on. Rather than create any fuss and bother, it is safer to say nothing. But since the gardens mean life or death to them, they return to them when the next opportunity arises. This time, the Nurep/GPK comes to meet them for the second time.

1. Settlement; 2. People go to the gardens; 3. Nurep/GPK make contact for the second time

At this second meeting, the Nurep/GPK explains:
  i That they have just received more help from the towns. To prove it, they show the people ammunition, clothes, medicines, food and so on. There is already quite a lot of this material, they say, being stored in caves. When the time comes, these supplies are going to be put to use, but for the time being, they are still wearing their old clothes.
  ii That former GPK members who have come down from the bush have already been able to create forces. In fact, the GPK *bot-bot* (leader) who was previously in the bush has now become a *bot-bot* in a town, and they are ready to go into action.
  iii That it won't be long now before they win victory. People who don't or don't yet support them will be brought before people's courts and punished with forced labour. Although people can still tend their gardens, they should remember that the gardens are located in territory that is under GPK control.

d. At the next meeting, the Nurep/GPK tells the people:
  i Propaganda about successes scored in other areas such as Los Palos, Manatuto, the western sector and so on.
  ii Propaganda as well about other victories, all of which arouses among the people feelings of confidence and fear.

e. Influenced by such propaganda, whether consciously or out of fear, the people then seek out friends in the settlement and create a force under someone's leadership. (In this particular experience, the leader was a sixth-form primary school pupil. The force included a company commander, a platoon commander as well as a team commander.)

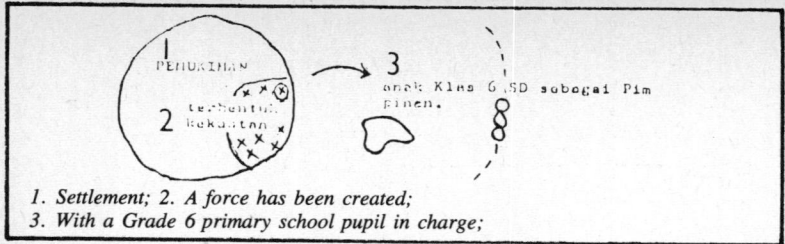

1. Settlement; 2. A force has been created;
3. With a Grade 6 primary school pupil in charge;

f. The GPK then instructs a member to surrender deliberately together with his weapons. Because this person has surrendered, he is treated well by the officer. After receiving guidance and having given good account of himself by taking part in an operation, the person is appointed commander of a *ratih* platoon. After a while, the schoolboy hands over leadership of the force that has been created to the GPK member who surrendered, and stays on himself as deputy leader.

g. When they consider that their force has become strong enough, they make plans to take over the settlement by launching a joint attack, combining outside GPK forces with the force that has been created inside the settlement.

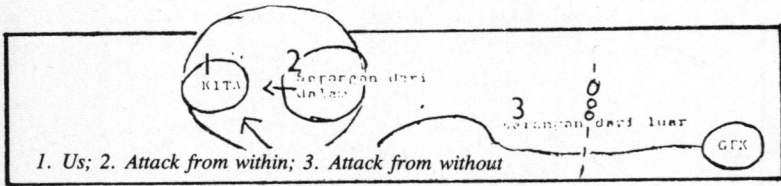

1. Us; 2. Attack from within; 3. Attack from without

h. Fortunately, this plan was soon exposed and the GPK underground support network was broken up. It turned out that 24 Ratih members were involved in the group.

III. Ways to protect people from the influences of GPK propaganda

An experience like the above, based on actual fact, must not be allowed to occur again in any settlement or town. In order to prevent this happening, the Kodim, Koramil and in particular the Team Pembina Desa (TPD) and Babinsa must carry out various activities, including:

1. Intensify control of the population.
Every single activity of the population must be known exactly, in the following ways:
a. Appoint reliable people as *Katuas** to help neighbourhood chiefs (RT). Arrange it in such a way that each *Katuas* takes responsibility for 10-15 families.

---

* *katuas*—'elder' in Tetum.

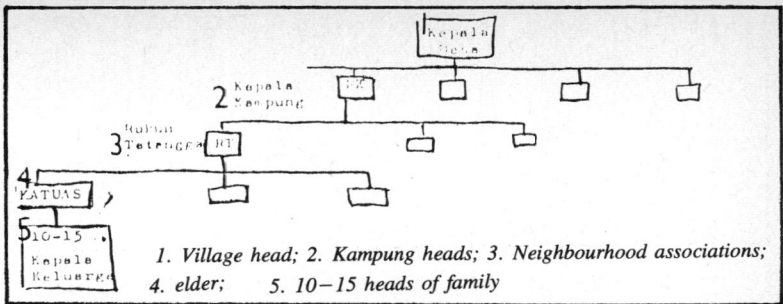

1. Village head; 2. Kampung heads; 3. Neighbourhood associations; 4. elder; 5. 10–15 heads of family

Each *katuas* must be able to know exactly the activities of the families under his guidance; for example, when they go to their field, go to collect wood, get permission to go to another village, to tend flocks, go to market and so on.

b. Appoint an 'informer' in each of these groups of 10-15 families led by one katuas. This informer should be able to follow, secretly, all the activities of these 10-15 families.

c. Every time anyone goes out of the village, he/she must have a travel pass (*surat jalan*), and every person who comes into the village from another village must report.

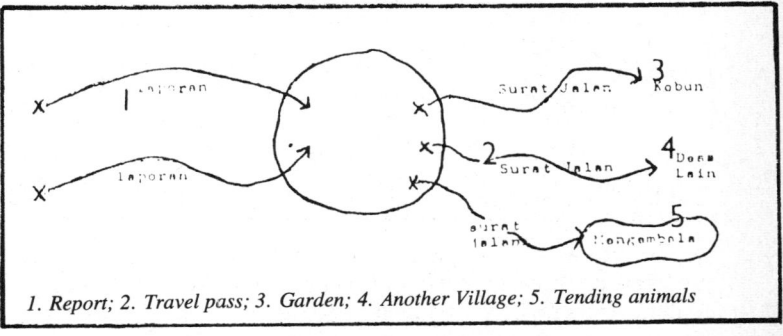

1. Report; 2. Travel pass; 3. Garden; 4. Another Village; 5. Tending animals

d. Inspection posts must be set up to keep a check on everyone who enters or leaves the village.

e. Maintain an element of surprise (*pendadakan*) by holding extraordinary roll-calls, or by having check-ups on the population by the katuas, to check whether anyone has left without permission or whether anyone has arrived from another village without reporting.

f. Take other actions, according to circumstances in each village, for the purpose of intensifying control over the population. For instance, house-to-house visits, and patrols inside the village to prevent illegal meetings from taking place there.

2. *Re-arrange the location of gardens and fields of the population.*

a. There should be no gardens or fields of the people located far from the settlement or village.
b. No garden or field of anyone in the village should be isolated

(situated far from the others). Arrange preferably for all the gardens and fields to be close to each other.

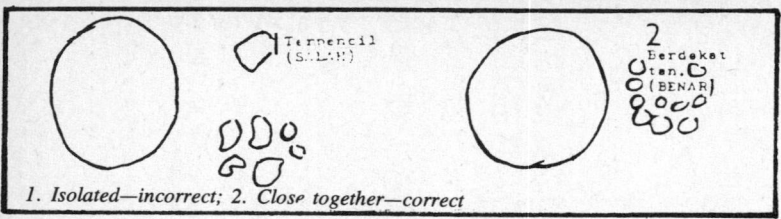
1. Isolated—incorrect; 2. Close together—correct

c. When people go to their gardens or fields, no-one should go alone; they should go and return together.

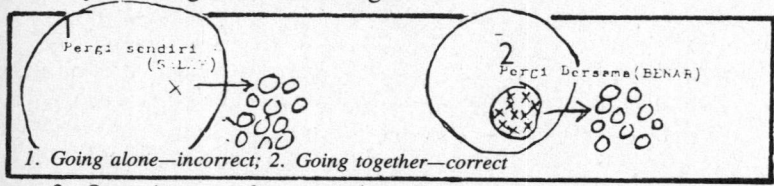
1. Going alone—incorrect; 2. Going together—correct

3. *Organise patrols round the village.*
a. Organise patrols round the village particularly in the vicinity of the gardens and fields of the people, so as to prevent any meetings between the *Nurep/GPK* and the population.

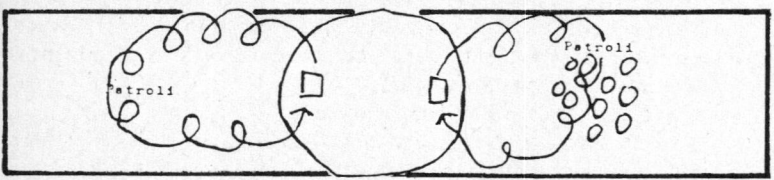

b. Go round during the night stealthily, particularly to the people's gardens and fields.

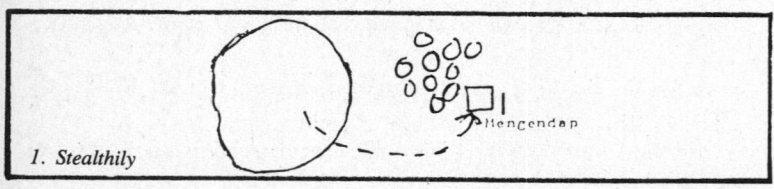
1. Stealthily

c. In addition to these patrols, send 'satellites' to places round the village where it is suspected that meetings between *Nurep/GPK* and the population might take place.

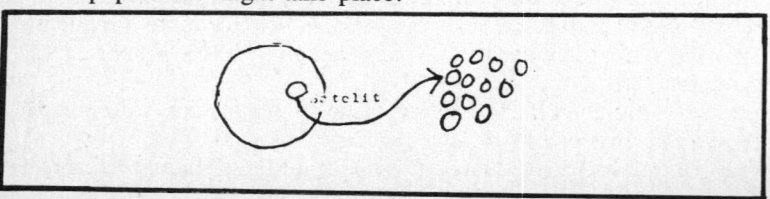

d. Protect the population's gardens and fields from disturbances/thefts/attacks by the GPK.

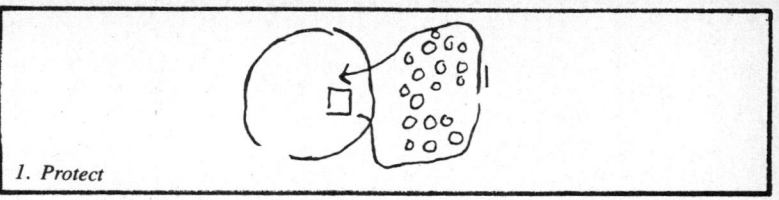

1. Protect

4. Consolidate Hansip and Ratih.

a. Get to know the members of Hansip and Ratih and their families one by one.
b. Carry out activities listed in Instruction Manual No. JUKNIS/06/IV/1982, April 2, 1982 regarding the activities of the Babinsa/TPD in promoting and phasing out trained people's resistance forces, under point 9c.2, namely:
    i by establishing a high standard of discipline, like the discipline in ABRI:
    ii give constant indoctrination about consciousness to defend the state and prevent infiltration of negative influences from GPK remnants. Explain that the GPK tries to influence them, as described above. (The process of setting up GPK support networks). Explain that everything the GPK says is untrue. This will ensure that Hansip and Ratih are not influenced by their propaganda.
    iii Keep strict control of weapons.
    iv Re-check so as to make sure that there are no GPK sympathisers among the members of the Hansip and Ratih.
    v Appoint as their leaders (team, platoon and company commanders) people who can be one hundred per cent trusted by us.
    vi Show appreciation to those who have achievements to their credit.

c. Provide opportunities for Hansip and Ratih to rest, so as to give them a chance to tend a garden or field.
d. Provide them with the opportunity for recreation, such as sports and so on.

5. Organise information work to neutralise GPK propaganda.

a. Kodim will try to send information teams consisting of community leaders and ex-GPK people who are now helping us, to provide information in the village, to explain that all the GPK propaganda is untrue.
b. In addition, efforts will be made to send films showing the government's efforts to develop East Timor.
c. Efforts will also be made to provide a Map of Indonesia, showing East Timor's location in the territory of Indonesia.

d. Whilst waiting for the above three points to materialise, each Babinsa/TPD will give information to Hansip and Ratih members, to the ex-GPK in the village, as well as to the inhabitants. The ways to do this include:

    i Supply information about the things that are to be explained to community leaders and ex-GPK who are now helping us. For example:
- That GPK propaganda is untrue.
- That the government, together with the entire people of East Timor, is now trying hard to develop East Timor so that the living conditions of the community improve.

    ii Train these community leaders and ex-GPK who are to become information experts to explain these matters in the presence of an interpreter who can be trusted.

    iii Gather the people together and instruct this information person to give a talk and instruct the interpreter to check that the person says the right things.

    iv Besides giving direct information in this way, carry out indirect information work by giving people who can be trusted the task of making home visits to the people of the village.

    v Give the best possible guidance to those ex-GPK people who have come down from the bush:
- keep them under special supervision;
- give them things to do to keep them busy;
- consider their living circumstances so that they get a better picture of life; for instance, consider providing them with a home, a garden or field, and so on;
- hold frequent discussions with them to fill their minds with the correctness of integration, so as to eliminate any remaining ideas from the time they were in the bush;
- tell them about the efforts being made by their comrades still in the bush to influence them, so that they remain vigilant and don't allow themselves to be influenced.

IV. Final Section

This Instruction Manual is issued to complement earlier Manuals, particularly regarding territorial intelligence. Because the Babinsa and TPD are the most 'advanced' territorial element, the success or otherwise of our efforts to protect people from the influences of GPK propaganda depends to a very great extent upon these Babinsa and TPD. Therefore, these instructions must be implemented as well as possible.

    All success to you in the performance of your duty, because God is on our side.

Issued in Dili, on 10th September 1982

Intelligence Officer
Williem da Costa
Infantry Major No. 24293

Document 6

Instruction Manual No. JUKNIS/06/IV/1982
Subject: Babinsa/TPD Activity in developing and phasing out Trained People's Resistance Forces.

[*Parts of this Manual are illegible. Several sections are concerned with treatment and rewards for members of the 'trained people's forces' and the Civil Guard (Hansip) who have been killed or wounded in combat. These latter sections are less relevant to an understanding of ABRI's strategies and tactics, and are omitted. The following translation therefore includes only extracts from this Instruction Manual.*]

I. Introduction

In support of operations for the restoration of security in East Timor, there are Wanra units (which we generally refer to as 'Hansip' or Civil Guards) in every *Koramil* (Sub-district Military Command)/Babinsa area. The members receive a regular monthly payment of 33 kilograms of rice (for operations and for their family) plus a sum of Rp. 11,500. In addition, every Koramil/Babinsa area has, since the *Operasi Kikis* (The 'Chipping-Away' Operation), set up Ratih (trained people's) units which receive support (rice or corn) only when out on operation. Instruction Manual No. JUKNIS/01/XI/1981 issued on 15 November 1981 concerning the keeping of Log-books on Data and Activity by the Babinsa, stated that the Wanra forces would in future be phased out step by step, whilst at the same time developing the Ratih forces. This is intended as a start towards developing a consciousness among the Timorese people of the need to defend the State, towards developing the realisation by every single citizen that he/she has the right and duty to take part without reserve in the defence of the State. Experience shows that Wanra participation in operations for the restoration of security is not yet supported by a profound consciousness of the need to defend the State. The members are driven by a variety of motivations, such as:

    a. Wanting to get back to normal quickly so that they can work calmly to build the region.
    b. Feelings of revenge because the person or his/her relatives were cruelly treated by Fretilin/GPK

c. Simply in order to get money, rice and so on.
d. They don't want their kampung or village, or their personal possessions to be frequently disrupted by the GPK.
e. They want to show themselves off as men of courage.
f. They have switched from supporting the GPK to supporting us after seeing that they can get a better life if they follow us than if they follow the GPK.

If not seriously dealt with, the plans to phase out Wanra and develop Ratih will cause unrest which has already been used as an issue by the GPK. [*The following sentence is illegible.*]

II. The Plan to phase out Wanra [Omitted]

III. Plan to develop Ratih

a. *The Present Situation of Ratih*
In accordance with Instruction Manual No. JUKNIS/03/XI/1981 on activities of the Babinsas during territorial operations, page 12, section 23.e, a Ratih unit has been set up in every village with a strength that conforms with the capabilities of the local population. These Ratih units were set up in the frame of bringing into being a system of village defence. As distinct from Wanra (normally known as Hansip or Civil Defence), Ratih members do not receive regular support. Support is only provided when they are out on operations and cannot therefore eat at home. What we expect from these Ratih members is a reasonably high level of consciousness about the need to defend the State, so that they are prepared to fight for and defend integration without reserve.

b. *The plan to develop Ratih*
In principle every person who has received training to defend the state is a 'Ratih'. However, in view of the limited logistical supplies available (even for operations), a procedure needs to be introduced about developing Ratih in step with the phasing out of Wanra (Hansip), as follows:
    i. Based on estimates about the level of security and troublesome-ness of the region, the Kodim will determine the number of Ratih needed (who can be supported during operations), and this shall be proposed to the Sub-Regional Command (*Korem*).
    ii Korem shall determine the number of Ratih members allocated for a period of operations (three months) based on the phasing out and transferral of Wanra members, bearing in mind the degree of troublesomeness in the Kodim area in question.
    iii The Kodim will divide out the Ratih forces permitted to them among the Koramils in accordance with the needs of each Koramil.

iv Korem will inform Hansip Regional HQ of Wanra reductions and the numerical increase in the strength of Ratih.
  v Hansip Regional HQ will keep administrative records of the changes in the strength of Wanra and Ratih.
  vi The increase in strength of the Ratih will come from:
  - Former Wanra members who have been phased out.
  - New members recruited from the community.

[*The next page does not follow consecutively from the above points. There then follow several sections regarding treatment of killed and wounded members of Wanra, which are omitted here.*]

Guidance of Wanra (Hansip) and Ratih

1. The Wanra (Hansip) and Ratih units in each village reflect the level of people's resistance, to implement and defend integration which has already been approved of by the entire people of East Timor. In general, these forces are armed and therefore comprise a force of strength. So as to ensure that these forces are really and truly directed towards our fixed target, namely the GPK remnants who are the enemy of the people of East Timor, it is necessary to give them continual guidance. Without such continual guidance, their weapons could be mis-directed, and could for instance be used to strike fear among the people or could even become a boomerang against the people and ABRI.

2. Babinsa/TPD Activities in giving guidance to Wanra (Hansip) and Ratih

> a. *Implant a high level of discipline, comparable to discipline in ABRI.* They should therefore be subject to the same laws that apply to members of ABRI, such as KUHPT and KUHDT. [*Special legal codes for the Indonesian Armed Forces*] In order to enforce this discipline, members of Battalion 745 have been deployed to assist the Babinsas.
> b. *Give constant indoctrination about the need for consciousness to defend the State and to prevent the infiltration of negative GPK influences.* Up to the present, GPK remnants are always trying to influence Wanra (Hansip) and Ratih forces, to get them to help the GPK and turn against the government. Such efforts must be foiled by every Babinsa/TPD by means of giving continual indoctrination.
> c. *Exercise careful control of weapons.* All weapons in the hands of Wanra (Hansip) and Ratih forces must be very well supervised and controlled. The best way is to have them stored away whenever they are not in use. They should only be handed out when operations are in progress.
> d. *Re-check to make sure that no members of Wanra (Hansip) and Ratih are GPK sympathisers.* Every Babinsa/TPD must be able to know them all one by one. Examine their background, their life

history and their motivation for joining Wanra (Hansip) and Ratih. If there are any indications that any members still sympathise with the GPK, these persons must immediately be taken into custody (withdrawn to Koramil/Kodim).

e. *Appoint as commanders (from team and platoon level upwards) of Wanra (Hansip) and Ratih forces people who we can trust one hundred per cent.* Exercise constant control over these commanders and fill their motivation with the defence of the State.

f. *Give proper rewards to those who have accomplishments to their credit.* Inform Koramil of any members with good accomplishments to their credit to be reported to Kodim. Kodim will give due reward, in accordance with its capacity.

How to handle the TBO

1. The TBO (*Tenaga Bantuan Operasi*—Operational Support Force) is also composed of trained people; they are outside Wanra (Hansip) and Ratih. They are the ones who normally go out with the troops on operations. Because they have mixed with members of ABRI for quite a long time, TBO or ex-TBO members are in some respects ahead: for instance they can speak Indonesian, their state of health is good, they are relatively young (between 12 and 35 years old) and they have a sense of loyalty towards ABRI with whom they have operated. Nevertheless, without proper guidance, these TBO members can themselves be a source of trouble. For instance, they have a very precise knowledge of the weaknesses and strength of the troops with whom they operate, and such information can easily be passed on to the GPK. There are plenty of experiences to show that TBO members have fled to the bush and joined forces with the GPK because of lack of proper guidance.

2. Babinsas/TPD Activities in giving guidance to the TBO

a. Try to ensure that former TBO members who are no longer used by the troops become members of the local Ratih.

b. Those of school age should be encouraged to go back to school, whilst those who meet the necessary criteria and are aged between 18-25 can become members of Ratih units and then members of ABRI.

c. Give them continual guidance so that they are not influenced by the GPK.

d. All units that need TBO forces must make a request to the local Babinsa/TPD and then return them [*some words unclear*] where the TBO were first requested. The return of TBO members must be accompanied by a nominative *(sic)* and administrative list, especially if TBO members have been wounded or killed.

Final Section

The Babinsa and TPD are in the forefront of our territorial apparatus.

Therefore, the success or otherwise of our efforts to organise these Trained People's forces depends to a very great extent upon these Babinsa/TPD. Keep this constantly in mind, implement all instructions as effectively as possible, and here's wishing you all the best in the performance of your duties. The Lord God is with you all.

Issued in Dili, on 10 September 1982

Chief of Intelligence
(signed)

Williem da Costa,
Infantry Major NRP no. 24293.

Document 7

Military Regional Command XVI, Udayana
Military Resort Command 164/Wira Dharma
Established Procedure for Conducting Razzias (Raids) on Settlement Areas (Protap/01/VII/1982)

I. Introduction

1. General

Anti-guerrilla operations which are now in progress in accordance with Instruction INSOP/02/XI/1981 and Protap 01 which is an instruction manual for territorial intelligence activities, are considered not to have achieved the operational targets set yet; it has not yet been possible to break up the clandestine organisations existing in the settlements. In addition, experience so far shows that guerrilla tactics of always getting close to the kampungs or villages, particularly when they are hard-pressed, mean that we have to devote far greater attention to the settlements. If our pursuit of guerrillas is to be more successful, there is a need to issue instructions about conducting razzias in the settlement areas so as to ensure that these areas and their environs will eventually be completely clean of the influence and presence of guerrillas.

2. Objective

This Protap is issued for the purpose of achieving uniformity of action particularly in conducting razzias in the settlement aeas so that ultimately the guerrillas will no longer use these settlements as hideouts, particularly at times when pursuit operations are in progress.

3. Scope

The scope of this Protap includes techniques for conducting razzias in the settlement areas and the target of these razzias. The systematic is as follows:

    a. Introduction
    b. GPK efforts to get close to the Settlement Areas.
    c. Techniques for dealing with the GPK.
    d. Conclusions.
    e. Final Section.

II. GPK Efforts to Get Close to the Settlement Areas

4. General

The fact the the GPK still exists and can continue to survive is made possible because there are still people in the settlement areas who help them logistically with information and by providing them with hideouts. This is the basis for the GPK's guerrilla tactics of getting close to the settlement areas in certain circumstances, which they do for the purpose of:

   a. Contacting their networks.
   b. Influencing the people.
   c. Waging terror and intimidation.
   d. Evading our operations.

5. Contacting their networks

Protap number 01 INSOP 02 explained how the GPK establishes organisational networks in the settlements to support their struggle. The territorial apparatus (*Apter*) and political apparatus (*Appol*) must always remain vigilant and suspect everyone in the community of the area for which they are responsible, and must strive to eliminate any GPK organisations that exist in the settlement. Once the GPK have managed to establish an organisational network in a settlement, they will go on trying to get close to and make contact with people who side with them, and this will ensure the GPK of continued survival and endanger life for the rest of the community.

Example:

In the region of Uatolari, the GPK has succeeded in establishing an organisational network. From the security point of view, the region is safe from disturbances by the GPK because the GPK will not create disturbances in a region that supports its operations, but GPK members continually come to this region or get close to it for all kinds of everyday needs and for their struggle.

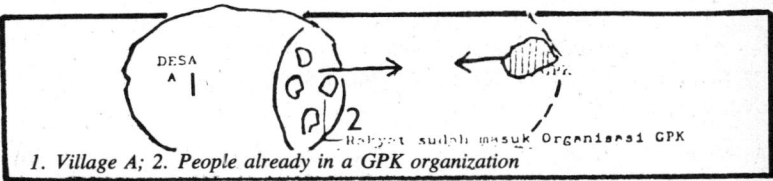

1. Village A; 2. People already in a GPK organization

6. Influencing the people

In those regions where they do not yet have an underground organisation, they use the method of trying to influence the people in the settlement to support them. In the first instance, this takes the form of simply having a meeting, and this subsequently develops into meetings for the purpose of obtaining help. Once this is proceeding well, efforts are then directed towards forming an organisation or at the very least influencing the people to side with them and not to report their presence in the settlement.

Example:
In Vinilale, in the first instance, they only met people who went to look for food in their former village. Eventually they were able, after several meetings, to develop the contact into the creation of a network.

7. Waging Terror and Intimidation
In regions where the community is consciously helping ABRI and community leaders fully support operations to restore security, the GPK wage terror and intimidation—robberies, murders and arson as well as kidnapping people or community leaders in the area. These activities are intended as a warning to the community or its leaders not to help ABRI.

Example:
The terror and intimidation they waged in Quilikai against a member of the Baucau Sub-Regional People's Assembly, their attack on Nunira Kampung when they also planned to kidnap the Ratih company commander in Nunira.

8. Evading our Operations
In the face of security operations conducted by ABRI together with *Ratih* and civil guard units, the GPK use a relatively small number of people to conduct guerrilla operations so as to elude our operations. They do this in a variety of ways, such as:

> a. Evading us and quickly merging in with the community in the settlement area. This is only possible if there are people in the settlement area who are on their side.

Example:
Kikis ('Chipping-Away') Operation 'C' in Laga region, on which occasion, the GPK were able when encircled to use Nunira Kampung as a hideout.

> b. If the GPK are not able to merge, the method used is to escape from the encircled area and stay in another region where the people are willing to accept their presence.

III. Techniques for dealing with the GPK

9. General
In dealing with the guerrillas, the best thing is to wage anti-guerrilla operations in which the basic activity is aimed at separating the guerrillas from the People supporting them.

In order to separate the GPK from the People supporting them, one way is to guard against or prevent the GPK from the entering settlement areas to hide. A good way of dealing with their efforts to hide in settlement areas is to conduct kampung *razzias*. These razzias can be conducted by:

> a. Conducting repeated razzias but at irregular intervals (irregular razzias).

b. Conducting razzias in settlement areas located in the vicinity where the target for an *Operasi Kikis* ('Chipping-Away' Operation) is located.

c. Conducting razzias in kampungs which lie close to the place where armed contact occurs.

10. *Irregular razzias*

By irregular razzias is meant conducting razzias suddenly and not according to a fixed time schedule, and conducting razzias on targets that have not been fixed in advance. These razzias can be conducted as follows:

a. *One at a time*
Conducted against several villages one after the other, in turn.
Example: In Quiliqai kecamatan there are seven villages of which four are suspected as hiding places for the GPK. Razzias can be conducted against each of these four villages in turn and at irregular times.

b. *Simultaneous*
Conducted simultaneously against all the villages in a kecamatan which are suspected as hiding places for the GPK, with the objective of ensuring that the GPK is not able to move from one place to another while the razzia is in progress.

11. *Razzias conducted whilst an Operasi Kikis is in progress.*

In conducting a razzia of this kind, it is hoped that the GPK will not be able to hide in villages in the vicinity of the target of the *Operasi Kikis*.

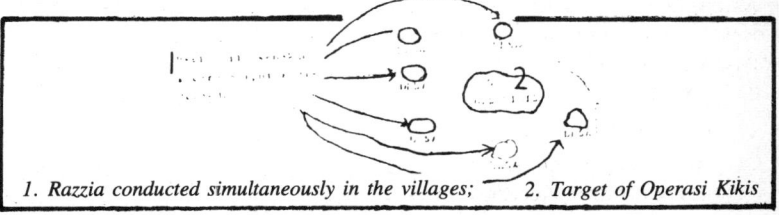

1. Razzia conducted simultaneously in the villages;   2. Target of Operasi Kikis

12. *Razzias in villages near the location of an enemy attack.*

This razzia is conducted after the GPK has waged an attack against a patrol (convoy) of ours, in cases where this attack was launched close to kampungs that can be used as hiding places. The purpose of this kind of razzia is to cut off the GPK's line of retreat.

13. *Razzia techniques*

In order to secure the maximum results, the following techniques can be used in conducting razzias:

a. The units which are to conduct the razzia should be taken from those troops not involved in the *Operasi*.

b. The razzia plan should be known only to the District Unit Commander and the Intelligence and Operational Staff Officers so that the plan does not leak to the Community.

c. If the razzia takes place at night, all the people are ordered not to leave their homes while the razzia is in progress; anyone who goes out of a house is regarded as being a GPK who is trying to run away.

d. If the razzia takes place in the daytime, all the men and women are gathered in one place to listen to a lecture whilst officers conduct the razzia by entering the homes for the purposes of razzia. Steps should be taken to prevent people's property from being lost as a result of the razzia; if property is lost, this can be used by the enemy and their supporters for propaganda purposes.

e. While the razzia is in progress, people are not allowed to enter or leave the settlement. Anyone moving round will be regarded as the enemy.

f. Place patrol posts round the settlement in question, particularly at night.

14. Other techniques

Another method for conducting a razzia in a kampung is for the kampung in question to be encircled first, particularly closing off the roads leading into and out of the kampung, and thereafter the razzia is conducted only against those houses that are under suspicion.

IV Conclusions

[Sections 15 to 21 of this PROTAP merely reiterate the headings and conclusions of the earlier sections, and stress the need for thorough comprehension and good understanding by all personnel throughout the apparatus, as well as the need for close and well-coordinated co-operation.]

Issued in Dili on 8 July, 1982

Commander
(signed)
A. Sahala Rajagukguk,
Infantry Colonel NRP No. 18805.

Document 8

**Military Regional Command XVI, Udayana
Established Procedure for the Interrogation of Prisoners.
PROTAP/01-B/VII/1982**

I. Introduction

1. General

Pursuit operations against GPK leaders and operations to destroy armed GPK groups can only succeed if we are able to detect and know the places which are the hideouts of the GPK groups. One of the ways to find out about these places is through captives who surrender. As soon as these prisoners are taken, the information obtained must be quickly processed as part of data-gathering activity. Data-gathering activity requires the skill or ability to interrogate people so that correct conclusions can be drawn about where the GPK leaders or units are hiding. Incorrect data-gathering methods will lead to wrong conclusions and will result in sending our troops in the wrong direction.

2. Aim

The purpose of this PROTAP is to ensure that the techniques of interrogating former GPK prisoners or of people who have just come down should be directed more effectively towards obtaining correct information and not directed towards confirming the interrogator's assumptions or in other words, interrogation results obtained by force.

3. Scope

This PROTAP deals with interrogation techniques, the aims of interrogations, and things that need to be avoided when interrogations are conducted. The points dealt with are as follows:

   a. Introduction.
   b. GPK efforts to eliminate their traces.
   c. The aims of interrogation.
   d. Techniques for the conduct of interrogation.
   e. Things to be avoided when conducting interrogations.
   f. Conclusions.
   g. Final Section.

II. GPK Efforts to Eliminate Their Traces

4. General
The GPK realise that, in the conduct of a guerrilla war in which their units are relatively small in number in comparison with ABRI units and the people, they cannot possibly win victory. They therefore pursue their guerrilla war by:

   a. Avoiding pursuit operations and encirclements.
   b. Spreading false reports so as to mislead efforts to discover their positions.

5. *Avoiding Pursuit Operations and Encirclements*
As soon as the location of one of their bases is discovered, pursuit operations must be launched, supported by encircling the region. To escape pursuit and to extricate themselves, the GPK adopt the method of dispersing themselves into small groups, thus making it difficult for those in pursuit to follow their tracks. By dispersing into small groups, the GPK gain the advantage that if one of the groups is caught or captured, the captured group will not know the direction taken by the other groups; it is therefore possible for them to avoid total destruction.

Example
During pursuit operations against the Ologari and Kalisa group in the Uaimori complex, pursuit was conducted by troops of Infantry Battalion 745 and Manatuto Ratih troops, and encircling operations were conducted by the Baucau Civil Guard and Infantry Battalion 509. When they were hard-pressed, the group dispersed into small groups so that when contact was made and one of their platoon commanders was shot in the leg, this person could not, when interrogated, say for sure which way the other groups had fled. This is one of the tactics used by the GPK to elude pursuit by other troops.

6. *Spreading false reports about the location of their bases, their plans to move and their hideouts.*
Besides moving in small groups and avoiding contact with us, the GPK also uses the method of spreading misleading reports, which are disseminated by letters and pamphlets as well as through people who have just come down from the bush. Elderly people, the sick as well as women and children who are felt to be a hindrance to their operations are told to go down from the bush and surrender, bringing various stories with them. They are even often threatened against saying anything about the true situation in the bush. Thus, for instance, when the GPK is going to move eastwards, they will tell these people that they are going westwards, and so on. Or, they threaten the people who are about to go down that if they tell the truth, they will be murdered. Such things are encountered among almost all the people who come down from the bush.

III. Aims of Interrogation

General

7. Before successfully conducting a security operation, the aims of the operation must first be clear. As we all know, the aim of all security operations is to smash the GPK remnants, their leaders are well as their armed units.

8. *Aims*
The aims of interrogation are as follows:

   a. To discover where the GPK leaders are.
   b. To discover the regions through which these leaders frequently move.
   c. To discover the regions often visited by the leaders, as well as their activities in these regions.
   d. To discover regions where armed GPK units operate, regions where they often travel, regions from which they get their logistical supplies, and regions often used as hideouts.
   e. To discover anything about GPK organisations, including those in the settlement areas.
   f. To discover the names of people in the settlements who are involved in these organisations.
   g. To find out about GPK plans.

IV. Techniques for Conducting Interrogations

9. *General*
In order to collect as much information as possible about the enemy, the interrogation techniques used must be good and correct so that the results will be really useful for operational plans and will not just consist of data or stories made up in the bush.

10. *Interrogation Techniques*
The interrogation techniques set out below are an improvisation (sic) between interrogation and on-the-spot implementation considered suitable when out on operations. The techniques are, among others:

   a. Give assurances of survival (life) to the person being interrogated. At the start of the interrogation, the person must be given a guarantee of his/her safety and survival so as to eliminate any idea that they will be killed regardless of whether they tell the truth or not. This is because of the stories and threats made to them by their leaders and commanders while they were still in the bush who told them: 'When you go down and are interrogated, they will kill you regardless of whether you tell the truth or tell lies, so you might as well tell lies, because you'll be killed all the same'. Another threat is that if they confess and then the soldiers go back to Java, Fretilin will come down and kill all those people who told the truth.

b. Let the people who have just come down or who have been captured know that we are well aware of the threats made by the GPK against the lives of those who tell the truth. We often forget to do this, or it is not done by the interrogator. Most of those people who come down or are captured are people who have never been to school; they therefore do whatever they have been told by the people in the bush. We must therefore approach them in the same way and say that we know all about the threats made in the bush as a way of cornering us, and we must urge them to speak the truth.

c. Give them the freedom to talk about anything they know. Once these people feel assured about their personal safety, the next step is to give them the opportunity to speak or give accounts about everything they knew while they were in the bush. We can then make our analysis and draw our conclusions from the things they tell us.

V. Things That Must be Avoided

11. General
To prevent the collection of inaccurate information through interrogations, there follows an account of some things that must be avoided during the course of interrogations.

    a. forcing the wishes of the interrogator.
    b. the use of violence and threats.
    c. drawing conclusions too hastily.

12. Forcing the wishes of the interrogator
A frequent mistake committed by interrogators is that, at the very start of the interrogation, the interrogator has already placed the person being interrogated in the position of being guilty. Consequently every question asked by the interrogator only remains to be answered, yes or no.

This method must stop since if the person under interrogation is [*not*?] given the chance to speak freely, anything he/she says that differs from the direction being taken by questioning will be ignored, particularly if accompanied by acts of violence.

13. The use of violence and threats.
Hopefully, interrogation accompanied by the use of violence will not take place except in certain circumstances when the person being interrogated is having difficulty telling the truth (is evasive).

If it proves necessary to use violence, make sure that there are no people around (members of TBO, Hansip, Ratih or other people) to see what is happening, so as not to arouse people's antipathy. The use of violence often results in the person under interrogation being forced to admit guilt because of fear, and thereafter he/she will just comply with all the wishes of the interrogator. Avoid taking photographs showing torture in progress (people being photographed at times when they are being subjected to electric current, when they have been stripped naked, etc). Remember not to have such photographic documentation developed outside, in Den Pasar, which could then be made available to the public by irresponsible elements.

It is better to make attractive photographs, such as shots taken while eating together with the prisoner, or shaking hands with those who have just come down from the bush, showing them in front of a house, and so on. If such photos are circulated in the bush, this is a classic way of assuredly undermining their morale and fighting spirits. And if such photos are shown to the priests, this can draw the church into supporting operations to restore security.

14. Drawing conclusions too hastily.
Interrogators must not draw hasty conclusions about the results of the interrogation. If necessary the interrogation should be repeated over and over again using a variety of questions so that, eventually, the correct conclusion can be drawn from all these different replies.

VI. Conclusions

15. When an Operasi Kikis is in progress, it will be more effective to know beforehand whether the aim is to get a leader or an armed unit. And in order to discover the whereabouts of the leader or armed unit, one of the ways is to collect data from information given by people or by GPK members who have come down from the bush or who have been captured.

[*The remaining points of the Concluding Section simply summarise the headings already given in the earlier sections of this Protap.*].

Issued in Dili on (?) July, 1982 [*the date is blurred.*]
Commander:
(signed)

A. Sahala Rajagukguk,
Infantry Colonel NRP no. 18805.

Document 9

Military Resort Command 164/Wira Dharma
Intelligence Section
Plan to Re-structure the Trained People's Forces (Ratih)

I. Introduction

1. Basis Oral command of the Commander of Korem 164/Wira Dharma, per voice (sic), on 5 May, 1982 regarding re-structuring Ratih throughout the Eastern Sector.

2. Objective This document is intended to give a picture of the plan to re-structure Ratih in the Kodim 1628/Baucau district which resulted from the face-to-face discussions between Muspida* Tk-II/Baucau (Baucau Second-Level Administration), the Chairman of DPRD Tk-II/Baucau (Baucau Second-Level Assembly), leaders of the community, the Commander of Hansip and commanders of Ratih, which took place at Flamboyant Aula from 5 to 8 May, 1982.

3. Scope The scope of this document is restricted to resolving problems relating to Ratih and its resolution in the form of re-structuring, together with other matters that were raised during the aforesaid face-to-face, and it is drafted with the following sections:

- a. Introduction
- b. The situation of Ratih at present
- c. Desired Objectives
- d. The Re-structuring Plan
- e. Other problems
- f. Conclusion
- g. Final Section

II. The situation of Ratih at present

4. The beginnings of People's Resistance
Prior to *Operasi Kikis* (Operation 'Chipping-Away') and while Operasi Kikis was in progress, people's resistance forces were set up in *Kodim*

---

*Muspida, the regional leadership consultative body, comprised all leading figures in the military, police and local government apparatus.

(Military District Command) 1628/Baucau, consisting of the *Hansip* (Civil Guard), and Partisans, Combat and Ratih units which were set up by *Nanggala* troops.* The forces of the people were however not fully involved. There were 520 civil guards, 60 Partisans, and about one hundred people in Combat and Ratih in Quiliquai and Baguia.

5. *The growth of Ratih*
Under the All People's Defence and Security System (*Sistem Pertahanan Keamanan Rakyat Semesta*), the people are organised in the defence and security system as follows:

  a. Basically speaking, the entire Indonesian people are fighters against the enemy, children as well as adults, the elderly, women as well as men. Elderly grandfathers or grandmothers can for instance wage resistance by supplying information if they meet the enemy, or by giving misleading information to the enemy. Children can participate in the resistance by reporting on any enemy forces they see while out tending animals. Women/mothers can participate by supplying logistics to their husbands who are out fighting.

  b. From among these people are selected a number of physically and mentally strong youths. They are given military training with emphasis on the 'five Ps'** and discipline. These are the people known as the Trained People's Forces (Ratih).

  c. People are then further selected from among these Ratih forces to be given training and skills so as to be able to protect the community against both natural disasters as well as the sacrifices of war. These are known as the Civil Guard (Hansip).

  d. A number of people are taken from this Civil Guard and given training for activity in community defence and security (*Kamtibmas*) so that they can assist the police force. These people are known as the *Keamanan Rakyat* (Kamra—People's Security).

  e. And from the civil guard, others are taken for training in defence and security so as to be able to assist operations conducted by the Armed Forces (ABRI). These people are known as *Perlawanan Rakyat* (Wanra—People's Resistance).

  f. And from the Civil Guards too, others are taken for training in defence and security so as to be able to assist ABRI, its land, sea and air forces, in the waging of military operations. These people are known as *Perlawanan Rakyat* (Wanra).

  g. From both Kamra and Wanra, people are further selected to be trained and educated to become members of the Armed Forces of the Republic (ABRI), both the police force as well as the War Forces of the Republic (APRI).

---

* *nanggala troops* are knife-killers of the paracommandos (Kopassandha).
** The 'five Ps' are troop regulations on discipline, protocol, marching, garrison service and internal affairs.

In this scheme of things ABRI is thus the nucleus of the defence and security forces, but basically the entire people are fighters against the enemy. The following diagram illustrates this:

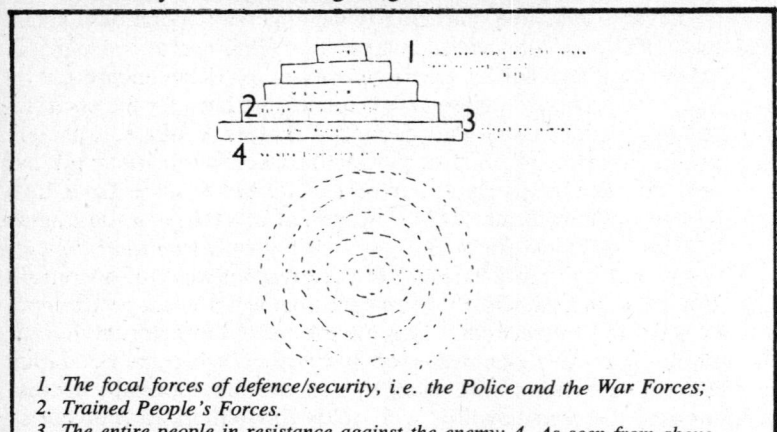

1. The focal forces of defence/security, i.e. the Police and the War Forces;
2. Trained People's Forces.
3. The entire people in resistance against the enemy; 4. As seen from above

In the developing people's resistance as pioneered during Operasi Kikis, Ratih units have since October 1981 been set up in every village in the District of Baucau. The strength of these units accords with the capability and circumstances of the population. Some villages have one platoon, whilst others have been able to create two platoons. Besides the Civil Guard and the Partisans, the Ratih units have a total of 2,392 members which are deployed as follows: [*Map with figures omitted.*]

Meanwhile, weapons for the Ratih are concentrated in the three troublesome Sub-Districts, Laga-Nunira, Baguia and Quiliqai. Thus for instance, there are 23 weapons in Laga, 164 in Nunira, 93 in Baguia and 93 in Quiliqai.

6. Problems Being Faced

a. *Some Ratih members still support the GPK*. Although there are no indications that Ratih forces in Baucau District include people who support the GPK, the fact is that in other areas, there still are Ratih members who support the GPK or who are at the very least double-faced. This is why preventive measures are needed by re-structuring the existing Ratih forces.

b. *Limited logistical support*. By contrast with the Civil Guard who receive routine support, Ratih forces do not receive routine support. They are provided with support only when they are in action. Support received by Kodim 1628/Baucau from the superior command amounts to [supplies for] 250 Ratih and 110 *Railakang* [possibly: *baterai mandala belakang* or rear- theatre artillery] forces. In view of the fact that this support is far less than the existing Ratih forces

(2,392), priority support has been established for three trouble-spot sub-districts (kecamatan), namely Laga-Nunira, Baguia and Queliquai, including *Railakang*. Other sub-districts are supported with whatever is available, particularly when pursuit operations against the GPK are conducted, against the GPK terror in Bahadik (Manatuto), also during special operations to Aitana undertaken by Ratih forces from Vemase and Venilale, and later for the encirclement operations along the red belt of Baucau-Venilale. Although priority has been given to supporting the three sub-districts, this has been provided in quite large numbers: *Railakang* (150) + Laga Ratih (150) + Nunira Ratih (242) + Laga Ratih (150) + Ratih Baguia (231) + Quiliquai Ratih (333) = 1,106 people [*the total only includes Ratih forces.*]. Because of the great intensity of operations and the large number of Ratih forces involved, the support provided is felt to be inadequate. This has created the impression that the Ratih forces are being neglected, particularly when the rice ration for those in action was replaced by a corn ration, especially because some of the corn supplied was moldy (broken and full of holes). So as to ensure that this limited logistical support can be more effectively utilised to the maximum, the need has been felt to undertake a re-structuring of Ratih forces.

III. Desired Objectives

7. Organisation
The formation of Ratih forces which are as effective and efficient as possible along the following lines:

    a. A small force but one which is capable of safeguarding the region's security because:
        i It is clean of GPK influence.
        ii It is physically strong enough to counter-balance the GPK.
        iii It has good capability to move about in combat terrain.
        iv It has good shooting skills.
        v It has good fighting techniques and tactics.
    b. The re-structuring process should not cause unrest.

8. Logistical support
The limited logistical support can be better felt by each Ratih member.

IV. The Re-structuring Plan

9. Organisation
From the existing Ratih forces, re-structured Ratih forces are to be organised, with an average strength of 150 for each sub-district excepting Laga which will have a strength of 300 people (Laga 100 and Nunira 200). In addition, there is the *Railalang* team of 150 people under the direct supervision of Kodim 1628/Baucau.

For this, a selection needs to be made, meeting the criteria listed under 7a. The village head and local community leaders are to be involved in this selection process. At the face-to-face on 8 May 1982, the Ratih commanders and community leaders gave guarantees that the Ratih forces to be set up would be clean of any GPK influences. Measures will be taken against any people who are clearly still under GPK influence because not only is this wrong according to the law, it is also wrong according to customs. As is now the case, village heads or community leaders will be commanders of the Ratih units and the sub-district (Koramil) commander or Babinsa will act alongside the commanders.

10. Weapons deployment
In view of the limited number of weapons, and bearing in mind the situation of the enemy/the GPK, priority in weapons deployment will be given to three trouble-spot regions: Laga-Nunira, Baguia and Quiliquai as well as the *Railakang* Team.

11. Logistical support
Whatever logistic support is received from the higher command will be used as effectively as possible, with priority going to the three trouble-spot sub-districts. But if we may presume to suggest, this logistical support should at the very least meet the requirements of 750 Ratih forces as follows: [*The diagram illustrating this is omitted*]

12. Operational plans
There is a need for operations to be conducted jointly. For instance, operations in Quiliquai should take place along with operations in Laga, Baguia, Kota and Vinilale. Initially it was suggested by the Ratih commanders that Ratih forces should be used in joint operations with Battalion 745 troops while other Combat Units should be used for the time being to guard security in the settlement areas. This is because many places are difficult for troops wearing shoes, whereas this is not a problem for Ratih forces. But when considered by the Muspida of Baucau, and since the task of the Combat Units is precisely to go in pursuit of the enemy, plus possible negative excesses if the Combat Units enter the settlement areas, as well as the lack of command control if Ratih forces go out on operations, agreement was reached that Ratih forces should continue to guard security in the settlement areas, doing this with more intensive techniques and tactics than previously, whilst the Combat Units should be the ones to obliterate the classic GPK areas.

13. Handling the remaining Ratih forces
Those Ratih forces who are not incorporated into this nucleus should continue to be Ratih members who are given tasks in development activity, in view of the heightened level of development work now underway in this Eastern Sector. In addition, they should, like the rest of the people, be called upon to participate in general activities such as guard duties, providing information and so on.

V. Other Problems

14. *Don't make promises*
In the past, many officials have made promises to members of the civil guard, partisans and community leaders, but these promises have not been kept. They include promises to appoint people as village heads, sub-district chiefs, and so on. It is to be hoped that the government will not make promises which are difficult to keep.

15. *Lack of information work*
Because of language/communication and other factors, many people are still not conscious over the question of integration and state affairs. There is therefore a pressing need for information work to be intensified. At present, Muspida Baucau is planning information work activities right down to the villages, making use of teams that were indoctrinated in Dili a short while ago, as well as people now undergoing indoctrination in Dili.

16. *Officials' wives should be closer to the local women*
Until now, the only ones to go down are male members of Muspida, without taking their wives. Yet, through the women, information work among the people can be far more effective. Plans are therefore being made to involve wives in going down to the villages together with their husbands, as well as in activities undertaken separately by Dharma Wanita/Dharma Pertiwi [women's organisations of government departments and the army.]

17. *Salaries for heads of villages*
As a result of all the unrest, many village heads have been replaced, whilst many new villages have emerged. Yet, the first-level administration still lists the old village heads. Further, the new villages have not yet been recognised. This has led to discontent over the distribution of salaries for village heads.

18. *Development of New Settlement areas*
The Laga sub-district has proposed the reconstruction/restoration of Soba village in Boleha and of Takinomata village in Samagua. If settlement areas are constructed in these two places, it will be possible to gain control of the region north of the Matabean mountain and the region of Susugua. Besides constructing the settlement areas, it will be necessary to build a bridge from Laga to the two settlements.

In old Quelicai (Afaca), a new settlement is being built.

Meanwhile, the Baguia sub-district administration has proposed that the village of [name indistinct] should be returned to its original location in the region of Bahatata whilst the village of Larisula should for the time being be re-settled in the region of Caidaua (name indistinct—Liquidiga—ricefield area). The opening up of these new settlement areas will open up the way to Uatuocarabau.

19. *Muspida statement on development*
In addition to the questions discussed above, Muspida has also explained

about development plans which are currently concentrated in the Eastern sector. The commanders of Ratih and community leaders are called upon to help safeguard these development plans from GPK disruptions. Nuclear Ratih forces will join in safeguarding their security, whereas the remaining Ratih forces will themselves participate in development work.

20. Conclusions
[*The points made in this section and in the following section headed Final Section are a reiteration of the points made in the main part of this document and do not need repetition here.*]

Issued in Dili, on 10 September 1982

Chief of Intelligence,
(signed)
Williem da Costa,
Infantry Major, NRP no. 24293.

Bibliography

Australian Council for Overseas Aid (ACFOA), 1982. *Dossier on East Timor*.
Australian East Timor Association (AETA), 1983, *East Timor betrayed but not beaten*.
Amnesty International, 1983. 'Submission to the UN Decolonization Committee'.
Anderson, Benedict R. O'G, 1980. Testimony on 'Human Rights in Indonesia and East Timor', at the Hearing of the Subcommittee on Asian and Pacific Affairs of the Committee on International Relations of the House of Representatives, 6 February 1980. (Mimeographed)
Araujo, Abilio, 'Revolution in liberated areas', in *East Timor News*, No.51, 22 March, 1979.
Araujo, Rui, 1983. *Timor? Timor?* Film commentary of 'Grande Reportagem', made for Portuguese Television (RTP).
'Timor: Where are the 116 Disappeared?', in *ABC*, April-May, 1983.
Australian Parliamentary Delegation to Indonesia, 1983. *Official Report* (Chairman, W.L. Morrison, MP.) Australian Government Publishing Service, Canberra.
Australian Senate Standing Committee on Foreign Affairs and Defence, 1983. *Report of the Inquiry into the Human Rights and Conditions of the People of East Timor*. (Chairman, Senator Gordon D. McIntosh) Australian Government Publishing Service, Canberra.
Verbatim Records (Official Hansard Report) of the Senate Inquiry, 1982-82.
Awanohara, Susumu. 'Falling into Step' and 'Flooded with Funds', in *Far Eastern Economic Review*, 6 August, 1982.
Center for Defence Information. *A World At War, 1983*
Clark, Roger S. 'The "Decolonization" of East Timor and the United Nations Norms on Self-Determination and Aggression', in *The Vale Journal of World Public Order*, Volume 7:2, 1980.
Do Rego, Fr. Leoneto, interview by *Voz do Povo*, published in *East Timor News*, No.60, Dec 79.
Dunn, James, 1983. *Timor: A People Betrayed*, The Jacaranda Press, Queensland.
'The Timor Story', Parliament of Australia, Canberra Legislative Research Service, 15 July 1976.
East Timor: Notes on the Humanitarian Situation', Parliament of Australia Canberra Legislative Service, 26 September 1979.
'Report on Talks with Timorese Refugees in Portugal', 11 February 1977.
East Timor News, No.47, Dec 28, 1978 and No.48, Jan 10, 1979. 'Timor Year IV: from resistance to revolution.'
Forman, Shepard, Testimony to the Subcommittee on International Organizations of the Committee on International Relations of the House of Representatives, 28 June 1977.

Freney, Denis, 'Fretilin Resistance Continues' in *Carpa Bulletin* No. 15, November 1983.
Fretilin, *Edicoes Comite 28 de Novembro (Lisboa): 'Anossa Vitoria e Apenas Questão de Tempo*. (Publication of the 28 November Committee, Lisbon: 'Our Victory is only a matter of time'), March 1978.
Relatorio da Delegacão do Comite Central da Fretilin em Missão de Servico no Exterior do Pais. (Delegation Report on the External Mission of the Fretilin Central Committee), March 1982, Maputo.
Fretilin Conquers the Right to Dialogue, June 1983, Lisbon.
Hadomi, Special Edition, 'A Critical Time'. 10 August 1983.
Hamilton, John. 'Inside Timor' (series) in *The West Australian*, 27, 30 April and 2, 3, 4, 5 May, 1983.
Hill, Helen, May 1978. *Fretilin: The Origins, Ideologies and Strategies of a Nationalist Movement in East Timor*. (Mimeographed)
Indonesian Government (Department of Information) 1983, *East Timor After Integration*.
Indonesia, Cornell Southeast Asia Program. No.36, October 1983 (editors). 'Current Data on the Indonesian Military Elite'.
Jenkins, David, 'Timor's Arithmetic of Despair', in *Far Eastern Economic Review*, 29 September 1978.
'Alive, No Longer Kicking' in *Far Eastern Economic Review*, 3 November 1983.
Jolliffe, Jill, 1978, *East Timor: Nationalim and Colonialism*. University of Queensland Press.
Kamm, Henry, 'Ravaged Timor Struggles Back from Abyss' 28 January, and 'Timor's Legacy, Useless Currency, Stranded People', 30 January 1980, *New York Times*.
Kohen, Arnold and Taylor, John, 1979, *An Act of Genocide: Indonesia's Invasion of East Timor*, Tapol, London.
Leifer, Michael, 1983, *Indonesia's Foreign Policy*, Routledge & Kegan Paul, London.
Lopes, Mgr. da Costa, interview in *Tapol Bulletin*, No.59, September 1983.
May, Brian, 1978, *The Indonesian Tragedy*, Routledge & Kegan Paul, London.
MacDonald, Hamish, 1980, *Suharto's Indonesia*, Fontana Books, Victoria.
McFetridge, Charles, 'Seskoad—Training the Elite' in *Indonesia*, Cornell University Southeast Asia Program, No.36, October 1983.
McIntosh, Senator Gordon, 'Address to National East Timor Activities Conference', 28 January 1984.
Metzner, Joachim K, 1977, *Man and Environment in Eastern Timor*. Development Studies Series Monograph No.8, Australian National University, Canberra.
Munster, G.J. and Walsh, J.R., 1980, *Documents on Australia's Defence and Foreign Policy, 1968-75*. Munster and Walsh, Hongkong.
National Times, The Timor Papers. (Dale van Atta and Brian Toohey), 30 May-5 June, 6-13 June, 1982.
Neobere interview in *Tapol Bulletin* No.58, July 83 and No.60, Nov 83.
Nordland, Rod, 'Hunger: Under Indonesia, Timor Remains a Land of Misery' in *The Philadelphia Inquirer*, 28 May, 1982.
Permanent People's Tribunal Verdict of Session on East Timor, Lisbon, 19-21 June, 1981.
Richardson, D.J., 'Report on Visit to East Timor'. September 1982. (Mimeographed)

Richardson, Michael, 'Timor pays for its invasion—in coffee' and 'Coffee boom too late for Timor', in *The Age* (Melbourne) 15 and 17 March 1977.
Rodgers, Peter, 'Horror on our doorstep', *The Age*, 1 November 1979.
Southeast Asia Chronicle, No.74, August 1980. 'East Timor: Beyond Hunger'.
Southwood, Julie and Flanagan, Patrick, 1983. *Indonesia: Law, Propaganda and Terror*. Zed Books, London.
Tanter, Richard, 'The Military Situation in East Timor, June 1976', Democratic Republic of East Timor Information Office, New York.
Tapol, *West Papua: The Obliteration of a People*, 1983. Tapol, London.
Timor Information Service, No.28, February 1980, 'East Timor: How many people are missing?'
Traube, Elizabeth, Testimony to the Subcommittee on International Organisations of the Committee on International Relations of the House of Representatives, 28 June 1977.
  'Statement on East Timor' to the Fourth Committee of the United Nations, 17 October 1980.
UN General Assembly, East Timor, Working Paper prepared by the Secretariat, 13 August 1982, New York.
US Congressional Hearings:
  'On Human rights in East Timor and the Question of the Use of US Equipment by the Indonesian Armed Forces', 23 March 1977.
  'On Human Rights in East Timor', 28 June and 19 July 1977.
  'On Famine Relief in East Timor', 4 December 1979.
  'On Human Rights in East Timor', 6 February 1980.
  'On East Timor', 10 June, 1980.
  'On Recent Developments in East Timor', 14 September 1982.
US State Department, *Country Reports on Human Rights Practices for 1983*, Washington.
Waddingham, John, Testimony to the Australian Senate Inquiry, *Verbatim Records* pp. 696-778, 29 June, 1982.
Wain, Barry, 'East Timor is being developed but local support eludes Jakarta', 'East Timor Governor fights Jakarta to remain in power', and 'Military seen behind firm controlling Timor's coffee', in *Asian Wall Street Journal*, 14 and 16 June 1982.
Walsh, Pat, 'Notes on the East Timor Issue Based on an International Visit', Action for World Development, Melbourne. 7 June—18 August 1980.
  'Church may hold the key to Timor's future', in *National Outlook*, Vol IV, No.1, January 1982.
  'Timorese People Support the Church in its Opposition to Indonesian Takeover', in *National Outlook*, Vol VI, No.11, November 1982.
Weatherbee, Donald, 'The Indonesianization of East Timor'. Paper to the 20th Annual Meeting of the Southeast Conference for Asian Studies, 24 January 1981.
  'The Situation in East Timor'. Institute of International Studies, University of South Carolina, 1980.
Wertheim, W.F. *Oest Timor, Westerse Medeplichtigheid aan Volkenmoord* (East Timor, Western Responsibility for Genocide), October 1982, Komite Indonesia, Amsterdam.
Xanana, Kay Rala, 'Message to the United Nations General Assembly', 14 October 1982. Reproduced in *East Timor News* No.78—80, Spring 1983.

Periodicals
East Timor Information Bulletin, BCIET, London.
East Timor Reports, ACFOA, Melbourne.
East Timor News, Sydney.
Funu, Lisbon.
ICRC Situation Reports, Geneva
Indonesië, Feiten en Meningen, Amsterdam
Tapol Bulletin, London.
Tempo (weekly), Jakarta
Timor Information Service, Melbourne.
Timor Newsletter, Lisbon.

Index

ACFOA (Australian Council for Overseas Aid) 41, 78, 96, 105
Aceh 45, 46
ACR (Australian Catholic Relief) 109, 120, 128
Aileu 104
Ainaro district 91, 142
Alkatiri, Mari 54
Amaral, Xavier do 34, 35, 36, 54, 59, 61, 63, 64, 65, 117
Amir Machmud 97
Amnesty International 131, 132, 134-5, 137, 145
Anderson, Benedict 79
Angola 13
APODETI (Associacão Popular Democratica Timorense) 5, 6, 16, 17, 18, 53, 97, 99, 101, 128
Araujo, Abilio dos Reis 54, 55, 65, 152
Araujo, Arnaldo dos Reis 98
Araujo, Rui 100, 126, 132, 136, 138
ASEAN (Association of South East Asian Nations) 8, 14, 147
ASDT (Asociacão Social Democratica de Timor) see Fretilin
Atabae 21, 22
Atapupu 17
Atauro 6, 39, 65, 115, 131, 132, 135-8, 145, 180, 213
Australia 8, 10, 13, 148, 149, 150, 151, 152, 154
    Allied campaign 4
    Ambassador 9
    Government 20
    Intelligence 20
    Labour Party 154
    military support 8, 17, 30
    Parliament 35
    Parliamentary mission 82, 85, 86, 89, 105, 113, 132
    press 20, 83, 120
    refugees 37, 125
    Senate Inquiry 32, 109, 110
Australian Catholic Relief see ACR

babinsa(bintara pembina desa) 82, 102, 172, 176, 179-82, 190, 191, 212, 213, 214, 222, 225-7
Balibo 20, 126
Batugade 19
Baucau 4, 22, 23, 25, 40, 42, 57, 65, 70, 74, 77, 80, 82, 84, 86, 88, 104, 115, 136, 137, 141, 144, 174, 183, 184, 185, 186-9
Belo, Carlos Philipe Ximenes 122, 123
benteng stelsel 44, 45
Bere Malay Laka 70
Bertin, Gilles 140
Bonaparte, Rosa Muki 56

Cape Verde 13
Carrascalao, Mario 72, 89, 99, 100, 105, 136, 138, 143
Casa dos Timores 54, 56
Catholic Church of East Timor 50, 51, 110, 117-124, 145, 194
Catholic Church of Indonesia 49, 122-3, see also Mawi
Chile 148
CIA (Central Intelligence Agency) 15, 17, 18, 20, 21, 51
    National Intelligence Daily 15, 17, 18, 20, 21
Civil guard see Hansip

250 Index

Coffee 98, 99, 100, 103, 104, 105, 106
Comarca Prison 136, 144
Conference of Non-Aligned States 13
Concelhos, 74, 96
Costa, Williem da 46, 130, 169
CRRN (Revolutionary Council of National Resistance) 62, 69, 71, 72, 129, 130, 131, 132, *see also* FRETILIN
CRS (Catholic Relief Service) 78, 90, 115
Cuba 13

Dading Kalbuadi 19, 20, 22, 28, 30, 35, 48, 119, 125, 146
Dare 38
Democratic Republic of East Timor (DRET) 3, 6
 declaration of independence 7, 156
 formal recognition 13
Denok 90, 103, 104, 105, 106
DGI (Dewan Gereja-Gereja Indonesia) 124
Dili 3, 4, 6, 8, 15, 17, 18, 22, 23, 25, 31, 36, 38, 39, 40, 53, 57, 60, 68, 70, 74, 75, 76, 77, 79, 81, 84, 90, 96, 97, 98, 103, 104, 105, 106, 107, 114, 115, 122, 128, 129, 131, 132, 135, 136, 137, 140, 141, 144, 145, 147
Dilor 86
Dom Boaventura 3
Dunn, James 4, 21, 55, 99, 128
Dutch 154, 155
 Dutch East Indies 4
 military support 8
 Government 30, 142, 152

East Timor
 administration 97-103
 agriculture 75-6
 chemical weapons 35, 36
 death toll 49-51
 education 109-13
 Indonesianization 96-126
 infiltration 5
 invasion 15, 27
 Japanese occupation 99
 livestock 85
 negotiations 45-7
 plantation economy 103-9
 propaganda war 7
 provincial government 101-3
 public health 114-6
 refugees 35, 46, 96, 125, 140, 142
 resettlement camps 43, 76-95
 security conditions 31
 self-determination 3, 153-5
 State organizations 96
 struggle 5-14
 Timorization 39, 40
 uprising 4
Ermera 4, 77, 104, 105
European Community 155

FALINTIL (Forças Armadas de Libertaçao Nacional de Timor) 18, 24, 25, 33, 36, 43, 46, 56, 57, 61, 62, 63, 64, 65, 67, 68, 70, 71, 72, 73, 141, 144, 151
 see also FRETILIN
fence-of-legs tactics
 see Operation Security
Fernandes, Alarico 36, 54, 61, 62, 64
Ford, Gerald 9, 21
Ford, Sir John 10
Forman, Shepard 74, 86
France 8
Freney, Denis 49, 58
FRETILIN (Frente Revolucionaria de Timor Leste Independente) 5, 12, 15, 18, 25, 26, 34, 36, 38, 44, 46, 47, 52-67
 Central Committee 33, 54, 56, 62
 clandestine groups 5
 clandestine networks 44, 201-2, 216-8, 229-30
 forces 20, 37, 38, 41, 48, 142, 170-1, 177-8, 202-4
 guerrilla strategy and tactics 26, 171-2, 183-4, 195-204
 leadership 27, 35, 36, 53, 66, 67, 69, 72, 117, 132
 liberated areas 58
 military skills 24
 new strategy 43, 68
 non-alignment 10, 151

Peace Plan 150, 151, 156
popular support 15, 24, 39, 57
Radio Maubere 24, 29, 35, 36, 58, 61, 76
report 78, 83-95
self-determination 12
social and political programmes 53, 54, 55, 56, 57
Fry, Ken 23, 30

Gama, Cancio de Sousa 82, 83, 88
Gama, Jaime 152
Golkar (Golongan Karya) 113, 114
Gonçalves, Guilherme 99
gotong royong 85, 91
GPK (Gerakan Pengacan Keamanan) 44, 82, 178-85, 187, 189, 193, 194-210, 212-4, 216-22, 224, 225, 226, 229-32, 233, 234-6, 240-2, 244
Grenada 13
Guinea-Bissau 13, 53
Gusmão, Kay Rala *see* Xanana

Hamilton, John 84, 86, 87, 89
Hamis Basarewa 59, 63
Hansip (Pertahanan Sipil) 71, 86, 91, 133, 134, 173, 184, 186, 187, 190, 191, 202, 213, 221, 225-6, 236, 239
Hastings, Peter 109, 120
Hawke, Bob 148
Hayden, Bill 148, 151
Hill, Helen 59
Holbridge, John 11-3
Horta, Jose Manuel Ramos 54, 64, 99
Ibnu Sutowo 26
ICRC (International Red Cross) 47, 77, 78, 94, 95, 101, 115, 136, 137, 139, 145, 152, 156
IGGI (Inter-Governmental Group on Indonesia) 8
India 13, 147
Indonesia
   Armed Forces 8, 19, 22, 30, 39, 45, 73, 102, 103, 106, 143, 151, 153, 169-70, 176
   attitudes 40
   bill of integration 96
   casualties 29
   Government 10

hostility 7
invasion 15, 17, 18
military adventure 24
military command 44, 45, 46, 169-70
military operations 18-20
military supplies 17, 19
propaganda 18, 104, 221-2
raids 228-32
regional revolt 4, 46, 47
troops 15, 18, 19, 24, 32, 43, 46, 47, 57, 65, 66, 72, 96, 103, 126, 140
war 22-48, 145-7, 173-5
International Red Cross *see* ICRC
International solidarity 154-6
Interrogation 179-80, 207-8, 233-7
use of torture 131-5, 236

Jakarta 4, 20, 26, 30, 46, 78, 97, 141, 143, 144
Japan 8, 148, 153
Jenkins, David 22, 31, 81
Jolliffe, Jill 10, 64, 152

Kalangi 98, 99, 100, 101, 103, 105
Kamm, Henry 124
Kilik, Wae Gae 65, 69, 196
Kissinger, Henry 9
Kohen, Arnold 26
Kopasgat (Komando Pasukan Gerak Cepat) 22
KOPASSANDHA (Komando Pasukan Sandi Yudha) 22, 24, 129, 140
KOSTRAD (Komando Strategis Angkatan Darat) 24
Kotis (Komando Takis) 102
Kupang 6, 99

Lakluta 40, 86, 113, 127, 128
La Rocque, Gene R 27, 51
Lere Timur 65
Lisbon 6, 35, 37, 46, 134
liurais 3, 96, 176, 205
Liquica 23
Lobato, Nicolau 36, 52, 53, 55, 65, 143
Lopes, Martinhu da Costa 35, 50, 79, 80, 108, 116, 117, 118, 119, 120, 121, 122, 123, 128, 129, 144, 149

Lopes da Cruz, Francisco 49
Los Palos 25, 41, 82, 94, 106, 136, 142

Macau 4
Majelis Waligereja Indonesia *see* MAWI
Malaysia 14
Maliana 31, 101, 107, 108, 115
Malik, Adam 5, 49
Manatuto 86-7, 136
Mambai, 59, 60, 75
Manufuhi *see* Same
Masters, Edward 31, 78, 79
Matabian, mountain range 31, 32, 33, 36, 66, 67, 89
Maubara 23, 108
Maubere 25, 58, 59, 60, 118
  Maubere people 33, 34, 37, 38, 67, 82, 150, 151, 153
Mau Hodu 65
Mau Hunu Bulerek Karatainu 67, 68, 69, 70, 196
Mau Lear 33, 54, 59, 63, 64, 65
Mauk Moruk Teky Timor 70, 196
MAWI (Majelis Waligereja Indonesia) 121, 122, 123-4, 137
McFetridge, Charles 145
Metzner, Joachim K 75, 107
Mochtar Kusumaatmaja 46, 149
Mondale, Walter 30
Morrison, Bill 82, 83
Mozambique 13, 53
Murdani, Benny 17, 22, 27, 28, 30, 37, 47, 48, 97, 121, 123, 128, 139, 140, 141, 142, 143, 145, 147
Murtopo, Ali 5, 17

Natarbora 32, 33, 142
Neobere 18, 35, 58, 114, 115, 116, 135
Netherlands *see* Dutch
Newsom, David 9
Ngudiono 101
Nicaragua 13, 147
Nordland, Rod 80, 81, 88, 126
Norway 149
nurep (nucleos de resistencia popular) 69, 82, 83, 171, 172, 178-81, 202-3, 206-7, 212, 216-8, 220

Ombai-Wetar Straits 10
Operasi Keamanan *see* Operation Security
Operasi Kikis 230-1, 238
Operasi Komodo 5, 17
Operasi Pembersihan 37
Operasi Persatuan see Operation Clean-Sweep
Operasi Sapu Bersih see Operation Clean-Sweep
Operasi Seroja 15, 22, 24, 36, 77, 146
Operation Clean-Sweep 47, 139-45
Operation Ganesha *see* Operation Security
Operation Security 40, 43, 45, 80, 81, 87, 115, 119, 120, 127, 135, 137, 174
Operation Skylight 36, 61, 130
OPMT (Organizaçao Popular de Mulher Timor) 56, 57
OPSUS (Operasi Chusus) 5

Pagar betis operations 41
Pancasila 102, 103, 111, 112
Panggabean, Maraden 17, 22
Papua New Guinea 21, 149, 154
Paraguay 148
Peace Plan *see* Fretilin
Perdido, Mount 84, 86, 87
Permanent People's Tribunal 155
Portugal 151-3
  administration 3, 116
  census 50, 51
  citizenship 101
  colonialism 3, 4, 106, 112
  colonial army 57, 62
  constitution 147
  refugees 35, 37
  secret police 53
  Timor 10, 19, 21
povoaçao 74, 76
postos 74, 75, 76, 115
Prabowo Soemitro 36
Pramuka 112
Provisional Government of East Timor 15
P.T. Denok *see* Denok
Purwanto 43, 44, 45, 46, 47, 48, 72, 83, 100, 115, 139

Queliquai 41, 42, 80, 81, 88, 89, 133, 135, 212

Radio Maubere *see* Fretilin
Rajagukguk, Sahala 44, 169
Ratih (Rakyat Terlatih) 181, 186, 187, 188, 190, 191, 221-2, 223-6, 236, 238-42
Reichle, Denis 28, 126
Remexio 31, 76
Ribero, Jose 117, 118
Richardson, D.J. 115
Richardson, Michael 13, 103
Rodgers, Peter 77

Sahe, Bieki 33, 54, 59, 63, 64, 65
Sao Tome and Principe 13
Salazar, Antonio de Oliveira 5, 10
Same 3, 78, 84, 91, 104
Sandalwood 3, 106
SAPT (Sociedade Agricola Patria e Trabalho) 105
Sekretaris wilayah daerah *see* sekwilda, *see* also Kalangi
Sekwilda (sekretaris wilayah daerah) 98, 99
Serakey 59, 67
Seroja *see* Operasi Seroja
SESKOAD (Sekolah Staf dan Komando Angkatan Darat) 145-147
Singapore 103
Soibada 57, 59, 62
Solarz, Stephen J. 11-13
State Department *see* U.S.
Suai region 18, 24, 76
Sucos 3, 74
Suharto 17, 19, 22, 28, 29, 31, 38, 46, 96, 103, 106, 121, 130, 141
Sukarno 19
Sulawesi 4
    Sulawesi solution 46, 47
Surono 17
Sweden 8

TAPOL 30, 108
Traube, Elizabeth 59, 75, 95
Tutuala 43

UDT *União Democratica Timorense* 5, 8, 17, 18, 53, 56, 98, 99, 102, 117
U.K.
    diplomats 10
    Government 11, 139
    interests 10
    military supplies 8
    Parliament 155

UN *see* United Nations
Unetim 56
União Democratica Timorense (UDT) *see* UDT
UNICEF 115
United Nations 4, 10, 47, 96, 97, 99, 147-155
    Charter 154
    Decolonization Committee 131
    document 51
    General Assembly 82, 95, 98, 138, 148, 149, 150, 152
    Peace-Force 150
    resolution 148, 150, 151
    Secretary General 148, 149, 150
    Security Council 21, 23, 150
U.S.A. 7, 9, 21, 107, 109
    administration 19
    Ambassador 9, 78-9
    bilateral relations 9
    Congress 155
    intelligence 20
    military supplies 8, 9, 17
    on self-determination 11-13, 148
    Pentagon 10
    State Department 9, 79, 109, 139
    Washington 9, 79

Vanuatu 147, 149
Vatican 117, 118, 119, 121, 122
Viqueque 25, 35, 65, 70, 74, 80, 84, 85, 106, 136, 139, 140, 141, 142, 144, 145

Walsh, Pat 119
Washington *see* U.S.
Weatherbee, Donald 80
West New Guinea *see* West Papua
West Papua 4, 102, 108, 140, 154
West Timor 5, 6, 7, 17, 18, 40, 143
Whitlam, Gough 120
Widodo 19
Woolcott, Richard 9

Xanana, Kay Rala 25, 29, 33, 37, 38, 39, 40, 43, 46, 47, 66, 67, 68, 69, 70, 72, 73, 129, 130, 139, 149, 150

Yusuf, Mohammad 29, 30, 31, 36, 45, 46, 47, 120

Zimbabwe 147